THE WHISPERINGS WITHIN

David Barash

The Whisperings Within

Harper & Row, Publishers

NEW YORK

HAGERSTOWN

SAN FRANCISCO

LONDON

1817

FIRST EDITION

Designer: Sidney Feinberg

Library of Congress Cataloging in Publication Data

Barash, David P
  The whisperings within.
    1. Sociobiology. 2. Social evolution.
  3. Psychology, Comparative—Social aspects.
  4. Nature and nurture. I. Title.
GN365.9.B38 1979   301.2   78-20155
ISBN 0-06-010341-8

79 80 81 82 83 10 9 8 7 6 5 4 3 2 1

To Genevieve, Waldeau and The Lump—
now revealed to be Ilona Anne

Contents

Acknowledgments

A first draft of this book was written while I was a Fellow at the Center for Advanced Study in the Behavioral Sciences, Stanford, California (1977–1978). I thank the director, Gardner Lindzey, and my fellow Fellows for providing an ideal personal and intellectual environment. Mrs. Irene Bickenbach cheerfully and expertly did the typing. I also thank the following persons for reading the manuscript and making valuable suggestions: Richard N. Adams, William Bernds, Warren Holmes, Eric Charnov, and Pierre van den Berghe. Nach Waxman, my editor at Harper & Row, challenged me on numerous points and made the final product much better than it would have been without him.

Finally, I thank Judith E. Lipton, friend, confidant, psychiatrist, lover and co-shareholder in my fitness, for everything.

When our intellect does not conform to the reality of things or is deaf to the world of nature, it wanders in the illusion of dreams and pursues a phantom. Between God and ourselves stands nature.

POPE PIUS XII

The ground aim of all science is to cover the greatest number of empirical facts by logical deductions from the smallest possible number of hypotheses.

ALBERT EINSTEIN

Descended from monkeys? My dear, let us hope that it isn't true! But if it is true, let us hope that it doesn't become widely known!

THE WIFE OF THE BISHOP
OF WORCESTER (19th century)

THE WHISPERINGS WITHIN

1

Introduction: Hottentot Gods and the Strange Case of the Plucked Ocelot

It may well be that we are born able to live a thousand different lives, but it is no less true that we die having lived just one. How many different lives could we really live if we had the chance? A thousand? Ten thousand? A million? Paradoxically, we are all the same in that we all share the capacity to be wonderfully different from each other. But we are also the same in that by virtue of our shared humanity none of us is all that different from anyone else.

Whether we are risen apes or fallen angels, our potential as human beings is undeniably very great, but it isn't infinite. We could never know life as an earthworm, as a crayfish or as a giraffe. Whether Pittsburgh steelworker, Iraqi farmer or Japanese fisherman, the stuff of our lives is drawn from the stuff of being human. In the pages to follow we will be looking at the makeup of that stuff, taking a look at the nature of human nature.

It is now more than one hundred years since Charles Darwin revolutionized our view of the living world, and we are finally beginning to use what we know about evolution to understand behavior. This fresh approach to an old subject is "sociobiology," the application of evolutionary principles to the social behavior of animals—and of human beings as well. It is a brand-new and wide-open field, with major discoveries taking place every day. Sociobiology offers dramatic insights into our own behavior, insights that some will find appalling and others, enormously stimulating. This book is an invitation to explore the latest findings of genetics and ecology as applied to human behavior. It is a speculative excursion into human sociobiology.

During this journey, I will be telling many animal stories, providing, perhaps, a somewhat novel perspective on the birds and the bees —stories of rape in ducks, adultery in bluebirds, prostitution in hummingbirds, divorce and lesbian pairing in gulls, even homosexual rape in parasitic worms. We'll talk too about why gorillas have small testicles while those of chimpanzees are enormous, and we'll see how coral-reef fish pretend to be more fierce than they really are, just to impress the ladies. But while these things are entertaining in themselves, my goal is not simply to be some racy modern Aesop; neither is it to discuss animals for their own sake, although that is surely a respectable enough undertaking.

What I hope is that the animals you'll meet in the following pages will help you know yourself better. But don't misunderstand; I won't be arguing that just because hairy-nosed wombats do something or other we should be inclined to do the same. The animals we meet may help reveal the way evolution operates on behavior, without necessarily prescribing the exact form the behavior will take. For example, male rabbits court females by urinating on them. They do this, in part, because it serves to cover the female with male scent, thereby enhancing the social bond between the mates. Obviously, human beings use different techniques to maintain their domestic tranquillity, and no one is suggesting that we act like rabbits, certainly not in this respect. But if we look beyond the specifics of what rabbits do and ask ourselves why they are doing it, we learn some interesting things. For example, male rabbits compete with other male rabbits for the sexual attention of females, and they use what is available in their rabbit repertoire to bring them success. If human beings turn out to be under comparable pressures, we might expect them to employ whatever is available from the human repertoire to accomplish their needs. That repertoire evolves over time, and the result is a series of uniquely human behaviors. By watching how evolution operates on the behavior of animals, it is possible we may begin to be able to identify general principles. Then, of course, we can take these principles and try them on ourselves, and if the shoe fits . . .

The real subject of this book, then, is human behavior, viewed from the perspective of sociobiology. We will explore the biological underpinning of human nepotism and altruism, the basis for families as well as a surprising and sure-fire prescription for conflict. We will analyze parental behaviors, the underlying selfishness of our behavior toward others, even our own children, and take a hard-headed (and undoubtedly unpopular) look at the evolutionary biology of differences between men and women, including a theory for the biological basis of the double standard. We shall consider aggression and competition, sex and gift giving, why only women have menopause and why men don't lactate, and whether Freud was right in claiming that deep down inside we all really want to kill our fathers and sleep with our mothers. Or vice versa. Some readers may be delighted with all of this, others infuriated; I hope none will be bored.

●

Biologist Joel Cohen points out that many of the sciences suffer from "physics envy," wishing that their disciplines were as firmly grounded as physics in the harmonious interplay of fact and theory. This is especially true of the specialties that have traditionally been concerned with understanding human behavior: psychology, anthropology and sociology. These social sciences have tended to assume that human beings are blank slates at birth and that as experience accumulates it writes on these slates, thereby producing a person. Change the writing and you change the person. Thus, the social sciences have seen their role as understanding the place of experience in determining human behavior, and while they have had their share of success, their accomplishments have been generally limited. Somehow, the "essence" of human beings has escaped their analysis, and indeed the social sciences have never been able to agree on even the most basic principles governing their work. They have much to envy in physics.

The real strength of physics, and to a lesser extent the other natural sciences, lies in their intellectual coherence. In most cases, good science derives from a small number of relatively simple but enormously powerful ground rules. Indeed, it is remarkable how simplicity and explanatory power often go together. By contrast, the social sciences have erected an incredibly intricate but rickety Tower of Babel. Theories have proliferated with almost the abundance of their expounders, and there have been over the years a succession of Spencerians, Durkheimians, Weberians, Marxists, Freudians, Adlerians, Jungians, Piagetians, Skinnerians—and countless others.

It may seem unfair to portray the social sciences as disheveled in contrast to physics, since physics is one science whereas the social sciences are many. However, that is just the point: physics undertakes the study of matter and energy, an incredibly broad agenda, but it still has a great deal of conceptual unity. The sciences of human behavior, on the other hand, are concerned with only a very small part of physics—the matter and energy that are put together as *Homo sapiens*—and yet they seem unable to agree on anything.

Perhaps such diversity is appropriate to the study of something as complicated as human behavior, and I certainly do not wish to imply that we should all abandon our heresies and embrace evolution. Truth is never so simple. Will Durant writes: "We are such microscopic particles in so immense a universe that none of us is in a position to understand the world, much less to dogmatize about it. Let us be careful how we pit our pitiful generalizations against the infinite variety, scope and subtlety of the world." Nonetheless, there are some especially valuable generalizations that help make sense out of the kaleidoscopic jumble that the world presents. Sometimes they even help us to see that not all variety is really "infinite." Evolution by natural selection is one of these generalizations.

Natural selection provides not only a unifying way of looking at the living world, it also explains the extraordinary sameness that underlies so much surface-level chaos. Out of the incredible number of possible arrangements of molecules, life uses only a small number. Virtually all living things use the same kind of molecule, DNA, for their genetic material, just as nearly all of them store energy in the same molecular form, called ATP. Similarly, if we were to survey every human society now living, or that ever existed, we would observe only a small proportion of all the theoretically possible interactions between people. Imagine a new Garden of Eden, starting again with Adam and Eve and all the plants and animals. Once the snake told them how, what kind of world would they create? One different from ours, certainly, with different groups of people in different places doing different things. But probably not radically different things.

Human beings are, after all, still human beings, and as such, there is a certain range within which their behavior will fall. They may develop distinctive customs of dress and adornment, perhaps parrot feathers in one place, strange patterns of head shaving in another, the ritual carving of deep scars on cheeks and foreheads in yet another, but some pattern of dress and adornment is always found. Similarly, marriage in one place might be sanctified by a ceremonial sharing of food, or maybe by the union of menstrual blood with semen, or by the payment of tokens from one partner to the other or by signing a document and uttering officially approved words, but some ritualized sanctioning of male-female association seems almost always to take place. In addition, we might expect some kind of procedures whereby people identified their relatives, even in total ignorance of scientific genetics and, furthermore, they would behave more favorably toward relatives than toward non-relatives. The inhabitants of our "second go-round" world almost certainly would differentiate into male and female roles, even though what is considered male in one culture might be considered female in another.

One of the things that we are trying to do in this book is to uncover some of these underlying human patterns. For, while it is true that culture makes people, people also make cultures, and there is much to gain by looking at what remains the same about people underneath their customs and habits.

Most students of human behavior are intensely aware of how variable that behavior can be, both when comparing individuals from different cultures and when watching the same individual change over time. Impressed as they are by the variety and flexibility of it all, they tend to feel that there can be no such thing as an inherent human nature. On the other hand, to the biologist looking at human beings as merely another species of animal, *Homo sapiens* shows a consistent pattern. We form societies in which, for example, age and power are closely allied, in which relatives are distinguished from non-relatives, in which men and women do predictably different things, in which exchange, barter and gambling occur, and in which there is some sort of formalized association between men and women. Some of these things show our similarity to other animals, others such as our use of language and our ability to carry out rapid culture change, show our uniqueness. But any way you slice it, human nature, diverse as it is, looks narrow indeed in the wider context of the diversity of living things.

No other animal does all the things we do and every species of animal does things that we don't. We lack the stable monogamy of gibbons, the programmed suicide of stinging bees, the social indifference of starfish. As great as the differences are between Laplander, Arab, Zulu and Bavarian, they are not nearly as great as those between any person and a garter snake, or even a chimpanzee. Considering how diverse we might be, but aren't, the biologist is bound to conclude that we have a definite "nature."

The true nature of human nature—it is no small topic, and it is crucial not only in biology and social science but is also a traditional issue in philosophy. Thus Aristotle felt that society was the product of the nature of human beings, while Plato maintained that human beings were the products of society. Sociobiology is closer to Aristotle, although any evolutionary theory of human behavior must certainly recognize an interchange between the nature of each individual and the nature of his or her society.

By stressing the inner, biological influences on human nature, a sociobiologic view of humanity seems to run counter to some of our popular ways of looking at ourselves. Simone de Beauvoir claimed that we are "l'être dont l'être est de n'être pas"—the being whose essence is having no essence. And Jean-Paul Sartre's credo of "existence precedes essence" tells us that whatever our inner nature—our essence—it is our responsibility as human beings to define ourselves by our actions—our existence. By doing so, we may transcend that essence, and we will experience our full humanity. An eagle can soar and a chickadee cannot, but however it may excite our admiration, an eagle can still do no more than be an eagle. Our question, then: what are we and what can we be when we are being human?

•

At the Seattle zoo there was once an ocelot who was literally tearing himself to pieces. He sat in his cage, ripping patches of fur and skin from his haunches, making himself a ragged, bloody mess, and driving his keepers frantic. Nothing seemed to help this beautiful, self-destructive cat—not vitamins, not a bigger cage, not even a lady ocelot. We knew, of course, that birds were the main food of ocelots in the wild, and someone finally noticed that the poor animal seemed to be using the same plucking motions on itself that free-living animals use on freshly-captured prey. So the ocelot was given a chicken instead of the usual horsemeat mixture, and it immediately began plucking the bird and stopped plucking itself!

Ocelots apparently have an innate need to pluck, and if this is thwarted by giving them, say, Alpo instead of whole chickens, the suppressed behavior emerges in some other way. It is unlikely that we humans have an innate behavioral pattern as specific and precise as that of the ocelot. But, just as an ocelot has ocelot nature, we have human nature. We are, perhaps, the most flexible animals in the world, but to be human is still something distinctive, and evolution offers us a look at what that something may be.

To some people, the thought that we might be reducing human behavior to biology is unacceptable, but we are not suggesting that biology explains behavior, only that it gives us some impressive insights about it.

We tend to fancy ourselves as special, the apple of God's eye, extraordinary creatures who control the world and not vice versa. In fact, it has taken us most of our history and not a little anguish even to recognize that we are a part of the world. Modern science shows a long progression of insults to our overblown conception of our own uniqueness, with the *Homo sapiens über alles* contingent digging in their heels every step of the way. This process began with the likes of Copernicus, Kepler, and Galileo and the shocking revelation that the earth—and by implication, our species—was not the focal point of the universe. We were kicked out of center stage and relegated to a small planet circling an insignificant star in a remote corner of an out-of-the-way galaxy. That was painful, but it was still hardly preparation for the mid-nineteenth century, when Charles Darwin argued that natural selection provides a mechanism for evolutionary change and showed the operation of that mechanism in most of the observable facts of biology. In *The Origin of Species*, Darwin scrupulously avoided references to man, but the implications were clear.

The book was an instantaneous best-seller. Again man's comfortable view of himself was shaken as our ancestry was linked to apelike primates and ultimately to all of life. Darwin wrote that "there was grandeur in this view of life," that all living things, from the humblest protozoan to *Homo sapiens* itself, were produced by the same universal process. But many of his contemporaries saw it rather differently. Indeed, living in an age that has grown up with evolutionary thought, it is difficult for us to appreciate the mental anguish created by Darwin's ideas. Howls of protest appeared everywhere. Prime Minister Disraeli announced that in the matter of apes versus angels, he was firmly on the side of the angels. And then, in one of the most famous person-to-person confrontations in the history of ideas, Thomas Huxley, a brash and brilliant defender of Darwin, debated Bishop Samuel Wilberforce. It was in 1860, at a meeting of the British Association for the Advancement of Science, and toward the end of the debate and a particularly stirring oration, Wilberforce turned to the much younger Huxley and with studied sarcasm asked whether it was through his grandfather or grandmother that he claimed to be descended from the apes. Huxley gave his famous reply:

> If the question is put to me would I rather have a miserable ape for a grandfather or a man highly endowed by nature and possessing great means and influence and yet who employs those faculties and that influence for the mere purpose of introducing ridicule into a grave scientific discussion—then I unhesitatingly affirm my preference for the ape!

Of course, Huxley had not only preference on his side but the facts as well. And those facts simply would not go away, so we lost much of our self-proclaimed pre-eminence in the animal world.

But even though we had admitted the animality of our bodies and the less than godly nature of our past, at least we still had our intellect —what the nineteenth-century Age of Reason hailed as the "crystal palace" of rationality—elevating us above the beasts. Then, in the early twentieth century, Sigmund Freud described the underlying power of the subconscious and suddenly we were stripped of our protective cerebral mantle, revealed as mere servants to the dark impulses of the irrational and the unconscious. So even the crystal palace had cracks.

Still, we continued to picture ourselves as largely under our own control, the products of whatever experiences we chose to design for ourselves. True, there were all sorts of things going on beneath the surface, but we comforted ourselves with the conviction that, by exercising judicious control over our experience, we could at least determine what occurred underneath. And now comes sociobiology, threatening yet another intellectual earthquake, revealing that our blank slate, the one assurance that we are running our own show, may have been somewhat prewritten after all.

Ever since Darwin, biologists have been exploring the implications of evolution for our understanding of life. And such is the explanatory power and persuasiveness of evolution by natural selection that Nobel prize-winning immunologist Sir Peter Medawar was led to write: "For a biologist, the alternative to thinking in evolution-ary terms is not to think at all." But, even while biologists were reveling in the insights that evolutionary theory provided for paleon-tology, anatomy, genetics and physiology, the study of behavior re-mained largely neglected. Now, however, encouraged by their other successes, biologists have finally started taking a new look at behav-ior. Crucial to this new look has been a massive, vitally important book pulling together fact and theory relating evolution and behav-ior. A truly encyclopedic work, *Sociobiology: The New Synthesis* was written by Harvard's Edward O. Wilson and was published in 1975.

Sociobiology is Wilson's name for what had previously been a loose amalgam of evolutionary theory, ecology and animal behavior. This new discipline has already been spectacularly successful in help-ing us understand the behavior of animals, but the real excitement and controversy lie ahead, in the ways that sociobiology may be applied to a very important but little-understood primate—our-selves. The intellectual traumas starting with Copernicus may have shaken our self-confidence, but they also helped us begin a process of self-revelation. Sociobiology, in the same tradition, may help us discover our own nature and allow us to eavesdrop on the whispers of biology within us all.

•

To many people, saying that a behavior is instinctive is equivalent to saying that it is "biological." The obvious alternative, of course, is for a behavior to be acquired by culture—that is, through learning—and therefore somehow "not biological." However, as we shall see, the distinction between "cultural" and "biological" is not really valid. And "instinct," the most misused term of all, has often served as a substitute for real understanding. One of sociobiology's real strengths is that it uses evolutionary theory to help us understand why behav-iors occur, without merely throwing up the smokescreen of "in-stinct."

Notions of instinct have been around for a long time, but most have been neither very plausible nor very useful. In 1924, Luther Bernard, a sociologist, read 500 books by social scientists and used them to compile a list of 5,759 distinct human instincts. Such calcula-tions served only to hasten the disrepute of human "instincts" among social scientists. More recently, the idea of human instincts has begun to regain some acceptance. Psychologist Salvadore Maddi distinguishes "core elements" from "peripheral elements" in determining human personality. In his scheme, peripheral elements result from experiences, impinging on the developing person and modifying him or her in complex ways. Core elements are the essential person, an entity bequeathed by evolution to each of us; they are the *us* upon which experience acts. The great strength of sociobiology is that its conception of the "core" is grounded in evolution, allowing us to interpret behavior according to the most potent single principle biology can offer.

Although it is not yet in the mainstream of today's social science, evolutionary thinking is not totally without allies. Since the 1960s, there have been a number of popularized accounts of human behavior, including *African Genesis, The Territorial Imperative* and *The Social Contract* by Robert Ardrey, *The Naked Ape* and *The Human Zoo* by Desmond Morris, and *On Aggression* by Konrad Lorenz. These books are similar to each other, and to this book as well, in that they view *Homo sapiens* as an animal, if a somewhat special one. However, sociobiology parts company with the Ardrey, Morris and Lorenz approach in that it is concerned less with the behavioral baggage of our primate past than with using the principles of evolution and natural selection to analyze and interpret our present.

Since understanding human behavior is of central interest, and not only to biological popularizers, it should be no surprise that a small band of anthropologists and sociologists have now begun to use sociobiology in taking a new look at their old subjects. Pierre van den Berghe of the University of Washington, Napoleon Chagnon and Jeffrey Kurland of Pennsylvania State University, Northwestern's William Irons, and the appropriately carnivorous-sounding Lionel Tiger and Robin Fox have argued that we should seek to understand the innate set of biologically-given rules that establish the boundaries of our behavior, what some call our "biogrammar." Just as the rules of our grammar let us generate an enormous number of possible sentences, the behavioral rules set in our biogrammar by evolution allow human beings to participate in an enormous number of possible behaviors. And just as grammar sets limits on language (every sentence, for example, must have subject and predicate), our biogrammar sets limits on our behavior.

There is no doubt that languages are learned and not innate. A

Kalahari bushman reared from infancy in the court of Louis XIV would have spoken impeccable French. The *capacity* for language, however, is innate and all languages conform to certain basic patterns. It is all too easy to get lost in the details of how people behave differently, thus missing the forest for the trees. What is important is that these are patterns common to all peoples, and a great deal of our behavior is but variation on a small number of themes set by evolution. It is noteworthy that all human societies have had some conception of the supernatural, although, as far as I know, only the Hottentots believed that God was a praying mantis.

Sociobiology offers some hope of going beyond the trees, of using our knowledge of the nature of trees to recognize the forest. Harvard anthropologist and sociobiologist Irven DeVore points out that by emphasizing the differences between human societies anthropology tends to look only at the icing, while ignoring the cake that lies beneath. Yet that cake is remarkably constant, among all peoples. Not only that but the nature of the cake may well constrain the possible range of icings. A chocolate filling makes it unlikely that tomato sauce will go well on top. And the process of evolution, operating on human beings, has produced a creature for whom certain behaviors just don't go at all, whereas others go very well indeed.

•

The Siriono Indians of the upper Amazon appear to think little of copulating in full view of others but may be shamed into exile if they are caught eating in public. We are very complex creatures, and in pushing evolutionary biology to explain human behavior we must not lose sight of the role of culture in making us what we are. A full picture of human behavior should include, eventually, an appropriate weighting of both environmental and biological considerations. This book cannot do the whole job, and, especially, it cannot give adequate, equal coverage to both social influences and biological ones. Ultimately, a balanced treatment should be written, but I am satisfied here to make the case for evolutionary biology, in hopes of redressing what seems to be, at present, an imbalance.

That imbalance may turn out to be more common among scientists than among humanists, many of whom are our most acute observers of human nature. Samuel Johnson claimed that Shakespeare's

genius, and the persistent success of his work, lay in its contact with
the wellsprings of humanity, transcending local norms and custom:

> His characters are not modified by the customs of particular places,
> unpracticed by the rest of the world; by the peculiarities of studies or
> professions, which can operate upon but small numbers; or by the acci-
> dents of transient fashions or temporary opinions.

And the French playwright Racine wrote:

> . . . the taste of Paris . . . conforms to that of Athens; my spectators have
> been moved by the same things which, in other times, brought tears to
> the eyes of the most cultivated classes of Greece.

Commenting on such thinking, anthropologist Clifford Geertz has
written:

> The trouble with this kind of view . . . is that the image of a constant
> human nature independent of time, place and circumstance, of studies
> and professions, transient fashions and temporary opinions, may be an
> illusion, that what man is may be so entangled with where he is, who he
> is, and what he believes that it is inseparable from them. . . . Men
> unmodified by the customs of particular places do not in fact exist, have
> never existed, and most important, could not in the very nature of the
> case exist.

In Geertz's view, which is shared by most psychologists and sociologists, there simply is no backstage where we can glimpse the
actors as they truly are, as real persons living their own private lives.
In fact, there are no actors, distinct from the roles they play.

One of the oldest and least productive debates in the history of
science has pitted "nature against nurture," "instinct against learning." This futile issue has been resolved to the satisfaction of all by
recognizing that it was a meaningless distinction in the first place, a
pseudo-problem. There is no behavior without "nature" (that is,
there must be an organism) and there is no behavior without "nurture" (all organisms grow up and live in an environment). Nature and
nurture work together at all times, and all behavior emerges from
the interaction of these two.

But this does not mean that nature and nurture are fictions, just
because we are unable to separate them clearly. Imagine two people
wrestling underneath a carpet. It may be impossible to say who's
winning and it may even be difficult to distinguish one person from

something is obviously going on.

there is no "us" located inside, beneath or
e are in danger of missing ourselves alto-
erned about human dignity I would happily
gical recognition of human nature grounded
xtreme social science view that people are
ting for culture to fill them up, ghostly actors

e. Whatever truth it carries is always relative
nts at particular times and, when it becomes
ably extinction. It is a sobering thought that
f the species that ever lived are now extinct.
But culture is no guarantor of success either. Consider this, from
social scientist Weston LaBarre:

> No morality is an absolute, the safely proven, the caught bird with salt
> on its tail. It is the chosen and hoped-for, a loyalty that is man's burden,
> his glory and his cross. For in the last analysis every culture is a moral
> geometry—a system not inalternatively embedded in the physical world,
> but a contingent means of triangulating one's course through reality. But
> a culture is also the immortality of dead men, a way in which their
> judgments and choices manage to coerce the living. Still, all men, includ-
> ing dead men, can be wrong.

Insofar as human beings share the same biology, we are all one,
and there should be a fundamental sense in which we all recognize
each other and understand each other's behavior. Culture contributes to this, enhancing communication among those of similar experience, helping them to develop the same vocabulary. But it has the
opposite effect between groups, increasing the behavioral distance
that separates people of different backgrounds.

Choose any two people at random. Except for identical twins,
they are bound to be different, carrying different genes even if they
grew up in the same culture. If these two people are from different
cultures, the differences between them will be greater yet, perhaps
even lethal. Incredibly, the atomic bomb may have been dropped on
Japan because a news agency incorrectly translated the word *mokusatsu* as "ignore" rather than "withhold comment (pending delibera-
tion)." This was the official diplomatic response of the Japanese cabi-
net to the Potsdam surrender ultimatum, and presumably it meant

that a decision, possibly a favorable one, would soon have been reached, whereas it was interpreted by President Truman as an outright rejection.

Biology and culture undoubtedly work together, but it is tempting to speculate that our biology is somehow more real, lying unnoticed within each of us, quietly but forcefully manipulating much of our behavior. Culture, which is overwhelmingly important in shaping the myriad details of our lives, is more likely seen as a thin veneer, compared to the underlying ground substance of our biology.

In William Golding's *Lord of the Flies*, a group of English boys, shipwrecked on an island, gradually descend to primitive—and violent—tribal ways. Interestingly, when a movie was made of this book, threats of violence developed among the young actors endangering their own safety as well as the progress of the film. In a strange case of reality following art, the boy playing "Piggy," a victim in the story, feared that he really would be killed. Director Peter Brook commented: "My experience showed me that the only falsification in Golding's fable is the length of time the descent to savagery takes. I believe that if the cork of continued adult presence were removed from the bottle, the complete catastrophe could occur within a long weekend."

Sociobiology will probably have little to tell us about why we select a blue necktie or a red one, but a great deal about why we choose to adorn our bodies in the first place; very little about why we vote Democratic or Republican, but a great deal about why we choose to have leaders in the first place; very little about the details of our lives, which are largely determined by learning, by chance, or by the whims of custom, but a great deal about why, underneath it all, we act like human beings.

Sociobiology has already been enormously successful in applying evolutionary thinking to the behavior of animals. And, while some feel that things should stop there, it may well be worth applying the same analytic tools to human behavior. Do we really know ourselves so well that no further help is needed? Those concerned with understanding our infinitely complicated species know full well that they need all the help they can get.

If those who apply sociobiology to humans seem arrogant in doing so, think of the greater arrogance of refusing such aid. Of course, we may end up hearing some things about ourselves we would just as soon not know. That's not sociobiology's fault, though. Its role is to help us understand our nature, not to legitimize our foibles. No claim is made that what is natural is therefore good. "Smallpox is natural," Ogden Nash pointed out. "Vaccine ain't." And there is very little good that anyone can see in smallpox.

Although science is ideally value-free, the motives of scientists are often less pure. In the years following World War II and the atomic bomb, many disillusioned physicists turned their attention to biology in the hope of finding a less destructive outlet for their talents. Max Delbruck, who later won a Nobel Prize in Physiology and Medicine, warned physicists in 1949 that they would probably be less successful at unraveling the living cell than they had already been at figuring out the atom, since "any one cell, embodying as it does the record of a billion years of evolution, represents more a historical than a physical event. . . . You cannot expect to explain so wise an old bird in a few simple words." If physicist-turned-biologist Delbruck was awed by the complex structures of single cells, how much more awesome are whole animals, let alone human beings? And then what of behavior, which is even more variable and mysterious? Delbruck was right: every product of evolution is a wise old bird, not easily understood. And we, even though our pedigree is not especially old, are perhaps the wisest and most complicated birds of all.

The fact of complexity is not a reason for despair. In the early 1950s, an eminent biochemist stated that, because heredity was obviously very complicated, it was useless to hope that a single type of molecule would be "the" genetic material. Less than eighteen months later, James Watson and Francis Crick announced the structure of DNA. We must, as Delbruck said, use more than just "a few simple words" to talk about human behavior, and we are not even going to undertake to explain it—at least, not all of it. But, just as cells are subject to the laws of physics, and physicists have been able to enrich our understanding of life greatly, so all living things, including human beings, are subject to the laws of evolution. Then it may well be that sociobiology can enrich our understanding of ourselves and why we do many of the things that we do. Anyhow, it seems worth making a try.

2

Where We Stand: Alcoholic Mice and Why Sugar Is Sweet

In the beginning was the gene.

It made its appearance about six billion years ago, sloshing around in what biologists call the "organic soup," a broth, rich in chemicals, found along the shores of the earth's ancient seas. From the geological record it appears that initially the soup's major ingredients were hydrogen, ammonia, methane and water vapor. Not a very appealing mixture; poisonous, in fact, to most living things today. But it was these chemicals that gave rise to us all. Experiments have shown that when they are combined in a laboratory, exposed to ultraviolet radiation (to simulate the early sun), and jolted by electric sparks (lightning), something important happens: organic molecules are formed, including some of the essential amino acids, which are the building blocks of proteins. And, under certain circumstances, even purines and pyrimidines, the components of nucleic acids—the basic units of heredity—have been formed.

In the primeval soup, the first organic molecules bounced continually against one another, absorbing energy from the sun, lightning, and possibly heat from volcanoes. Often they broke apart, then reunited, only to form again what they had been before. But occasionally they combined in novel ways, perhaps joining fragments never connected before and thereby producing something new and infinitely more precious—life. It is not at all clear at what point such complex molecules became "alive." However, since all living things can reproduce (in fact, the ability to do so is one of the consistent defining properties of life), a complex organic molecule began, in effect, to live when it began to reproduce.

There are many ways in which primitive life could have made copies of itself. Consider one: let us picture a complex molecule as A–B–C–D, with the letters each representing different components of the molecule and the dashes representing linkages (chemical bonds) between them. Some of the components the same as themselves. They have, however, even stronger affinity for certain other specific components, which we will identify here as the letters adjacent to them in the alphabet. These patterns of affinity occur in part because of the shapes of the molecular components and in part because of the way their different electrical charges attract and repel each other.

So, then, imagine that we have one molecule of A–B–C–D, floating around in our primeval alphabet soup, along with many other loose As, Bs, and so on. Some of the loose components begin to join with others, perhaps forming long, dull chains such as A–A–A–A or B–B–B–B. But occasionally a loose one, say a C, may come blundering by and be snapped up by A–B–C–D, which thereby becomes A–B–C–D. Some time later, a loose A may be-
$$\begin{array}{c}\text{A–B–C–D}\\ \quad\;\;|\\ \quad\;\;\text{C}\end{array}$$
come incorporated, thus forming A–B–C–D. Eventually, all the avail-
$$\begin{array}{c}\text{A–B–C–D}\\ |\quad\;\;|\\ \text{A}\quad\text{C}\end{array}$$
able spots in our initial sticky molecule become filled. As a result, the molecule A–B–C–D has become A–B–C–D.*
$$\begin{array}{c}\text{A–B–C–D}\\ |\;\;|\;\;|\;\;|\\ \text{A B C D}\end{array}$$
But there is still more to the story, as all components have a very strong affinity for the next ones in sequence. So the A–B–C–D ar-
$$\begin{array}{c}\text{A–B–C–D}\\ |\;\;|\;\;|\;\;|\\ \text{A B C D}\end{array}$$
rangement becomes A–B–C–D. Now, we know that the components
$$\begin{array}{c}\text{A–B–C–D}\\ |\;\;|\;\;|\;\;|\\ \text{A–B–C–D}\end{array}$$
tend to have stronger bonds with the next ones in sequence than with identical copies of themselves—that is, A sticks more strongly to B than it does to another A. So, when there occurs some sort of jarring of the system—physical agitation, perhaps, or ultraviolet radi-

*Of course, many other arrangements might also arise, such as
$$\begin{array}{c}\text{A B C}\\ |\;\;|\;\;|\\ \text{A–B–C–D}\end{array},\text{ or}$$
$$\begin{array}{c}\text{A–B–C –D}\\ |\;\;|\;\;|\\ \text{B C D}\end{array}$$
with D.

ation or electrical sparks—the weaker A–A, B–B, C–C and D–D bonds rupture, leaving two A–B–C–D molecules where we had started with one. Diagrammatically, this is what occurs:

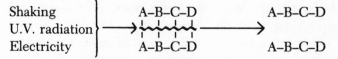

Something terribly exciting has happened: We have the essential ingredient of life. British zoologist Richard Dawkins calls these early molecules "replicators." As time passes, some of these replicators will prove to be more efficient than others at making copies of themselves and, therefore, their numbers will increase in the soup. Of course, changes in the makeup of these replicators will occur from time to time, as, unavoidably, errors are made in the matchups. There are other components floating around—E, F, G and so forth—so that A–E–C–D may appear, if a parent A–B–C–D makes a mistake and a B accidentally sticks to an E instead of another B. This new combination will probably be less stable than A–B–C–D; but it may persist for a while. So diversity arises from simplicity. Some of the new replicators are successful, some aren't. The poor combinations disappear, the better ones become dominant and are evolutionary success stories. What makes a replicator better? A good guess would be its ability to attract loose molecules, to break and reform bonds appropriately and relatively rapidly, and to copy itself accurately.

So far in our story, each new molecular individual is functioning pretty much on its own, devouring a little bit of the organic soup in the process of copying itself. But there hasn't been much in the way of pushing or shoving. Eventually, however, something nasty—but no less natural—begins to intrude on this idyllic scene: competition. As the free components are incorporated into the different molecules, shortages begin to develop. Our old friend A–B–C–D, for example, may begin to compete with B–C–D–E for the dwindling supply of component C. There need be no active fight about it, but nonetheless one type could be consistently more successful than the other. If this happens, we can say that natural selection is occurring, and the winners—the forms that persist and increase over time—are those that are better "adapted."

Adaptation is a very important concept in evolutionary biology. It refers to the ability of a living thing to function well in its environment. And the ultimate measure of such functioning is how successful an individual is in replicating itself, while others are trying independently to do the same. Eventually, however, the competition must have become more direct and less gentlemanly. If you are molecule A–B–C–D, and there is a shortage of C, why shouldn't you capture it directly from a B–C–D–E or C–D–E–F that happens to cross your path? A molecule that does so will be replicating itself more successfully than one that doesn't.

But let's not get lost in a symbolic world of letters, for this is no dry, intellectual game—it is the blood-and-guts reality of life itself. The model just presented is only one possible scenario for the origin of life, but however it really happened, it seems clear that nonliving molecules somehow aggregated themselves and began reproducing. Initially, they lived like scavengers, simply using up the organic soup of which they were a very special part. Then, at some point, as the soup became thinner, some of these molecules found themselves with the ability to break up other molecules and to use their chemical components—that is, to "eat" them. Since we are now dealing with living things, we can correctly say that these destroyer molecules "killed" other molecules. They were the first animals, since they obtained their basic materials by breaking down other molecules.

Of course, not all the potential prey remained helpless. Some were able to defend themselves, and, in evolutionary terms, those that did had an advantage over those that did not. There were many defensive techniques, of which perhaps the simplest was for the molecules to encapsulate themselves within a protective shell, likely made of protein. Although walled off from the surrounding world— once nurturing, now become dangerous—the replicators still had to meet their needs of nutrition and reproduction. Those that succeeded did so because they gradually incorporated the necessary materials and survival mechanisms within their walls. These new-style molecules had tiny pores in their sheaths to allow nutrients to flow in and waste products to flow out; sensors to detect favorable or unfavorable aspects of the environment; tiny hairs or lashing whips to make movement possible; and even devices that enabled some of the replicators to combine with others and produce new individuals.

The first cells were formed, and sex reared its complicated head. Replicators competed with other replicators to house and protect themselves, and occasionally to attract other replicators. Eventually, these individual, one-celled survival machines combined with other similar units, and these multicellular plants and animals were often more successful yet. In his book, *The Selfish Gene,* Richard Dawkins describes the consequences with appropriate drama:

> Was there to be any end to the gradual improvement in the techniques and artifices used by the replicators to ensure their own continuance in the world? There would be plenty of time for improvement. What weird engines of self-preservation would the millennia bring forth? Four thousand million years on, what was to be the fate of the ancient replicators? They did not die out, for they are past masters of the survival arts. But do not look for them floating loose in the sea; they gave up that cavalier freedom long ago. Now they swarm in huge colonies, safe inside gigantic lumbering robots, sealed off from the outside world, communicating with it by tortuous indirect routes, manipulating it by remote control. They are in you and in me; they created us, body and mind; and their preservation is the ultimate rationale for our existence. They have come a long way, those replicators. Now they go by the name of genes, and we are their survival machines.

So life probably started as simple molecules that joined to form more complex molecules, some of which eventually began replicating themselves. In the ensuing melee (which probably lasted several billion years) certain replicating molecules were successful because they enclosed themselves in protective structures that we now identify as plants or animals—even that very special kind of animal, human beings. And the replicators are now called genes.

They are still playing the old game, of course—making copies of themselves—although the rules keep changing as they reappear through the generations in newer and newer models off the evolutionary assembly line. But nothing in nature is perfect, and sometimes, even now, one of these genes will make a mistake when it copies itself (as with the A-B-C-D molecule that accidentally produced A-E-C-D). This sort of mistake is a mutation, and in most cases it is harmful to the other genes and to the body on which they all rely. Mutations generally hurt rather than help, because genes and their bodies are highly nonrandom, descended as they are from combinations of elements that are proven successes. They have maintained themselves despite the many stresses of competition and unintentional efforts of the nonliving world to break them down. So, introducing a random change into this highly-organized system is like kicking a television set to improve its performance: an act unlikely to be beneficial. On the other hand, just occasionally, such a random act might help a loose connection make contact and sharpen the picture. A successful organism is one that is more successful at reproducing its genes. Most mutations do not enhance gene reproduction, and we say these are selected against, but some, occasionally, are helpful, and we say they are selected for.

As time goes on, living things jostle with each other more and more to excel in passing on genes. Or, to describe it from the gene's viewpoint, genes that are able to construct bodies with characteristics that make them successful will themselves be successful. New genes arise by mutation, are reshuffled with other genes during sexual reproduction, and appear in a wide variety of combinations every time a new living thing is produced. Some of these living things are more successful in reproducing themselves than are others, and, to some extent, the difference in success between these individuals will be due to the differences in the genes they are carrying. Just as an all-star team is composed of the best players at each position, living things come to be composed of individual genes each of which tend to have consistently high batting averages in the game of reproduction.

The sifting and winnowing that occur over time as some bodies are more successful than others in perpetuating their genes we call *natural selection*. The result of this process is a change in the nature of the genes and the bodies in which they appear from one generation to the next. We call this change *evolution*.

•

As Samuel Butler pointed out, a chicken is but an egg's way of making more eggs. A more modern view might be that a chicken is a device invented by chicken genes to enhance the likelihood of more chicken genes being projected into the future. People are similar devices—temporary, skin-encapsulated egos, serving as complex tools by means of which their potentially immortal genes replicate themselves.

Natural selection is happening whenever some individuals produce more successful offspring than others, which is another way of saying that some genes are making more copies of themselves than are others. In other words, individuals and genes differ from other individuals and genes in their *fitness*—how successful they are at projecting copies of themselves into future generations. Those that are more successful we call more "fit."

The fit—not the meek—have already inherited the earth. This is not to espouse cutthroat competition or dog-eat-dog nastiness. The fact is that fitness may be achieved in many different ways, of which the most important are probably the least eye-catching—keeping the body going, avoiding temperature excesses, getting enough to eat and so on. Although success in all these activities requires a great deal of complex organization, and although a clear-cut goal is achieved— maximum fitness—neither the genes nor their carriers need have any picture of what they are doing, or why. They simply do their job, and natural selection does the rest. A gene that produces gills would be more fit in a fish than in a human being.

One of the new insights of sociobiology is that fitness, mediated by natural selection, is not limited to such relatively simple factors as the structure or functioning of a body. It also includes complex social behaviors, such as courting, fighting, associating with friends and caring for offspring. It turns out that, in general, individuals that function better socially are better perpetuators of their genes (that is, are maximally fit) and are more favored by natural selection than those that don't.

Notice that the focus in all our discussions is intensely selfish, focusing on the individual and not on the species. This emphasis runs counter to most people's conception of evolution: that it proceeds for the benefit of the species. This is a crucial point: it does nothing of the sort. It proceeds because some genes, organized into individuals, are more successful in reproducing themselves than are other genes, organized into other individuals. Picture two individuals of the same species, faced with the same predicament—let us say, a dangerous predator has appeared and is attacking others of the species. What will our hypothetical individuals do? They can help their species by rushing to the aid of their colleagues or they can help themselves, by rushing in the other direction. Since fighting with a predator involves a real risk, individuals that do so will, on average, be less fit than others that selfishly look out for themselves. From the gene's perspective, those genes which induce their bodies to benefit the species but at some net cost to the genes themselves will leave fewer copies of themselves in the next generation than will the selfish ones. In this sense, evolution is an extraordinarily selfish process. As we shall see throughout these explorations, this fundamental selfishness has profound implications for human behavior.

Imagine that one's genes are like playing cards, ace through king (in reality, there are something like one million such cards). Now let us deal out hands to two individuals, such that each gets two aces, two deuces and so on, up to two kings, a total of twenty-six cards per person. The rules state that each hand of cards must contain two of each rank, but the suits may be the same or different. This is analogous to our genetic system, in which everyone has two sets of chromosomes (forty-six in all), each chromosome having a space for one ace, one deuce and so on, up to one king, while its matching chromosome also has one matching space for each denomination. These cards are in competition with each other, the king of clubs, for example, struggling with the kings of diamonds, hearts and spades to project copies of itself into future generations—that is, into the next hands to be dealt out. As you might expect, some are more successful than others.

Picture the scene: the king of clubs influences its carrier to do something that contributes to the carrier's success in reproducing— let us say, it makes it better able to capture prey, or defend its young, or attract a mate. By contrast, the kings of hearts, spades and diamonds are able to exercise a less favorable effect. What happens? In our example, since individuals holding the king of clubs are more successful at capturing prey, defending their young or wooing mates, they are also more successful at reproducing. If we were to look at many such hands dealt out over a long period of time, we would find that the king of clubs would become increasingly abundant, since those combinations including the king of clubs were reproducing more successfully than were those combinations lacking that card.

In other words, natural selection will favor those genes that operate to increase their own numbers in succeeding generations. The prevailing strategy of each gene is to make the best deal it can to insure that copies of itself will occur in the future. Indeed, when we consider living things, we find only those individuals whose genes have been successful. Of course, the simplest way to insure this success is to reproduce and to reproduce well. By "well" I do not simply mean in large numbers, since a larger number of inadequately cared-for—and hence feeble—offspring may represent a losing strategy compared to the production of a smaller number each of which is better endowed and hence more likely to succeed.

Even with the production of fine, robust offspring, living things are not guaranteed evolutionary success. Fitness is always relative to the environment and the environment is always changing. For example, in a frequently cited case, a delicate light-gray moth was abundant in English forests for thousands of moth generations. It blended in beautifully with the light-gray tree trunks. Black mutants occurred occasionally, and, because they didn't blend, were almost invariably eaten by birds. Then, with the Industrial Revolution, things changed: soot darkened the tree trunks, revealing the formerly protected light-gray moths to their sharp-eyed predators, while the black forms —now well camouflaged—were suddenly the fit ones. In less than one hundred years, light-gray moths virtually disappeared from industrial areas of Britain, as evolution quickly favored the black ones. More recently, the pendulum has swung once more: with increasingly effective air pollution control since the mid-1960s, British forests are regaining their pristine gray trunks and natural selection is once again favoring the light-gray moths.

The point is that evolution is always becoming and never arriving. Certainly it all started many millions of years ago, but it hasn't stopped since. As the Red Queen pointed out to Alice, so long as the world is changing, we have to keep moving, just to stay where we are. And if we want to get anyplace, we must go even faster yet.

As do all other living things, people get ahead in evolution by passing on their genes to the next generation. Every time a person reproduces, he or she passes on half of its genes to the child. Using our earlier analogy, one ace, one deuce and so on are chosen at random; the hand combined forms an egg or a sperm. When these genes unite with the packaged genes from an individual of the opposite sex, somebody new is produced, carrying one-half of the replicated genes from each parent. There is only one way that natural selection can get a handle on the success of our genes: by the success of the bodies that carry them. Evolution is a process of gene replication, and it has no interest in what we do, except insofar as our behavior contributes, either positively or negatively, to this replication. And, in fact, everything we do, from relaxing, to working, fighting, eating—indeed, everything we do—does have consequences for reproduction, even though sometimes these consequences may seem small and almost inconsequential.

By reproducing, we replicate our genes. Parental behavior, then, in all animals—including humans—occurs because it represents the successful strategy of constituent genes in reproducing themselves. A genetic basis for intentional childlessness would have a dim evolutionary future indeed!

The plain fact is that genes have been selected for success in looking out for themselves, and they accomplish this by making copies of themselves. Making babies is their major way of doing that— although not the only way, as we will see in chapter five. Even reproducing is merely a special case of the more general evolutionary requirement of selfishness. Parental love itself is actually but an evolutionary strategy whereby genes replicate themselves. They do so by inducing the parents (their bodies) to behave in ways that enhance the success of their offspring. That is, the love of parent for child is one way that genes look after copies of themselves, encapsulated within other bodies, called children. Of course, our genes don't think, much less plan strategies. But they act as though they do.

We humans are self-conscious animals. Accordingly, we have difficulty conceiving of processes affecting us intimately which are neither conscious nor motivated. Yet most things in nature happen without anybody willing them, including a great deal of our own behavior. No one consciously tells his or her heart to beat or stomach to digest. Similarly, genes need not know what they are doing in order to function effectively, and—here is the painful part—neither need we. We can spend a whole lifetime serving their purposes without ever knowing it.

A guiding principle of sociobiology is that individuals tend to behave in a manner that maximizes their fitness. The result is a very strange sort of purposefulness, in which a goal—maximization of fitness—appears to be sought, but without any of the participants necessarily having awareness of what they are doing, or why. This is because the genes housed within each person have been selected to be maximally effective in projecting copies of themselves into the future. Those that were less effective fell by the wayside of evolutionary time, while those that were more effective kept right on going. Whether they knew it or not.

•

In general, there seems to be something artificial about separating the individual from its genes. After all, the two really are the same living thing. On the other hand, as the minds of certain Yoga masters reputedly can, genes can literally go outside their body; in that sense, they have an independent existence. They are not only potentially immortal, they may also be stubbornly cantankerous in their pursuit of their own maximal fitness.

Medical genetics provides a striking—and tragic—example of the fitness-enhancing strategies of genes. Huntington's chorea is a hereditary disease which in its best-known form strikes people around age twenty-five or older. It is a terrible affliction of the nervous system in which the victim's brain almost literally dissolves over time. And it is invariably fatal. One of its best-known sufferers was the great American folk singer and writer Woody Guthrie. As it happens, Huntington's chorea is produced by a single gene (technically known as an "autosomal dominant") so that, on average, one-half of a sufferer's offspring will contract the disease and therefore die themselves. Since the gene arises very rarely by mutation, and since it is ultimately fatal, we would expect it to disappear eventually in any population—it should be selected against, and strongly.

However, here is the striking finding: before they begin to reveal symptoms of the disease, people carrying the Huntington's gene are often sexually promiscuous. This may help explain why male Huntington's patients tend to have higher reproductive rates than normal people, and also why copies of the gene persist in the population. It is an unpleasant story but a dramatic and pointed case of a gene inducing its carrier to behave in ways that increase its own opportunities for replication. The Huntington's gene is disadvantageous to society, the species, even to the afflicted individual. It is dangerous to everything except itself. But that reproductive self-benefit has been sufficient to keep it around. It looks after its own fitness.

The Huntington's gene is stuck in the same rat race as all our other genes, the eternal evolutionary struggle to get ahead. This is a consuming task, with no greater purpose than to keep playing. We are all sitting at a cosmic poker game in which the house has an infinite supply of chips. Neither we nor our genes can ever really win, since we can never cash in our chips and go home. As for the compulsive gambler, there is nothing but the game, and since it has been going on for a long time, only the best players are left. It is an existential game, the only one in town, and all we can do is stay in as long as possible. We are all playing, so perhaps we may as well enjoy it. Certainly we should understand it.

●

When Zeus was struck in the forehead with an axe, the goddess Athena leaped forth, fully armored, brandishing her sword and shield. Some people think of behavior that way—residing somehow "within" a gene, ready to spring out, fully armed and ready to go. It doesn't work that way. Behavior patterns develop gradually, through an interaction between the instructions encoded on an organism's genes and the environmental realities that it encounters.

If you had been a biologist several centuries ago, the chances are you would have been either a "spermist" or an "ooist." Spermists believed that a tiny human being—a homunculus—lived within each sperm, and was released when contact was made with the egg. Ooists disagreed: the miniature person was obviously in the egg, waiting to escape when the sperm punctured its membrane. Both, of course, were wrong. Living things develop after the union of genetic material from sperm and egg, via constant interaction with their environment. So there is no homunculus, sealed off from the rest of the world and developing on its own. Rather, life is a process—a constant interaction between potential (genes) and the reality they experience (environment).

Genes are merely blueprints, and sometimes remarkably incomplete ones. This is because in the evolution of life genes have progressively given up direct control of their affairs. They no longer float freely, naked in the organic soup. Quite early, the world got far too rough for that. Instead, as we have seen, genes began to produce devices we call bodies to look out for their affairs. Their evolutionary fate is now determined by the bodies they have helped to create.

Actually, there are only two things genes can do: provide directions for the manufacture of proteins, and make more genes. Since proteins are the basic stuff of every animal body, by directing the structure of the body, genes can contribute to accomplishing their second goal—reproducing themselves. This they do by supplying the blueprints that lead ultimately to the form and functioning of such important adaptive structures as heart, lungs, teeth, liver—indeed, all the components of a living thing that we identify as "it." Clearly, these structures are important if the genes are to survive and replicate themselves: nutrients must be pumped around efficiently, waste products removed thoroughly, and so forth. The body must be kept whole and functioning, if the evolutionary game is to be played well, or indeed at all.

But good bodies alone do not guarantee evolutionary success. Bodies must also *behave* in the right way—that is, adaptively. They must do the things that increase their fitness through promoting successful reproduction by offspring or others of the species carrying similar genes. Living things must behave adaptively—select good mates, reproduce successfully with them, care for their young, look out for relatives, avoid predators, help certain individuals and be helped in turn, compete when it is in their interests to do so, and do a host of other crucial things.

But how can genes do all this? Out in the real world where bodies live, it is individuals who behave, ñot genes. But, just as genes provide a blueprint for the production of heart, gonads, liver and kidneys, they also code for the manufacture of the human brain. The path from genes to structure is tortuous and never a simple, straight line, but there *is* a path, and the one from genes to brain is not different from any other developmental path. Behavior arises from the functioning of the brain and the rest of the nervous system. When the brain works, we behave, just as when the teeth work, we chew, when the eyes work, we see, and when it all stops working we die.

When we say that bone structure is somehow "in our genes," we mean that genes carry directions for producing bone structure, although with considerable room for modification depending upon the environment encountered during the building process. When we say that a behavior is "in our genes," we mean exactly the same thing, except that bones depend largely on the distribution of certain compounds of calcium and phosphorus and brains depend largely on the distribution of nerve cells. There is a big difference, though. Once bones are completed, that's that, the job is more or less finished. But, when the brain is completed, it still must do a great deal in order to carry out its function. It must help the body to behave, bones and all.

In a sense, our genes speak to our behavior second hand—through the medium of our bodies. Sometimes the path from gene to behavior may be relatively simple, as with the blinking in response to a loud noise or the knee-jerk response when the patellar tendon is struck. In other cases, the path may be very diffuse, and environmental influences may play a major role, as in the development of artistic sense or one or another personality trait. Once again, individuals behave, not genes, but the behaviors reflect strategies that the genes have evolved for replicating themselves: find food, of the right sort and the right amounts; find mates, also of the right sort and the right numbers; care for your children and compete with others, if that suits your interests. Any way you choose to see it, the fact is we tend to do things that maximize our fitness. This is the central principle of sociobiology: insofar as a behavior reflects at least some component of gene action, individuals will tend to behave so as to maximize their fitness.

Of course, this principle applies only when a behavior occurs in circumstances similar to those in which it originally evolved. For this reason, we are relying here more heavily on the findings of anthropology to describe human behavior than on either sociology or psychology. Our species evolved very slowly, during the millions of years before agriculture, technology and writing. We lived in small groups close to nature, probably relatively isolated from other groups. By and large, psychologists and sociologists study modern, industrialized peoples—those of us living in new, complex worlds to which we are likely to be biological strangers. Anthropologists, to be sure, also study modern people, but they are generally more aware of our diversity and, hence, in a better position to identify underlying common patterns, the so-called behavioral universals that are the heritage of all *Homo sapiens.* In addition, it also seems intuitively reasonable that the behavior of Australian aborigines or Kalahari Bushmen, for example, is more indicative of earlier humanity than is the behavior of the Pentagon or General Motors.

It should surprise no one that we lack an instinctive avoidance of X-rays even though too much radiation causes cancer, or that most of us ride elevators even when it may be better for our hearts if we use the stairs. X-rays and elevators simply were not part of our evolutionary past. Nonetheless, evolution almost certainly has important consequences for our behavior—right here and right now.

•

Sociobiological theory says that a decision about behavior should be made by considering its potential consequences for the fitness of the one making the decision.* Of course, this evaluation is not conscious or intentional; it comes from the fact that in the past a variety of individuals existed, representing a variety of genes. As a result, a variety of different "decisions" were made. Those who decided correctly left more copies of themselves (that is, were more fit) than did those whose decisions were less inspired. As evolution proceeds there will automatically be an increase in any genes that code for behaviors that will give them an advantage over other genes. The upshot is that populations tend to become composed of individuals each of whom is inclined to "good" decisions—that is, they are descended from combinations of genes that made fitness-enhancing decisions in the past.

Recent work by Daniel Janzen, one of our most creative ecologists, emphasizes that evolution does not require any conscious intent on the part of the individuals involved. Janzen has pointed out that even plants "perform courtship displays, rape, promiscuity, and fickleness just as do animals." This is no mere whimsy by a plant lover. For example, plants with male flowers will "attempt" to achieve as many fertilizations as possible. How is this done? Among other things, they bombard female flowers with incredible amounts of pollen, and some even seem to have specially evolved capacities to rape female flowers, by growing a pollen tube which forces its way to the ovary within each female. At the same time, female flowers may possess defenses which insure that only the best pollen is successful. What is in this for the female? In other words, why is she so "fussy"? As we shall see in the next chapter, just as sexual aggressiveness is generally to be expected among males, sexual persnicketiness is generally to be expected among females, and plants are no exception.

Even germs behave in ways that maximize their fitness. In a research report entitled "Why Fruits Rot, Seeds Mold and Meat Spoils," Janzen shows how the noxious characteristics of rot, mold and spoilage are produced by microorganisms that generate unpleasant and often poisonous chemicals. Have you ever asked yourself

---

*In a sense, this is analogous to what cyberneticists (specialists in the mathematics of decision theory) call "feed-forward" control—a situation in which something is influenced by the *expected* consequences of some particular act. Of course, in practice, "knowledge" of these consequences has accumulated over evolutionary time, as different responses have been tried by different organisms, with the successful (that is, the fit) persisting and the unsuccessful being selected against.

why rotten meat is bad for you? Why do bacteria and molds bother to make chemicals that taste bad and make us ill? The answer is simply that by doing so they keep us from eating their food—and themselves. Bacteria genes "want" to live and reproduce in that old, stale pot of soup.* Our genes, naturally, have other plans; they want their host bodies to eat the soup, that is, to convert it into more of themselves. If enough bacteria get there first, they do what they can to keep us from getting into the act.

Plants that commit rape and bacteria that spoil food are following evolutionary strategies that maximize their fitness. And, clearly, in neither case do the actors know what they are doing, or why. We human beings like to think we are different. We introspect, we are confident that we know what we are doing, and why. But we may have to open our minds and admit the possibility that our need to maximize our fitness may be whispering somewhere deep within us and that, know it or not, most of the time we are heeding these whisperings.

For example, consider one of the most important decisions anyone ever makes: "Who should be the father (or mother) of my children?" Let us make the simplifying assumption that from the viewpoint of a woman's fitness all men can be divided into two categories —those who will contribute to her producing successful offspring, and those who will not. Let us assume further that there is some genetic influence (however slight) over that woman's choice. It is easy to compare the evolutionary fate of those women (and their genes) who choose the fitness-enhancing man with those who choose men in the other category. Women who choose men who enhance their own fitness will necessarily have more successful offspring than will the others. Accordingly, more of their genes will also be found in the next generation. Therefore, women should evolve a preference for mating with those men who will most contribute to their (that is, the women's) fitness. Of course, a similar process should also apply to men. As we shall see in the next chapter, there are in fact many traits in a prospective mate for which we expect men and women to be especially attuned. In other words, there

*It should be clear that bacteria don't really "want" anything, although they behave as though they do. Because evolution produces apparently purposeful behavior without necessarily producing conscious purposefulness, it will often be convenient to use short-cut words that suggest rational motivation or desires. Such anthropomorphisms are for simplicity only.

seems to be a biological wisdom in what "turns us on."

It should be apparent by now that sociobiology is somewhat unusual in the way that it explains things. Take its approach, for example, to the question "Why do people have children?" That seems simple enough, but not only is the answer complicated, even the question can be interpreted in several different ways. Thus we could say that we have children because a sperm fertilizes an egg, or because we love and want children, or because we can't help it, since copulating produces children and copulating is all a matter of hormones. And we would be right in every case. However, all these are proximal explanations—they deal with immediate causes. We should also be interested in considering the evolutionary reasons for a behavior—in this case, having children.

Why do people have children? An evolutionary answer would start by pointing out that we are all the offspring of parents who themselves had children . . . and so did their parents, and their parents before that, and so on. Indeed, if we trace back the ancestry of anyone alive today (or who has ever lived) we find that he or she is bound to be the offspring of parents who successfully reproduced. A guaranteed unbroken line. No one was ever the child of someone who didn't reproduce. Accordingly, any genetic tendency to reproduce would be strongly selected.

This particular example does not actually provide us with much intellectual leverage for understanding ourselves, except it does suggest that Planned Parenthood, Zero Population Growth, and other organizations concerned with curbing the world's population may have tackled an even bigger problem than they appreciate.

Let's try again. Why do we breathe? There are several different proximal explanations: because an increase in carbon dioxide in our blood is sensed by our brain; because that part of our brain communicates with our diaphragm and chest muscles; because we are so large that our body cells cannot exchange oxygen and carbon dioxide directly by minute tubes leading directly to the outside, as do insects. Once again, these explanations are all correct. But what about the adaptive explanation of breathing? In this case, it's easy: Why do we breathe? Because our body requires oxygen and is poisoned by an excess of waste products, an efficient system for exchanging these substances has been strongly selected for. That is the adaptive significance of breathing—it has a lot to do with our fitness.

We will be encountering more controversial examples during our explorations ahead. For now, it is enough to know that sociobiology involves a different way of thinking about things, a way that is novel for most of us.

"Very nice," says someone looking at an abstract painting, "but is it art?" Looking at modern sociobiology, the observer might well ask, "Very nice, but is it science?" Yes, it is. Aristotle wrote that falling objects accelerate because they become more "jubilant" as they approach the earth. Newton improved on this with his laws of gravity. When social scientists ask people the reasons for some particular behavior, they often get the answer "Because it is the custom," and although researchers tend to disdain this explanation, they frequently explore the matter no further themselves. In many ways, "custom" has become in modern social science the equivalent of Aristotle's "jubilation," and it is one of sociobiology's goals to improve on this.

Western science tends to be reductionist, always seeking to explain things by breaking them into smaller and smaller parts. This is a good way to proceed, but it is not the only way. Reductionism is why we presently know so much more about cells than about ecosystems, perhaps to our peril. Sociobiology reverses the perspective, looking outward toward the larger world and seeking to place behavior in its context of evolution and the complex, interacting network of life.* Proximal analysis deals with the immediate factors that operate within an individual to produce a particular behavior. Evolutionary analysis asks about the behavior's adaptive significance: why do the proximate mechanisms occur in the first place? The great astronomer Johannes Kepler said: "We must understand why things are as they are, and not otherwise." As sociobiologists view behavior, there may be many different proximate means to the same ultimate, evolutionary end, which is the maximization of fitness.

•

Among the Azande of Africa, male witches inherit their "witchcraft substance" from their fathers and women get it from their mothers.

---

*It might be argued that sociobiology also is reductionistic in that it looks for a cellular—in fact, a genetic—basis for behavior. However, sociobiology is typically more concerned with the adaptive significance of the genetically-influenced behavior (the *why*) rather than the proximal question of *how* that behavior is produced, which is the realm of genetics.

It is, according to the tribesmen, a "round, hairy ball with teeth," and it is invariably found in the intestines of a witch. (Unfortunately, the diagnosis is always by a post-mortem!) Modern biologists take a somewhat different view of the inheritance of behavior. The study of behavior genetics is crucial to sociobiology, since sociobiology is the study of natural selection's influence on social behavior, and natural selection can only have such influence if that behavior is at least in part the result of genetic action. More precisely, natural selection can only act on a behavior if individuals differ concerning that behavior, with that difference being at least in part the result of genetic differences between them.

For example, imagine a group of apemen, ancestral to modern humans. To start with, they may all have had rather small brains, but eventually they gave rise to our big-brained selves, because individuals with slightly bigger and better brains were relatively more successful in leaving offspring—presumably because they behaved in a more adaptive manner: maybe they were good at killing mammoths, escaping from saber-tooths or rearing children. Picture the alternative: what if adaptive behavior had no genetic underpinning linking apeman reproduction to the nature of each individual's brain? There would have been no evolution of large brains, since the reproductive success of some individuals vis-à-vis others would not have had any effect on the brain size of their descendants.

In other words, for evolution to operate on behavior, or indeed, on any trait, that trait must be influenced at least in part by genes. Note, there is no requirement that it be rigidly controlled by genes. Nothing derives from genes alone, just as nothing comes from environment alone. However, there must be some connection, however slight.

What direct evidence is there for genetic influences upon behavior? We cannot ethically conduct behavior genetics experiments upon people, and even if we could, probably very few scientists would have the patience to do so, since several generations are usually needed before any results are obtained. For similar reasons, we know very little about the genetics of behavior among elephants and nothing about it in blue whales. Fortunately, however, we do know quite a bit about other, faster-breeding animals, and the results are unequivocal. There *is* a field called behavior genetics, because there are numerous, incontrovertible examples of direct effects of genes on behavior.

Let's look at some examples, starting with the lovebirds, close relatives of the parrots. One species of lovebird has a peculiar way of carrying nest-building material: it tucks pieces of grass and twigs into its rump feathers, then flies home, pulls out the stuff and weaves it into the nest. Another species is more traditional, simply carrying things in its beak, as we expect a bird to do. When William Dilger, a biologist at Cornell University, crossbred individuals of these two species, he came up with hybrids that were greatly confused; they would pick something up, start to tuck it into their feathers, then stop midway, hesitate as though not knowing what to do, perhaps drop it, then pick it up again, then grasp it with their beak only to drop it again moments later, and so on. They had inherited a weak dose of each behavior and wound up doing a poor job at either.

In another study, biologists at the University of Nebraska succeeded in hybridizing mallard ducks with pintails, which are close relatives. As with most ducks, both mallards and pintails normally engage in rather peculiar, ritualized behaviors as part of their courtship. For example, mallard drakes normally perform a distinct series of stereotyped courtship gestures that ethologists (biologists who study animal behavior) identify as "bill shake," "grunt whistle," "nod swimming," "up-downs" and so forth. Normal pintails exhibit some of these behaviors but lack certain others, replacing them by rituals unique to pintails, such as the rather indelicate "burp." Hybrids between these two species revealed the strong but complex role of genetics in their courtship activities: behaviors normally shown by both mallards and pintails were found to occur normally in the hybrids. However, behaviors normally found in only one species were often either absent or only weakly developed in the offspring. There can be no question about it: heredity bore significantly on behavior in these animals.

In addition to such hybridization research, there have been many studies that have looked at the effects of selective breeding upon some behavior—in other words, artificial selection. For example, psychologists at the University of California at Berkeley were able to produce "maze-bright" and "maze-dull" rats by repeatedly choosing the best and the worst maze learners, then selectively breeding the best with the best and the worst with the worst. When descendants of this experiment were tested many generations later, the two strains still showed real differences in their abilities to learn the maze. But surprisingly, when the two strains were tested in a different maze, there were no differences between the two groups in their performance. One possible explanation is that the two strains of rats came to differ genetically over some remarkably precise behavioral tendencies—for example, a tendency to turn right at the second choice point, perhaps, rather than left. Indeed, it may well be that what the researchers thought was a generalized maze intelligence was actually much more specific and limited. In any event, the trend conclusion, which has been confirmed repeatedly, is clear: we can make evolution "happen" to the behavior of animals simply by choosing some individuals and letting them have more offspring than others. There can be only one explanation—genes have a great deal to do with behavior.

Animal breeders have been aware of behavior genetics for a long time. Horses, for example, have been bred for war, for show, for speed or for strength. Pigs have been bred for laziness (since energy not used running around is turned into meat or fat), and throughout much of the world roosters are bred for success in cockfights. Dogs provide innumerable examples of selective breeding for behavior: pointers like to point—they will stand stockstill, pointing at a grouse or pheasant; and a Doberman really is more apt to bite you than is a golden retriever. I have a female Newfoundland. She has never had a course in lifesaving, but when she first saw my children swimming in a pool, she became terribly agitated, and when one of them yelled —in high spirits, as it happened, not distress—she immediately jumped in and dragged him out of the water. It is hard to discourage a 120-pound dog intent on saving you, whether you need it or not! As you may have guessed, Newfoundlands were bred for water rescue, and they are still used as lifeguards off the coast of France. Similarly, a friend's babysitter always brought along her pet Border collie—it did a marvelous job of herding the children from room to room.

The role of genetics in behavior often shows up in unintended ways. Picture this true scene. A raccoon had been trained (by being given food whenever it did the right thing) to deposit coins in a piggy bank as part of an exhibit featured in a bank window. It was to be a lesson in saving. But at crucial moments, rather than inserting the coins, he would obstinately insist on rubbing them together in his paws, looking for all the world like a penny-pinching miser who couldn't bear to part with his wealth, rather than projecting the bank's hoped-for image of a cheerful depositer. Why this peculiar behavior? Raccoons typically manipulate their food a great deal before eating it in nature—indeed, doing so under water gives them an even better "feel," thus contributing to the myth that they wash their food. In any event, handling food-related objects is an important instinctive behavior in these animals, and even intensive training using modern psychological techniques has been unable to eliminate traces of this genetically-influenced tendency.

Behavior geneticists have identified the effects of a number of specific, individual genes on behavior, and in fact there are dozens of such traits now recognized. There are mice that waltz when they hear a particular sound, dogs that refuse to bark, rats that will fight almost anything in sight, and even strains of mice, evolved in the laboratory, that would rather drink an alcohol solution than water. The point, I think, is clear: *there is a real connection between genes and behavior,* and this has been found to be true for every animal species at which anyone has seriously looked. What about us, then? Unless we seriously wish to claim that there is a radical biological break—a true qualitative chasm—between human beings and other animals, we should accept the likelihood that our genes influence our behavior as well.

This is not to say that we necessarily carry genes "for" competition, say, or altruism, courtship, child care or group identification. But it is similarly true that there are no genes "for" arms or legs; our limbs develop out of a complex interaction between our genetic makeup and our environment. When embroyos are exposed to thalidomide, their genes and their products may function peculiarly or not at all. Under normal circumstances, however, our genes guide our development to produce a recognizably normal human being. They also guide our behavioral development, producing, it is true, many different people who do many different things. But all of those people are distinctly human.

It is also worth noting that genes for particular behaviors can disappear from a population just as they can increase. Ask any chicken farmer: it is very difficult to find a "broody" hen these days. That is, hens, at least in the United States, are less and less inclined to sit on their eggs. The reason is clear and significant— nearly all American chickens are reared in huge, automated factories in which incubators replace hens. (The hens are more valuable producing additional eggs than sitting on those they have already laid.) As a result, genetic tendencies favoring broodiness no longer confer a selective advantage and they are steadily being lost. In less-industrialized societies, hens still brood their own eggs. Those that don't aren't very fit. Of course, a variety of new traits are being selected in our technologized chickens—for example, the ability to lay many eggs, to produce a lot of meat on little feed, and so forth.

Homo sapiens may similarly be losing certain traits and accumulating others. Thus, the availability of insulin doubtless enables diabetics to survive and reproduce, whereas in earlier times this was much less likely. (I am personally rather glad of this evolutionary innovation: my paternal grandmother was diabetic, and without insulin I would have been different from what I am now—or, to be more accurate, one-quarter different. Similarly, someone with my eyesight during Paleolithic time would probably not have survived to reproduce; more likely, he would have been stepped on by a mammoth.) In any event, we are clearly monkeying around with our evolution, and no one knows the consequences. A nonbroody hen would be unfit in a traditional barnyard, just as a diabetic would be unfit without insulin or a severely myopic college professor would be unfit without eyeglasses.

●

I have been making this case for behavior genetics in order to justify looking at the influence of evolution on our behavior. And I will continue throughout to be an advocate, marshaling theory and evidence in support of this position. There is some danger, of course, in giving a one-sided view of human potential. We are the products of biological evolution and are, accordingly, the thinking, feeling, sweating embodiments of genes interacting with environments. In some dimensions, our horizons are probably quite narrow. Others have yet to be reached or even glimpsed.

Consider the following medical case: You are the doctor. A woman comes to you for advice. She has tuberculosis and her husband syphilis. Their first child was blind, the second died, the third was deaf and dumb, and the fourth has tuberculosis. Now the woman is pregnant with her fifth child. Should she have an abortion? What would you say? If you agree with me, then congratulations, we have just eliminated Beethoven!

●

Why is sugar sweet? Because it contains sucrose, of course. But why do we experience it the way we do? What is the evolutionary explanation for sugar's sweetness? Clearly, just as beauty is in the eye of the beholder, sweetness is in the mouth of the taster. To anteaters, ants are "sweet"; anteaters may even find sugar bitter—certainly they don't like it as we do. The reason is clear enough: we are primates, and some of our ancestors spent a great deal of time in trees, where they ate a great deal of fruit. Ripe fruit is more nutritious than unripe, and one thing about ripe fruit is that it contains sugars. It doesn't take much imagination to reconstruct the evolutionary sequence that selected for a strong preference among our distant ancestors for the taste that characterized ripe fruit. Genes that influenced their carriers to eat ripe fruit and reject the unripe ultimately made more copies of themselves than did those that were less discriminating.

Just as we find sugar sweet, we find certain behaviors to be sweet as well. This means that, at least in part because of evolution's handiwork, we are inclined to do certain things rather than others, and it should be no surprise that in general our inclinations are those that contribute to our fitness. "Evolution," the eminent physical anthropologist Sherwood Washburn has pointed out, "builds a relation between biology, psychology and behavior." Sociobiology points out more precisely how that relation is built.

Of course, we are not talking here about genetic determinism, but rather genetic influence. This is the difference between shooting a bullet at a target (determinism) and throwing a paper airplane (influence) . . . in a strong wind. Environment is that wind, and certainly for human beings culture, our major environmental fact of life, does a great deal to modify our genetically-influenced predispositions. Thus, the patrons of sophisticated singles bars are not normally found copulating wildly under the tables, no matter how subdued the lighting. This is not because the inclination isn't there but because it is susceptible to being modified, in this case inhibited, by our culturally-induced perceptions of what is acceptable public behavior and what is not. At their core, most human beings probably agree on what behaviors are sweet; however, we satisfy our sweet tooth with a wide range of ingredients and the special recipes of cultural diversity.

•

As with sociobiology, the science of ethology deals with behavior, also in an evolutionary context. Ethology is largely concerned with careful descriptions and analysis of the rather stereotyped, automatic responses that characterize much of animal behavior. Ethologists have discovered, for example, that male stickleback fish possess a very strong genetically-influenced tendency to attack other males, whom they recognize by the red chest they display during the breeding season. In fact, males will attack just about anything that is red. Nobel prize-winning ethologist Niko Tinbergen reports that one of his sticklebacks, when placed near a window, used to threaten the British mail trucks passing by outside. We probably don't experience anything quite as mindlessly automatic as that. No doubt from time to time we feel vague and diffuse inclinations to behave in certain specific ways, but such notions can generally be overridden by our conscious mind and modified drastically by our experience. Still, there is something there, some impulse underneath—a whispering.

Not surprisingly, much of being human consists of contributing to the success of our genes just as being a kangaroo, or even a dandelion, involves contributing to the success of kangaroo or dandelion genes. It was not exactly what he meant, but Freud was right: much of our behavior has to do with sex.

We humans are susceptible to stimulation of all sorts, some of the most effective stimuli being exaggerations of normal sexual traits: lipstick that amplifies normal redness, brassières and silicone implants that modify normal breast shape and size, beards that make the aggressive chin even more so, and a variety of male clothing styles, from padding to military epaulets, that appear to enlarge the shoulders. We transmit many subtle signals and respond to them too, all unconsciously. Experiments have shown that our pupils dilate when we see something we like and they contract when we see something less pleasant: the pupils of young women dilate when they are shown pictures of young men. And, predictably, young men's eyes widen when they see pictures of young women.

Although we seem to be unconscious of sending these signals, we may be quite aware of receiving them ("There was something in her eyes . . ."). The bazaar merchants of the Middle East may owe some of their reputed astuteness to their "reading" of a customer's real interest, by means of his pupil size. It is probably no accident that many Turkish rug dealers wear dark glasses—all the better to hide what they are really thinking, or better yet, feeling.

As with unconscious signaling, the influences of evolution on our complex social behavior are probably so subtle and pervasive that they cannot be easily noticed. Sociobiology is particularly concerned with such unnoticed things, the things that all human beings take for granted: our love of children, nepotism (favoritism toward relatives), male-female behavior differences, competition and aggression, the exchange of goods and services, and so on. Isaac Newton revolutionized science when he took a fresh look at the world, questioning what others were taking for granted: why do things fall? Similarly, Einstein asked the astonishing question: what would the world look like to someone riding on a beam of light? Sociobiology's groundbreaking inquiry is, Why do we do what we do? Why are some behaviors "sweeter" than others?

Humans are unique among animals in that our behavior appears to be liberated from the tyrannical demands of our biology. We are not ocelots, constrained to pluck ourselves if we cannot find any chickens. We do what we want, we say, following our personal satisfactions and the teachings of society rather than the imperatives of natural selection. Or do we? Perhaps we should look harder at those behaviors that we find personally satisfying and ask just why we should find them so. The comfortable feeling after eating, the sense of well-being that follows a good rest, sexual satisfaction, the pleasures of healthy movement, personal autonomy, the respect of others, the accomplishments of ourselves and our offspring—all these we find pleasurable. And, it's interesting, all these pleasures contribute in one way or another to our own fitness. We have been selected, naturally, to engage in them. We find them sweet.

We even derive pleasure from behaviors that seem to be a waste of time and energy—organized athletics, for example. But the fact is that sports are an excellent source of exercise and provide opportunities to learn important skills and experience being part of a group. Not only that, all people seem to enjoy showing off. Anthropologist Napoleon Chagnon writes about the public dancing of the

Yanomamo Indians, who live in the rain forests of the Brazil-Venezuela borderlands:

> The enchantment of the dance issues from the dancer's awareness that, for a brief moment, he is a glorious peacock that commands the admiration of his fellows, and it is his responsibility and desire to present a spectacular display of his dance steps and gawdy accouterments. In this brief, ego-building moment, each man has an opportunity to display himself, spinning, prancing about the village periphery, chest puffed out, while all watch, admire and cheer wildly.

Can anyone doubt the adaptive significance of such pleasures, especially when we consider that many of the watchers are female, and that some Yanomamo get to have many wives whereas others wind up with none at all?

Of course, the Yanomamo is not a peacock, even when he is dancing. Unlike peacocks, which can never exceed their feathery peacock nature, humans can at least occasionally go against their human natures. We can force ourselves to drink something bitter, for example, but we cannot go entirely beyond our biological capacities and think or behave like a seahorse or a giraffe. Every species has its limits. A giraffe cannot write a symphony, celebrate Yom Kippur or be schizophrenic. But giraffes do find it sweet to do what is appropriate for giraffes. We find it sweet to do what is appropriate for humans. What's striking here is that neither the giraffes nor we bring very much in the way of insight to our inclinations.

Even obviously adaptive behavior may not necessarily be accompanied by a great deal of insight. The Eskimo who were perhaps the most technically ingenious of all non-industrialized peoples are a case in point. For example, they invented the igloo, with its super-efficient hemispherical shape, its tunnel entrance (imitated by modern mountaineering tents), and its adjustable door of snow blocks, which can be moved precisely to allow in exactly the correct amount of cold air that will quickly be warmed by a seal oil lamp and then rise and escape through another adjustable aperture, this one in the ceiling. Yet, after spending many years with the Eskimo, explorer and anthropologist Vilhjalmur Stefansson found that they could not accept any general statements about the theory from which this engineering marvel was derived—not even the notion that hot air rises. According to these people, the behavior of the world is governed by

gods and spirits, not by laws of cause and effect. Nonetheless, hot air
does rise and although the Eskimo may not "know" this, they certainly behave as if they do. Could Eskimo ingenuity be a model for
much of human behavior? Could it be that we do many things that
are adaptively "correct" . . . even without knowing why?

•

But what about our pride and joy, the crowning glory of human
uniqueness, our brain? We certainly do have unusually large and
complex brains, but the fact is their basic anatomy and physiology
remain the same as we observe in other, less cerebral beasts. In *The
Dragons of Eden*, Carl Sagan suggests that something of great evolutionary importance may have happened at the point when the
amount of information stored in our brains exceeded the amount
stored in our genes. Our genes discovered then that they could best
perpetuate themselves by throwing in their lot with a conglomeration of nerve cells that was extraordinarily flexible in its operation
and capable of modifying its activity as a result of past experience.
This conglomeration—the brain—is, from one viewpoint, simply a
very efficient device for maximizing the fitness of weak-bodied animals (or their genes) living in a hazardous and unpredictable world.
Far from freeing us from the demands of evolution and natural
selection, our brain became a dramatic example of one way that our
genes "made do" in the evolutionary race.

•

J. B. S. Haldane, one of the founding giants of evolutionary biology,
was once being interviewed on BBC radio by the Archbishop of
Canterbury, who asked him: "Given your life-time study of the Creation, what would you conclude as to the nature of the Creator?" The
response was immediate: "An inordinate fondness for beetles!"
    Haldane's point was well taken. More than 85 percent of the
world's animal species are insects, and most of these are beetles. We
are only a very small part of the natural world. We are, however, very
special. Haldane again: "Only man can swim a mile, walk 20 miles
and then climb a tree." But this is only our physical equipment,
which after all is probably the least remarkable thing about us. We
also have culture, and as anthropologist W. Laughlin points out: "A
man can run down a horse in two or three days and decide whether

to eat it, ride it, pull a load with it, wear it, or worship it." The decision will probably be strongly influenced by cultural considerations, although once again evolutionary demands will almost certainly play a role.

How large a role? A very difficult question, since the two are very tightly entwined. It would be naïve, though, to assume that biology is somehow more important than culture. Let's consider an apparently straightforward example. Most American women report discomfort associated with menstruation—for some it is extreme while a small minority report no difficulties whatsoever. We have the same report for women in Samoa. This seems to be a clear example of biology having its way. After all, think of all those hormones, the uterus and so on. Very biological. But among the Arapesh of New Guinea, Margaret Mead writes, menstrual pain is not recognized at all. Are Arapesh women biologically unique? Perhaps, but as Mead suggests, Arapesh culture may also have something to do with it, "possibly because the extreme discomfort of sitting on a thin piece of bark on the damp, cold ground in a leaky leaf-hut on the side of a mountain, rubbing one's body with stinging nettles, obscures any awareness." Take that, biology!

I don't know why Arapesh culture prescribes that women behave like this when they are menstruating, but we can't attribute their lack of menstrual pain to either biology or culture, acting alone.

It is possible, I suppose, that evolution imperiously pulls the strings of our biology and we dance helplessly like marionettes. On the other hand, maybe culture is the puppeteer. Most likely, the answer lies in between: it is as misleading to blame biology for all that we do as it is to cry "culture."

When we look at our behavior, without preconceptions in either direction, it is striking how many parallels may be seen between our cultural lives and the behaviors that natural selection favors. Most likely, this fitness-maximizing component to human behavior is a large part of our human nature. It seems we are products of direct biological imperatives, tempered by a flexibility that inclines toward adaptive use of our environment.

Students of animal behavior must constantly beware of anthropomorphism. But the opposite, zoomorphism, is equally likely, and misleading, as Margaret Mead has cautioned. Similarly, the great evolutionary biologist Julian Huxley warned us to beware of "nothing butism," the notion that just because we are animals we are nothing but animals. And, again, the opposite is equally misleading: beware the notion that we are "nothing but" the products of social learning. For too long social science and biological science have pursued "nothing but" approaches. Sociobiology may just help redress that imbalance.

Anthropologist Ruth Benedict once observed that "culture is personality writ large." A sociobiologist might say, "Culture is biology writ fuzzy." But, despite its complexities, the writing of evolution seems to be legible, and we may be groping our way at last toward a Rosetta Stone. Biology whispers deep within us, and if we use our knowledge of natural selection to eavesdrop, we may yet hear those whisperings and discover something new and something terribly exciting about ourselves.

3

Sexism: Strategies of Reproduction, or When Is Beeswax Like a Ferrari?

Generations of Tom Sawyers and Huck Finns set out on their boisterous adventures and come home covered with mud, while we chuckle indulgently. Little girls, though, are made of sugar and spice. "Boys will be boys," we're told, but "nice girls don't do that." "Vive la différence," echoes the French Parliament. *La différence* is one of sociobiology's most important concerns.

There has been no human society that has not distinguished the sexes, by their anatomies and by their behavior. But we tend to focus on the superficial differences—dress, hair length, body shape—and most of us don't really know what makes a woman female and a man male.

We all know how a human male differs physically from a female. Likewise for male and female chimpanzees, elephants and lions. But how do we differentiate birds, for example, which generally lack a penis or vagina? And what about oysters? Not much visible there, but biologists, at least, are absolutely confident in distinguishing the sexes. What is the underlying biological meaning of male and female?

The answer is quite simple. In almost all living species there are two different kinds of sexual individuals. One kind, the female, produces a relatively small number of large sex cells, called eggs. The other kind, the male, produces a relatively large number of rather small sex cells, or sperm. In many cases, the difference between male and female sex cells is dramatic. Birds may lay eggs that weigh 25 percent or more of their total body weight, while their mates produce only a few drops of sperm. Mammals seem to be exceptions to this, since their eggs are quite small; a human egg is only about the size of a pinhead. But the sperm are even smaller; a single male ejaculation produces enough of them to fertilize every woman in North America. Zoologist Richard Dawkins points out that the exploitation of women by men probably began very long ago, when the smaller, more active sperm began to take advantage of the rich food reserves present in the larger, less active eggs.

The biological consequences of fertilization and pregnancy are immense, falling only on the woman. Eggs are fertilized by sperm, not vice versa. And women become pregnant, not men. It is the woman who must produce a placenta and nourish her unborn child; who must undergo the metabolic and hormonal stresses of pregnancy; who must carry around an embryo that grows in bulk and weight, making her more and more ungainly as her pregnancy advances; and who, when the child is born, must nurse it.

Because women become pregnant, they simply cannot produce as many children as can men. We may regret this fact, glory in it or simply accept it, but it remains, nevertheless, an indelible part of our biology. Although Priam's wife Hecuba, the queen of Troy, was said to have had more than twenty children, twelve or so is a more realistic maximum for one woman, and in most societies, six or seven children is considered quite a few. By contrast, there is little in their biology that limits the number of children that men can produce. For instance, Ismail, a seventeenth-century king of Morocco, is reported to have fathered 1,056 offspring.

In some ways, Western society is a great equalizer. By our promotion of monogamy, we have narrowed the reproductive gap between men and women. We are even less likely to tolerate a modern-day Ismail than a Hecuba, and, with the exception of successful sperm donors, most men today really have little opportunity to father more children than women have to mother them. However, we are still perfectly good mammals, and the biology of maleness and femaleness continues to apply to us, just as it does to a mouse or a monkey. There is good reason to believe that we are, in fact, primed to be much less sexually egalitarian than we appear to be. We may not be entirely comfortable with *la différence*, but we had better try to understand it.

The biological difference between men and women is absolutely crucial to comprehending sociobiology's arguments for the behavioral differences between them. Natural selection dictates that individuals will behave in ways that maximize their fitness, so, clearly, different strategies will be appropriate for the two sexes, given their dramatically different biological characteristics.

Sperm are cheap. Eggs are expensive. Accordingly, females have a much greater stake in any one reproductive act. Biologist George C. Williams points out that in virtually all species males are selected to be aggressive—sexual advertisers—while females are selected to be choosier—comparison shoppers. Again, these behaviors follow directly from the biology of what it is to be male or female. For males, reproduction is easy, a small amount of time, a small amount of semen, and the potential evolutionary return is very great if offspring are produced. On the other hand, a female who makes a "bad" choice may be in real evolutionary trouble. If fertilization occurs, a baby is begun, and the ensuing process is not only inexorable but immensely demanding. In certain species of flies, copulating with a male from the wrong species results in the death of the female. The male, however, loses little. Among birds, a comparable error by the female in choosing a mate can lead to the production of sterile eggs —a potential wastage of one-fourth of her body weight. She may also be unable to breed again for a full year. The cost to the male? Again, little, if anything. Small wonder that females in virtually every species are more discriminating than males in the choice of sexual partners.

The evolutionary mechanism should be clear. Genes that allow females to accept the sorts of mates who make lesser contributions to their reproductive success will leave fewer copies of themselves than will genes that influence the females to be more selective. Accordingly, genes inducing selectivity will increase at the expense of those that are less discriminating. For males, a very different strategy applies. The maximum advantage goes to individuals with fewer inhibitions. A genetically influenced tendency to "play fast and loose"—"love 'em and leave 'em"—may well reflect more biological reality than most of us care to admit.

According to Zorba the Greek, God has a very big heart, but "there is one thing that He will not forgive—when a woman calls a man to her bed, and he will not come!" Presumably, had the situation been reversed and a man called a woman to his bed, and she demurred—that He *would* forgive. Sociobiology helps us understand why this should be so.

In a well-known custom of medieval Europe, when a serf got married, the lord of the manor had the right—the *droit du seigneur* —to spend the wedding night with the new bride. Intolerable to today's morality, perhaps, but it probably did wonders for the lord's fitness. And why was it the lord who slept with the bride and not the lady of the manor who slept with the groom? Such a practice would probably not have helped milady's fitness and, not surprisingly, there never was a *droit de la madame.*

•

When we introduce a female mammal to a sexually-aroused male, there is a flurry of copulation, which eventually subsides. If we remove that female and replace her with another, copulation frequency rises again, only to subside once more. The coupling keeps occurring until male sexual performance finally "exhausts" (to use the apt scientific term). This phenomenon, known to psychologists as the "Coolidge effect,"* probably occurs in humans as well. According to pioneer sexologist Alfred Kinsey: "Among all people everywhere in the world, the male is more likely than the female to desire sex with a variety of partners." Clearly, this preference is also consistent with natural selection, since males can enhance their fitness with each new copulation while females are unlikely to do so.

Of course, evolution does not simply favor utter profligacy by males. Their sexual activity may be limited by other demands on their time, such as defending territory, feeding themselves and offspring already produced, or simply recovery from their exertions. Most significantly, they are limited by the activities of other males, with whom they compete for access to females. Nonetheless, sociobiological theory predicts dramatically different reproductive strategies for males and females. The differences are nearly universal. Primitive turbellarian worms are hermaphrodites, meaning that each individual is simultaneously both male and female, each having

*President and Mrs. Coolidge, according to the story, were given separate tours around a model farm. The First Lady noticed a large group of chickens in a yard and commented: "That rooster must be kept quite busy." She suggested that the fact might be mentioned to the President when he came by. Later, when the presidential group arrived, the guide explained, "Mrs. Coolidge wished me to point out that our single rooster must copulate many times each day." "Always with the same female?" "No sir." "Well," said Coolidge, "tell *that* to Mrs. Coolidge." Hence, the Coolidge effect.

both testes and ovaries. Yet the worms fertilize each other, not themselves, and the active individuals will force copulation with passive ones. Indeed, the same individual will eagerly and promiscuously inseminate others, but it will exercise more discretion when allowing others to inseminate it! These worms are active and aggressive when seeking to discharge their sperm, demure and discriminating when their more valuable eggs are at stake. Thus, a single individual has a "split personality," depending on whether it is looking out for its maleness or its femaleness.

If you walk through a marsh during the springtime in the southeastern United States, and if that marsh contains bullfrogs, you may be in for a demonstration of sociobiology in action. The chances are good that you will emerge from the marsh with a male bullfrog tightly clutching the toe of your boot, perhaps one on each boot, in a posture known as "amplexus." This grip is used by males to clasp females in the early stage of mating. Males will clasp almost anything that doesn't clasp them first. Occasionally we even run across an amphibian *ménage à trois,* with a single ripe female clutched by two eager males, one behind and one in front. The male bullfrog's sexual assertiveness is an adaptive part of its reproductive strategy: "If it moves, mate with it." By contrast, a female bullfrog will only release her precious store of eggs when clasped in just the right way by the right species of male at just the right time. She is much fussier, and appropriately so.

A mule is a cross between a female horse and a male donkey. While it may represent a good investment for the farmer, it is also sterile, and therefore a total evolutionary loss for its parents. And this loss is not borne at all equally. It has cost the male donkey only a bit of time and energy and a few drops of semen, which can easily be replaced. But the mare has devoted nearly eleven months of her life to carrying the fetus; she has also had to nurse her offspring afterward, during which time she was not able to breed again. All for what? Her genes will not go beyond the sterile mule, who cannot pass them along any further. The mule is a bad deal for both its parents, but a much worse one for its mother.

It may wound our vanity, but the reproductive biology of human beings does not differ dramatically from that of donkeys and horses —and perhaps even bullfrogs. It should surprise no one that women almost always are sexually coy relative to the more "available" men.

This pattern holds cross-culturally, as well. Margaret Mead has observed of Polynesian societies:

> It is the girl who decides whether she will or will not meet her lover under the palm trees, or receive him with necessary precautions in her house, or in her bed in the young people's house. He may woo and plead, he may send gifts and pretty speeches by an intermediary, but the final choice remains in the hands of the girl. If she does not choose, she does not lift the corner of her mat, she does not wait under the palm trees. A mood, a whim, a slight disinclination, and the boy is disappointed.

It is no accident that female prostitutes greatly outnumber male prostitutes, or that "girlie" magazines are many times more popular than their "beefcake" counterparts. A recent study of sexual attitudes among American teenagers found that two-thirds of the males but only one-fifth of the females thought sex was "all right with someone known only for a few hours."

In a similar study, three hundred unmarried West German workers were polled on their attitudes toward premarital sex. The results:

> Of 20-year-old virgin women, the significantly most frequent opinion is that they're waiting for true love, that they're decent or living properly. Of abstinent males, however, it is held that they're afraid, that they can't find a girl, or that they're not a real man. Women who have many coital partners are significantly more often criticized than promiscuous men as follows: they'll get a bad reputation, no one will want to marry them, and they should be ashamed. Of promiscuous men, the opinion is significantly more often: they're doing it right, they're enjoying life, these are real men.

Women are choosier, it seems, and for good evolutionary reasons.

•

Almost invariably, throughout the animal world, it is the male that defends a territory. It is the male, too, who performs bizarre and eye-catching behaviors intended to intimidate other males and to attract females. Male birds sing, while females rarely do. Male elk bugle and grow large antlers, using them to frighten off and fight other males, and to entice females. Time after time, in species after species, males are nearly always more aggressive than females. The list is punctuated by only a very few exceptions, where the "typical" reproductive roles are switched.

Some animals will mate monogamously. This arrangement is especially true of many species of birds, whose nestlings grow so fast that both male and female are kept busy feeding their offspring. I recently pulled a nasty trick on some mated pairs of mountain bluebirds, a monogamous species of western North America. Interested in testing the proposition that animals act so as to maximize their fitness, I designed the following simple experiment: while the male was away getting food, having left his mate at their newly constructed nest, I attached a model of another male bluebird to the tree, close to the nest and to the female. I was curious as to how the male would respond when he returned and discovered the "adulterous" couple. In particular, I wanted to compare the male's behavior when he caught his female *in flagrante* during the breeding season with his response later in the year, once the eggs were already laid. Early in the season, when breeding was taking place, all hell broke loose when the husband returned; as expected, he attacked the dummy male quite aggressively. But—and this I found especially interesting—he also attacked his own mate, in one case even driving the suspected adulteress away. She was eventually replaced by another female, with whom he successfully reared a brood. What happened when males were presented with the identical situation *after* the eggs had already been laid? There were still attacks on the intruding male, but of much lower intensity, and no further aggression was directed toward the female.

The male bluebird's actions are an almost diagrammatic example of reproductive behavior having been finely honed by natural selection to maximize individual fitness. It is certainly adaptive for the male bluebird to respond aggressively to male intruders. They are always competitors for food, and, even more serious, competitors for access to his mate during the breeding season. It is also adaptive for the male to drive away his mate if he has reason to "doubt" her fidelity, as long as she can be replaced with someone more trustworthy. (Rephrased in gene language: genes that cause their bodies to drive away unfaithful mates and replace them with more reliable ones leave more copies of themselves than do those who are cuckolded.) However, later in the season, when his genes are safely tucked away in his mate's eggs, the defending male's fitness is no longer threatened by his female's dalliance, so there is no reason to drive her away. In fact, any male who did so would be unable to rear another brood, for the breeding season is very short in the bluebirds' mountain homes and there simply isn't sufficient time to start breeding again midway through the summer. The mountain bluebirds' strategy is clearly appropriate to maximizing their fitness; furthermore, it is a distinctly male strategy.

Compare these two situations: (1) you are a male animal, paired with a single female, and your "wife" goes around copulating with other males; (2) you are a female animal, paired with a single male, and your "husband" goes around copulating with other females. In which case is your fitness likely to be lower? In the first situation, if you (as male) remain faithful to your "swinging" spouse, she will eventually conceive offspring via other males, and you will have lost out in the evolutionary sweepstakes. However, in the second case, if you (as female) remain faithful to your mate, you can still breed successfully despite his philandering, provided he includes you among his girlfriends. This is the basic biology of the double standard: males are expected to be sexually less discriminating, more aggressive and more available than females. They are also expected to be more intolerant of infidelity by their wives than wives will be of infidelity by their husbands. Frankie may have killed Johnny because he "done her wrong," but that was only a song. As far as I know, in all human societies, adultery by the wife is much more likely to lead to violence by the "offended" husband than vice versa. Almost invariably, it is a mortal offense to seduce another man's wife. Not surprisingly, the cuckolded husband is often the object of pity or derision, and human males typically invest a great deal of time and energy trying to protect themselves against being cuckolded by another man. Even the likely origin of the word "cuckold" indicates its biology. The European cuckoo deposits its eggs in the nest of another bird, leaving the unwitting foster parents to further the fitness of the cuckoo, rather than their own offspring. For good biological reasons, we don't wish to be like the cuckoo's victim.

In some polygynous societies, adultery is a civil crime, not a criminal one. Transgressors must give the "injured" husband set amounts of money, cattle and other goods, which he can use to obtain additional wives. It's all very civilized. To the sociobiologist, it also seems very fit.

•

In her book *Against Our Will*, Susan Brownmiller claimed that only human beings engage in rape. The facts are otherwise. Rape is common among the birds and bees, and is epidemic among the mallard ducks.* In fact, large groups of drakes sometimes descend on an unsuspecting female and rape her repeatedly, often causing death, as the victim's head may be held under water for a long period of time. What's going on here? When mallards pair up for breeding, there often remain a number of unmated males, since there are more males than females in most such species (probably owing to the risks involved in defending eggs against predators). These bachelors have been excluded from normal reproduction, and so they engage in what is apparently the next best strategy: raping someone else's female.

What about the victim's "husband"? Clearly, his fitness is threatened when his mate is raped, and we would expect him to do something about it. He does, and once again his behavior is remarkably consistent with sociobiological theory. He tries to intervene, beating the attackers away with his wings. However, if his mate is the victim of a gang rape, his chances of success are low and the likelihood of his being injured in the attempt are high, so he usually just stands by. Furthermore, if the rapists indicate by their behavior that the rape has been successful, the victim's mate does a most remarkable—and ungentlemanly—thing. He proceeds to rape the just-raped female himself! His mating is not quite as brutal as the initial violation of the female, but it clearly differs from the usual copulations of mated pairs, with their rather drawn-out courtship rituals. In this case the male simply forces himself upon his hapless and exhausted mate, without even the by-your-leave of "head pumping," *de rigueur* in mallard boudoir etiquette.

Again, what is going on here? Once more, the mallard drake is maximizing his fitness. If he can prevent the rape, well and good. If he cannot, either because he is outnumbered or because he is simply too late, the next best thing he can do is to introduce his sperm as quickly as possible, to compete with that of the rapists. Of course, behavior of this sort does not require any awareness by the drake that

*Some people may bridle at the notion of rape in animals, but the term seems entirely appropriate when we examine what happens. Among ducks, for example, pairs typically form early in the breeding season, and the two mates engage in elaborate and predictable exchanges of behavior. When this rite finally culminates in mounting, both male and female are clearly in agreement. But sometimes strange males surprise a mated female and attempt to force an immediate copulation, without engaging in any of the normal courtship ritual and despite her obvious and vigorous protest. If that's not rape, it is certainly very much like it.

he is maximizing his fitness. Any genetically influenced tendency to respond in such a fashion will be favored by natural selection, and this behavior will ultimately become characteristic of the species.

Compare the behavior of a mallard drake whose female has just been raped with the response of a male mountain bluebird who has been led to suspect that his mate had been adulterous. The mallard does not seek to drive away his female, whereas the bluebird does, at least early in the season. This difference in reaction is not simply one of greater tolerance, understanding or nobler character among mallards. Rather, it simply reflects the cold, unyielding calculus of evolutionary fitness. On Mount Rainier in Washington State, where I conducted my study, there is an apparent surplus of unmated female bluebirds. Accordingly a suspect female can be replaced, and the male is well advised—that is, most fit—to do so. Female mallards, by contrast, are in short supply, so that even after a female has been raped she is still too valuable a mate to drive off, since it is unlikely that the male will get another. Besides, he may have successfully fertilized her. Selection among mallards therefore favors male behaviors that lead to retention of the mate, and maximum protection of the evolutionary investment.

Rape in humans is by no means as simple, influenced as it is by an extremely complex overlay of cultural attitudes. Nevertheless mallard rape and bluebird adultery may have a degree of relevance to human behavior. Perhaps human rapists, in their own criminally misguided way, are doing the best they can to maximize their fitness. If so, they are not that different from the sexually excluded bachelor mallards. Another point: Whether they like to admit it or not, many human males are stimulated by the idea of rape. This does not make them rapists, but it does give them something else in common with mallards. And another point: During the India-Pakistan war over Bangladesh, many thousands of Hindu women were raped by Pakistani soldiers. A major problem that these women faced was rejection by husband and family. A cultural pattern, of course, but one coinciding clearly with biology.

●

It may seem by now as if evolution—and human culture—have given males an overwhelming reproductive and personal advantage over females. Not so. Remember, whenever a given child is produced, it is still a product of just one male and one female. The child is their triumph, their ticket to evolutionary success. When King Ismail of Morocco fathered 1,056 children, it was at the expense of 1,055 other Moroccan males. While he was reproducing, they weren't. On balance, the two sexes are equally successful, always. However, *individuals* of the two sexes need not be and, in fact, rarely are. In most animal species, there is a rather large variation in the number of offspring that different males produce, that is, in their fitness. Some males (the King Ismails) father many children, while others (the eunuchs, either literally or figuratively) have few or none. Among females, however, there is much less difference between the most and the least fit. No woman could produce 1,056 children, but most women are successful in bearing a rather small number. Certainly, the difference between the "haves" and the "have-nots" is less significant than among males.

A useful theory of male-female differences bearing on this point has been developed by Harvard's Robert L. Trivers, who has proposed the notion of "parental investment," defined as any expenditure of time, energy or risk that a parent makes on behalf of its offspring. Every expenditure of this sort carries a cost along with it, and an element in this cost is a reduction in the ability of the investing parent to rear additional successful offspring. As with everything in life, investing in a child is a double-edged sword. Give a child food and you have less for yourself and your other children; defend it from a predator, and you run the risk of losing your own life, along with any chance of breeding again. It is clear that women (indeed, females of nearly all species) necessarily invest more in each child than do men, quickly reaching a point where they exhaust their potential and can invest no more. But men have the biological potential to do more, and evolution favors those who attempt to do so.

Trivers's theory of parental investment emphasizes that, because of the high cost of offspring to women, they are limited in how many they can produce. During the nine months that she is pregnant, a woman cannot reproduce again—she is already occupied. A man continues to produce perfectly good sperm during that period. Furthermore, after the child is born, a woman is biologically primed to nurse it, often for several years. Her parental investment is "taken" and will not be available to her husband again for quite a while. In most animal species, therefore, the best reproductive arrangement for males is that they be mated to many females. As long as the females are also fulfilling their reproductive potential, this arrangement is satisfactory to their fitness as well.

Biology dictates that women provide more initial investment in their offspring than do men, and in the technical language of sociobiology, the sex investing more becomes a limiting resource for the sex investing less. For human beings, this means that men will compete with other men for access to women much more often than will women compete with other women for access to men. After all, the reproductive success of men is limited largely by the number of women they inseminate—more wives or lovers, more children. The reproductive success of women, however, is only rarely limited by the number of men with whom they copulate. For a man to be successful in making his sperm an evolutionary success, he must obtain, at a minimum, a woman's investment of an egg and placenta not already in use. This may not always be easy. What a woman needs to project her genes into the future is only a small contribution from the opposite sex, and it is unlikely that she will be unable to find a man willing to oblige.

The difference between male success and failure is likely to be enormous, resulting in strong selection for competition among males, for whom the payoff is so great. Because the payoff for females is much less, competition is also much less. As might be expected, this difference has wide-ranging consequences for the behavior of males and females.

Certain animal species exaggerate male-female differences with particular clarity. Among elephant seals, sea-going mammals that breed off the California coast, the adult males are truly elephantine, weighing about three tons, while the females are less than one-quarter of that size. Typically, these seals breed in large harems, presided over by one or a few adult males. If the harem is a small one, fifty females or so, a single male, the harem master, usually does most of the breeding. In larger harems, because a single male is hard-pressed to service all his females and also to defend them from the advances of other males, several other males may also father some pups. A successful harem master may well father 150 pups in a single year, a phenomenal evolutionary achievement.

Of course, success by the harem master is balanced by failure among the other males; harems make for many bachelors who do not

father any offspring. There is no payoff for being such an evolutionary failure and males therefore engage each other in titanic battles
with high stakes and high mortality. Adult females do not fight. As
with the males, their fitness is maximized by breeding, but, unlike
the males, they are virtually guaranteed the opportunity to do so.
Their successes, of course, are more restrained. There is simply no
such thing as an evolutionary jackpot for females, who do well to
produce a single pup every year. Since she may live twelve to fifteen
years, a female can hope to produce no more than 12 offspring or so
during her lifetime. (Compare that ability with 150 offspring in a
single year for a successful harem master.)

Burney LeBoeuf, a biologist at the University of California, Santa
Cruz, has recently begun observing the behavior of elephant seal
pups during their month-long nursing stage. Male pups, he finds,
grow faster than females, nurse longer, and are larger when weaned.
Even among the newborns, males and females behave differently.
For one thing, males may attempt "milk thievery," stealing milk
from adult females other than their mothers. Since these other
females have their own pups to nurse, and since there is no evolutionary return in nourishing an unrelated pup, we can expect strong
resistance to such theft. Being a milk thief is, in fact, quite risky, as
females bite and may seriously injure or even kill larcenous pups. But
the payoff is also high, since obtaining extra milk almost certainly
increases the chances that the thieves will not only survive the coming winter, but (and this is especially important for males) that they
will eventually be large enough and strong enough to compete successfully with other males and perhaps even be harem masters someday.

Female pups do not attempt milk thievery. The return for them
isn't worth the risk. Being female guarantees that they will breed,
which is not the case with males, who are born into a system in which
they might fail utterly and which therefore rewards risk taking. Interestingly, male pups do not develop canine teeth as early as
females. Of course, by the time they are needed for fighting other
males, these teeth are well in place. But milk thieves are better off
without canines, since if they are gentler on a female's nipple—
rather like the light touch needed by a good pickpocket—they are
less likely to be discovered and attacked.

Occasionally pups die before they are weaned. This situation frees a large potential source of milk—the bereaved and still lactating mother—for any pup willing to run the risk of getting it. Mothers who lose their pups will generally permit other pups to nurse, but the procedure is a delicate one for the pup. The foster mother will often attack would-be nursers, sometimes quite viciously, before she comes to accept them (mistakenly) as her own. However, the return for the pups is high. Such successful pups are, in LeBoeuf's colorful terminology, "double-mother-suckers," and they will go on to be "super weaners," weighing almost twice as much as their age mates who received milk only from a single mother.

The pattern is clear. Female elephant seals enjoy a high probability of modest reproductive success and, even as pups, they refrain from behavior that is risky, even if potentially rewarding. Most males, on the other hand, will be reproductive failures, but those who succeed will really strike it rich. Their strategy, therefore, is one of blatant fitness maximization—striving, despite heavy risks, to be super weaners and evolutionary stars.

•

People aren't elephant seals, of course, but we do share the same mammalian reproductive biology. And there may be reason to suppose that, through most of our evolutionary history, we ourselves were harem makers and that even today we carry indelible signs of this heritage in our bodies and perhaps, as well, in our behavior.

It is recognized increasingly that there are real differences between little boys and little girls, behavioral differences that begin early in life and that derive at least in part from our biology. For example, boys tend to be more active and more aggressive than girls. Girls accidentally exposed to testosterone, the male sex hormone, while still in their mother's uterus were found to be "masculinized" as children. They often developed into tomboys, favoring rough-and-tumble outdoor play, and were generally more active than other, "normal" girls, even though their parents seemingly did not treat them any differently. In fact, the parents of such children were so disturbed by their daughters' "boylike" behavior that the children were brought to a doctor—the basis of the discovery of the testosterone exposure.

The biology of male-female differences suggests a reason why little boys are more likely than girls to climb trees, get into fights, get covered with mud and wander far from home. Their behavior is more risky and more flamboyant. Natural selection and parental investment theory make intelligible much of what seems to be going on.

There are many possible predictions of differing male and female behavior that can be made and that would be worth testing. For example, male-male competition is likely to be greater when harems occur than when all of a group's members are monogamously mated. The reasoning is that harems are likely to leave some males sexually disenfranchised, but in situations where every male gets mated, there is little call for sexual competition. We also expect, and find, a greater male-female difference in behavior in harem-forming species, since reproductive success in males requires fighting success as well. It would be interesting to learn whether male-female differences in children's play are greater in polygynous than in monogamous societies. Such findings would not necessarily suggest a genetically influenced difference between males in the two types of societies, but if risky, aggressive behavior is more valued and more rewarded in one society than in another, we might expect that that society would be the polygynous one.

It has been observed that infant boys seem to be more "colicky" than girls. Perhaps they have more gastrointestinal distress, or simply a greater "need to cry," but whatever the cause, one result is that they receive greater parental attention, perhaps even more food and nursing. Such behavior can be risky, since it may backfire and anger the parent, but, as with the elephant seals, boys have probably been selected to take such risks.

●

Bizarre it may be, but homosexual rape is a fact of existence in some animal species. Moreover, this behavior seems to contribute to fitness maximization, by means of male-male competition. Consider a bug with the revealing scientific name *Xylocaris maculipennis*. In this species, males rape other males, even while the victim is himself copulating with a female. As a result of the rape, the victim's sperm storage organs are filled with the sperm of the rapist, so that the next time the victim copulates, he transfers the rapist's sperm, in a sort of fitness maximization by proxy. The adaptive significance and the evolutionary mechanism should both be clear. In another example, we might look at certain acanthocephalan worms, parasites that live in the intestines of vertebrates, including rats. Males of this species copulate with females within the close and untidy confines of their host's gut. Following normal copulation, males secrete a cementlike substance, known as a copulation plug, which they insert in the female's vagina. This plug serves a dual purpose, keeping the sperm from leaking out and preventing that of other males from getting in.* The plug is important in male-male competition, but there's more to come. When a male worm gains an advantage over another male, the aggressor applies his cement gland to the victim's sperm opening and cements it closed. The victim is thus made effectively sterile, and a potential competitor is removed. The rapist has increased his fitness by making it more likely that he, and not another male, will be able to copulate with available females. Such antisocial but clearly adaptive behavior is obviously not a case of mistaken identity by the attacker. When males copulate with females, sperm are always transferred first, followed by the plug. But, when males subjugate other males, only the plug is transferred, with no sperm. Evolution "knows" exactly what it is doing! And so does this peculiar beast, despite its scientific name, *M. dubius.*

If the significance of homosexual rape is not yet clear, ask yourself why female dubius worms don't treat other females the way males deal with their male competitors. Remember, the best evolutionary deal that a female can make for herself is to insure that all her eggs get fertilized, which, of course, can be easily accomplished by a high-quality male. Females that went around plugging up the vaginas of other females would probably waste a great deal of time and energy without greatly increasing their own evolutionary suc-

*Copulatory plugs are found in many different animals, including the primates. In many species it is easy to determine whether a female has copulated recently because of the telltale white material visible in her vagina. Presumably, if a human observer—obtuse by monkey standards—can tell, the chances are that other monkeys are at least as well informed. So the plug may also serve as a male calling card, indicating that "this female is already taken." Similarly, the largely nocturnal wombats generate a more visible rubbery-red plug.

But counter-strategies may occur. Anthropologist Jeffrey Kurland reports that among Japanese monkeys adult males occasionally terrorize females, often without provocation. This puzzling behavior actually makes genetic sense, because part of the female's terrified response includes loud cries and muscular convulsions of her abdomen, during which she occasionally "pops her plug." It isn't clear whether males then copulate with the newly available female, but evolutionary biologists wouldn't be surprised.

cess, since the biological nature of male and female virtually guarantees that each female will have all of her eggs fertilized. As a
result, females simply aren't very competitive, and they lack the
structures that would allow them to "rape" other females. (Of
course, if there were a danger that males could not fertilize all
available females, selection would doubtless favor female-female
competition for access to males. In this circumstance, one of the
possible adaptive mechanisms might include putting other females
out of commission.)

Don't be misled; these examples have nothing whatsoever to do
with human homosexuality. I have described them because they
reveal so starkly how evolution generates male-male competitiveness. Most people are already familiar with such male-male competition as the titanic battles of grizzly bears, antler clashing among bull
elk, and dramatic mid-air head butting among mountain sheep.
However, male competition is sometimes a good deal more subtle.
Chimpanzees, for example, live in large, loose social groups consisting of many adult males and many females. They display very little
male-male aggression and virtually no sexual rivalry; males will literally wait their turn while a female in heat copulates with them all.
But this does not mean that male chimps don't compete. They do
compete, but not by fighting. Their competition consists of producing larger amounts of sperm. Chimpanzee testicles are six times
larger than those of a gorilla, even though their bodies are only
one-third the size.

Male gorillas, as with the males of most harem-forming mammalian species, are much larger and fiercer than females, and compete vigorously with other males for control of the females. Gorilla
social groups consist, typically, of one adult male, perhaps one or
several younger males, and several females and their young. The
older male is the undisputed leader of his harem, for once he has
achieved dominance, gorilla social structure assures that he will be
the only one to mate. He has no need for oversized testicles; he has
competed successfully by using other parts of his body.

It is interesting that, while chimps can mount, thrust, ejaculate
and dismount in about seven seconds, gorillas are much more lei-
surely, and may take up to twenty minutes to do the same. By the
time copulation takes place, the dominant adult male gorilla has
already succeeded in eliminating the competition. He did so when

he originally gained control of the group—and its females.*

Sociobiology demonstrates that male-female behavioral differences are consistent with the basic biology of maleness and femaleness. Because they make such a small investment in their sex cells, males are generally selected to be less fussy and more promiscuous than females, and to compete with other males for access to females. This disparity explains why male elephant seals seek to be double-mother-suckers, why male *M. dubius* rape other males, why chimpanzees have large testicles while gorillas have small ones, and why, on the whole, men are generally more aggressive than women.

•

Before the spread of Western ways began the present homogenization of world culture, more than 70 percent of the world's people were polygynous. This does not mean that men were harem keepers like the elephant seal, or even like King Ismail. Human harems were more modest, in fact, with most men remaining monogamous. At the highest levels of society, older and particularly successful men had several wives, in many cases accumulating them over time as they accumulated wealth and status. As a result, many younger men remained bachelors. Polygyny, in some cases, reached spectacular extremes, creating a social milieu that probably led to especially strong selection for competitive traits among males, suiting their greater sexual availability.

Among the South American Yanomamo, a single headman, Matakuwa, had 42 children, one of whom fathered an additional 33. Some 45 percent of the population of 10 Yanomamo villages were descended from Matakuwa's father. Given the vigorous male-male competition this sexual oligopoly suggests, it should be no surprise that the Yanomamo were intensely warlike, calling themselves "the fierce people." Matakuwa regularly incited his followers to raid other villages and carry off additional women. Many similar instances have been reported. A chief of Brazil's Xavante Indians fathered 23 offspring, who comprised one-fourth of all the children in the village. An able and elderly hunter among the Anaktuvuk Eskimos of Alaska

---

*In some species, males compete largely by copulating for a very long time. Dogs, for instance, form mating "locks" which may last for hours, during which time they cannot be pulled apart. The great mammalogist R. F. Ewer once observed a marsupial mouse, which arose in heat one night and copulated for twelve hours with a single male. The next night the same pair performed for eight hours straight.

contributed one-fifth of the total living population of his tribe. Anthropologist Weston LaBarre comments quite explicitly on the extensiveness of this pattern:

> When it comes to polygyny . . . the cases are extraordinarily numerous. Indeed, polygyny is permitted (though in every case it may not be achieved) among all the Indian tribes of North and South America, with the exception of a few like the Pueblo. Polygyny is common too in both Arab and Negro groups in Africa and is by no means unusual either in Asia or in Oceania. Sometimes, of course, it is culturally-limited polygyny: Moslems may have only four wives under Koranic law—while the King of Ashanti in West Africa was strictly limited to 3,333 wives and had to be content with this number. The custom of concubinage, official or unofficial, or the taking of secondary wives and concubines, is also very widespread in both Asia and Europe and elsewhere.

There is even direct evidence from our anatomy and physiology suggesting that polygyny is the biologically "natural" state of *Homo sapiens*. Except for our genitalia, the physical differences between men and women are much more associated with fighting than with copulating. Among animals, monogamy is almost invariably found among those species that have little difference in size between the sexes. Foxes, coyotes, eagles, geese, swans, ducks, sparrows, bluebirds and warblers all tend to be monogamous, with males and females growing to approximately the same size. If we consider some polygynous species—elephant seals, deer, elk, moose, gorillas —the typical social system is one male mating with several females, and, not surprisingly, the males are considerably larger than their consorts. Among human beings, although some women are larger than some men, there is no question that, on the whole, men are the larger sex.

It is also instructive to compare the age of sexual maturation: among polygynous animals, males mature later than females. Actually, we might have expected the opposite to be true. Given that reproduction places greater stress on females than on males, it seems appropriate that females delay breeding until they are large and strong enough to do it well. However, male-male competition, it appears, overrides any tendencies to early male maturation. Polygyny, as we have seen, requires this sort of competition, and it's the larger, wiser males who tend to win. Strength and experience come with age, though, so it should be no surprise that, while elephant seal cows begin breeding at two or three, the bulls don't mature until they are at least five. Below that age, the bulls are simply unable to compete with the battle-scarred, veteran behemoths who control the harems. They are better off lying low until they are big enough, wise enough, and tough enough to "make their move." Consider that in our own species girls reach puberty several years earlier than boys. Sociobiology finally makes sense out of this undeniable fact of our biology.*

Monogamy is a rarity among mammals, and for good reasons. Since female mammals have breasts which produce milk, they are uniquely adapted to nourish their own young. Males are not particularly important as parents and may even constitute undesirable competition for food that would otherwise go to the mother and, through her, to the offspring. It is understandable, therefore, that among some mammals, such as bears and hamsters, the female chases the male away after mating. In other situations, notably the large hoofed mammals such as buffalo, antelope and zebra, males do contribute to their own fitness by defending the group against predators, but, even here, a prolonged bond between male and female is not adaptive and is rarely found.

Some carnivorous mammals, such as foxes and coyotes, are, in fact, monogamous. In these cases the males are useful as providers, bringing meat to their females. Meat, it should be pointed out, is a concentrated nutritional source. It would be very inefficient for an animal to carry grain or vegetables back home to eat, and I know of no cases where males of a vegetarian species bring plant food to their families. Males either bring home the bacon, or nothing at all.

To sum up our observations thus far: monogamy is rare in mammals, almost unheard-of in primates, and, despite our Judeo-Christian fondness for the "nuclear family," it appears to be a relatively recent invention of certain human cultures. Our biology may permit

*At this point, my editor asked me, "Can't little men fight with each other?" Of course they can, but under the conditions of our evolutionary past they were likely to be defeated by the older and larger men. Genes finding themselves in a male body were more fit if they caused it to mature later, when that body was big and experienced enough to make it likely that those genes would be passed on to new bodies in future generations.

this social form, but it certainly doesn't demand it—and may not even like it.

●

Consider the following question from the viewpoint of any adult mammal: Will I be more fit if I produce boys or girls? In general, either sex is an equally good evolutionary investment. Suppose we have a population of 20 individuals, consisting of 10 males and 10 females. If the society is monogamous, males and females are both equally successful as reproducers. But, surprisingly, the same *overall* result is found even if the society is highly polygynous. If we suppose that only one male mates with all 10 females, the other 9 males will remain disappointed bachelors. Since every female breeds successfully, parents that originally produced these females receive a guaranteed evolutionary return, with each set of parents neither more nor less successful than another. Any given set of parents that produced male offspring stand a 90 percent chance of losing out in the evolutionary lottery, since 9 out of their 10 male children don't breed at all. However, any given male also has a 10 percent chance of being wildly successful—10 times more so than any female. On the average, it all balances out. It is an equally good strategy, overall, to produce males as to produce females, although the former choice is a much riskier way to play the game. This may be another way of understanding why males often engage in "riskier" behaviors.

Parents are therefore equally fit producing males or females, so long as they have no idea whether their offspring are likely to be successful in competing with others. Any advance information they may have does change the situation a great deal, and there is every reason to suspect that parents can, in fact, "estimate" the likelihood of their offspring's success, even before it is born. For example, a child born to a socially dominant female is more likely to be dominant than a child born to one who is retiring and deferential. This might be due to the particular genetic characteristic of the parent, the social advantages enjoyed by the child, or some combination of the two. In any event, offspring of different sets of parents are not likely to be equally successful as adults. Another example: offspring born to a mother who is strong, healthy and in good physical condition will probably be strong, healthy and in good physical condition themselves, and, as a result, are likely to be more successful socially.

With a sufficient head start, individuals have a greater than average likelihood of achieving reproductive success—being a harem master, having many wives, etc.

The biologists Trivers and D. E. Willard have predicted that, among polygynous species, females who are socially dominant or are in especially good physical condition are expected to produce more male than female offspring, whereas subordinates or those in relatively poor condition should tilt toward producing females. In other words, the females should use the riskier strategy when the odds are stacked in their favor; otherwise, they should play it more conservatively. Remarkably, this "gamble" is just what seems to occur. Deer, mink, pigs and a number of other species bias their reproduction to favor males when they are healthy and females when they aren't. Although we don't know what mechanism these animals use to vary the sex of their offspring, there are numerous possibilities. The sex of the fetus is determined by which type of sperm fertilizes the egg (X sperm produce females, while Y sperm produce males). It would not strain the adaptive ingenuity of the female reproductive tract to vary the chemical environment of the vagina so as to favor survival of either X or Y sperm, depending on the mother's social or physical condition. Humans have already begun experimenting with choosing the production of boys versus girls by douching with either baking soda (the alkalinity of which is conducive to Y sperm survival) or vinegar (whose acidity is more hospitable to the X sperm) before intercourse.

Another possible mechanism for adaptively varying the sex of offspring is for the body to abort male embryos in preference to female ones when the mother is undergoing social or physical stress. Such spontaneous abortions may also occur in humans, but in a surprising way. It is common medical knowledge that male fetuses have a higher mortality than females. If a pregnant woman is ill or injured and has a miscarriage as a result, the still-born child is more likely to be male than female. This higher male mortality has traditionally been explained by some sort of generalized "weakness" of males, due, perhaps, to the effect of their carrying the more vulnerable Y chromosome. Sociobiology suggests that the greater susceptibility of male fetuses to stress may represent an adaptive, fitness-maximizing strategy by the mother, who jettisons her unborn male offspring when he ceases to be a good investment. A weak or injured male infant is a bad investment—even worse than a disadvantaged female, since competition between females is likely to be less severe than that between males. The sooner the old fetus is rejected, the sooner the mother can breed again. She may produce a girl next time, of course, but it may also be that conditions will have changed enough to make a boy a good bet the second time around.

Animal breeders arrived at this evolutionary wisdom long before sociobiologists. Breeders with top-quality stock prefer males, which are often very valuable for stud, while those with lower-grade stock prefer females, since low-grade males are virtually worthless for breeding purposes in a system in which a single high-quality stud can inseminate many females. We can predict that among humans high-ranking women may be more likely to invest in boys than in girls, and that infanticide (a common procedure in many human societies) may be directed more toward girls in such circumstances. Of course, the opposite prediction might be made for low-ranking women.

We might also predict that the expected correlation between high status and male preference would be greater in polygynous societies than in those more inclined toward monogamy. The more polygynous a society, the greater the payoff for the especially fit male, the greater the likelihood of being totally left out if one is less than excellent. If you were a parent in a society in which only one male breeds each generation, would you prefer to have boys or girls? If you choose boys, you are taking an enormous risk and are likely to be less fit than your neighbor who plays it safe and has girls. All of those girls will probably reproduce, while your boys almost certainly will not—unless, of course, you have reason to think that one of your sons will be *the* grand harem master. Polygyny should therefore lead to bias toward male offspring only among the best-endowed parents.

There is good evidence that preference for either boys or girls has had results which are gruesome, but which fit the predictions of sociobiology. In Chinese society, upper-class parents traditionally discriminated against girl infants and infanticide was common. Lower-class girls married upper-class men, who received dowries along with their brides. Upper-class males obtained both wealth and women, while lower-class men wound up with neither. This system resulted in greater reproductive success for those wealthy parents who followed the strategy of preferring males to females, since a successful Chinese male child was likely to sire many children by many wives.

We might predict that the lower classes would in turn actively discriminate against sons, since their daughters were likely to be successful while their sons would generally be out-competed by upper-class sons. However, the facts here are not clear. It is clear, however, that a similar strategy of upper-class preference for sons prevailed also in traditional Indian society. There, wives were taken from the lower castes, so that upper-class Hindus put all their parental resources into the raising of sons. In fact, the elite Punjabi priestly caste, the Bedi-Sikhs, were known as the *Kuri Mar*—the daughter killers.

•

There are a few human societies and a few animal species that practice polyandry, a mating system in which one female forms a reproductive bond with several males. This is a very rare and fascinating institution, which will be discussed in fuller detail in chapter five. However, it should be pointed out here that the existence of polyandrous animal species means, reassuringly to some, that females don't necessarily have to be less aggressive than males, and that, instead of sharing one male with several other females, they can enjoy a bevy of adoring consorts. The jacana, called in South America the Jesus Christ bird (because its long toes enable it to stand on lily pads, thus giving the impression of walking on water) provides one example of polyandrous mating. The female of the species defends a large territory within which there may be several males, each tending its own nest. The proprietor female goes from nest to nest, mating with each male, laying eggs in each nest. The male rears the young, with little or no maternal assistance.

Polyandrous species provide convincing support for the theory linking parental investment with competition: individuals of the sex investing less are thought to compete among themselves for access to individuals of the sex investing more. Usually the former are males and the latter are females, but among jacanas the situation is reversed. Since males build the nests and provision the young, they invest more than the females, and we therefore expect the females to show the effects of selection for competitive ability. This they do: they are much larger than the males and sport bright plumage, while the males are drab. Female jacanas are also quite aggressive, while the males stay home and quietly look after the domestic chores.

The origin of polyandry is obscure. Once systems of this sort became established, however, they could easily be maintained by natural selection acting on the different patterns of parental investment. But what originally produced these patterns? One possibility is suggested by the observation that in some species the female takes a short vacation after laying her eggs, leaving her mate to begin incubation while she gets a few good meals to make up for what was lost in producing the eggs. Such females occasionally gain enough weight to lay another clutch, and, if they are fertilized, will do so. This "double clutching" is possible only when food resources are abundant. The second clutch may be incubated by the female, or perhaps by another male; if the latter takes place often enough, it could be the gateway to true polyandry. But, even if this theory proves correct, it should not be mistaken for social or political liberation. Evolution is a tyrant, and while it works in different ways on the two sexes, it never gives up. In no cases are individuals of either sex entirely free of it. Certainly neither is more free than the other. The polyandrous female, for example, is simply "freed" to produce another clutch of eggs; if truly liberated, she gets the privilege of evolving large size, aggressiveness and the need to compete with other females who are selected for similar traits. She will probably have a shorter life span as well—a trait that is nearly always characteristic of the more competitive sex. (And the human species is not exempt —who lives longer, women or men?) She will be caught, in short, like all living things, in the forced labor of fitness maximization, whether eating, sleeping, courting, copulating, parenting . . . whatever she is doing.

•

What theories are available to account for the differences between men and women, both in sexual proclivities and in aggressiveness? The few that exist are woefully unconvincing. One theory proposed by Sigmund Freud has, for better or worse, been highly influential. According to Freud, most of our adult behavior derives from sexual impulses redirected early in life, with male-female differences proving no exception. Just as the mythical Greek Oedipus is supposed to have murdered his father and married his mother, little boys are believed to develop an early sexual yearning for their mothers. This potential incest is inhibited only because the mother is "already taken" by the much larger and more formidable father. The healthy male must work out his Oedipal conflict by identifying with his father and by seeking out other women who will ultimately substitute for the forbidden mother. In the process, of course, he may compete with other young males and may further act out his frustrated inability to dominate his father.

And little girls? As infants, they too are sexually inclined toward their mothers but soon make the shocking discovery that they (the little girls) don't have a penis. They develop "penis envy," and may resent their mothers for having irreparably castrated them. They cannot achieve their original goal—possession of the mother—because they are the "wrong" sex, and unfortunately father is also unavailable, because mother is around. So girls are resigned to a passive acceptance of their unhappy lot, producing babies as a "penis substitute."

Another theory, common in social science, is that boys act as they do because such behavior is taught to them, and the same for girls. There is no question about it, we do do a great deal to inculcate gender identity among our children. Girls are more likely to be given dolls to play with, and boys tend to receive toy airplanes. Much of this early conditioning may be quite unconscious, even by the most sexually unstereotyped parent. For example, we tend to hold girl babies differently—often, more tenderly—than boys, and we are more inclined toward rough-and-tumble play with boy babies. These differences, which almost certainly contribute to differences among adults, are not limited to Western societies. Among the world's warlike non-industrialized societies, boys are treated quite unlike girls. Beginning in infancy, they are rewarded for intemperate, aggressive behavior, which doubtless makes for intemperate, aggressive men.

This point is significant and carries a real message if we are to ameliorate our own sexist society. Dick-and-Jane books must show Jane doing exciting, interesting things too, if real-life Janes are to grow up believing that they can do so. But as an all-encompassing explanation for male-female differences, early social experience is simply insufficient. If we are to believe that there are no real male-female differences in behavior, and that such differences as we see are simply a result of the differential experiences that society provides little boys and little girls, we must also explain why such differences are promulgated independently by every society on earth. Anthropologist Marvin Harris has written: "Not a shred of evidence, historical or contemporary, supports the existence of a single society in which women controlled the political and economic lives of men."* It strains belief that around the globe and throughout history women have been the victims of a coordinated and sustained plot by churlish males who have conspired to manipulate the social structure to exploit women by forcing them into unwanted roles.

Granted, human societies tend to "make" girls distinct from boys. In addition, different societies do so in different ways and to different degrees. But *they all do it,* and the most reasonable explanation is that, at least to some extent, such differences express something of the biological dissimilarities between males and females. Such a conclusion is unavoidable. Society may exaggerate sex differences between people but it does not create them. Lionel Tiger and Robin Fox have pointed out that we learn aggressiveness as we learn love —easily. The same may well be true of sex role differences.

Another common explanation of male-female differences holds that the two sexes differ in their hormone levels, with testosterone prevailing in men and estrogen in women. Certainly, male-female hormone variations are very real, and no farmer needs to be told the difference between a bull and an ox, a stallion and a gelding, or a rooster and a capon. But endocrine action is an immediate, proximal cause, not an ultimate, evolutionary one. To say that men are more aggressive because of testosterone is like saying that internal-combustion engines are noisier than electric motors because of gasoline. In a sense, the statement is true, but a deeper fact is that internal-combustion engines use gasoline and other combustible (that is, noisy) fuels because that is the way they are designed. We are inquiring here into the design features of human behavior—in the present case, why we respond to testosterone in the way we do, and why men secrete more of it than women. Why is sugar sweet? Ask evolution.

Actually, there are two other biological factors that might contribute to the differences between men and women. Greater male size

*However, I don't wish to misrepresent Harris, who then provides a rather standard social science approach: "The appropriate response . . . is an investigation of the cultural conditions that have nurtured and sustained male sexism . . . Male supremacy is not a biological imperative or a genetically programmed characteristic of the human species."

and aggressiveness may also be due in part to a long evolutionary history of selection for male ability to defend the group and family against predators and enemies, as well as for the ability to hunt successfully. While these notions are fine up to a point, they don't explain such other phenomena as greater male sexual availability. Furthermore, they beg the question of why males were selected for defense and/or hunting in the first place. Perhaps this was because males are biologically the more expendable sex.

The fact remains: in all animals, human and otherwise, males are selected for a reproductive strategy different from that of females. In nearly all of these cases, males compete with other males for sexual access to females, as a consequence of their biologically defined maleness. Among some species, the contest is open and rather brutal. Elephant seals, elk and mountain sheep rams must defeat all rivals to win their harems. Females in these species are passive; they maximize their fitness by acquiescing to the results of the male contests, just as the males maximize their fitness by contesting. In other species, however, competition is often much more subtle. Males and females must still engage in fitness-maximizing strategies, but the male may either have to gain control of important environmental resources or make himself attractive to the female. This sort of self-advertisement introduces a whole new exciting dimension to reproductive strategies—female choice.

•

It is spring. Marshes throughout North America are alive with the burbling of red-winged blackbirds as males sing lustily and fight with their neighbors, each trying to establish a territory. These males have returned from their winter homes in the south several weeks earlier than the females in order to establish themselves as residents and therefore be attractive as mates when the females finally arrive. When the long-awaited day arrives, each female settles down in the territory of a male, mates with him and rears her young. However, not all males are equally successful: some wind up with as many as five or six females, while others mope through the spring without a single mate. Why should such a maldistribution occur? Why should any female elect to become the fifth or sixth mate of a particular male when she could have been the only mate of another? Such a choice is especially puzzling since by electing harem status the female surrenders any real possibility of aid from her male in provisioning her offspring. Males with five or six mates simply don't have the time or energy to help with the domestic chores of each of their females. A male with only one mate would be able to devote considerable attention to his single female.

Gordon Orians, the world's foremost authority on blackbirds, has offered an explanation. Essentially, the females make their choices based on evolutionary considerations—that is, they do what maximizes their fitness. Everything else being equal, a female might well be more fit if she were monogamously mated, since she would then be the object of undivided attention. However, all other things rarely are equal. In this case, something not always equal is the quality of the territory controlled by the male. Territories differ in many ways: some may offer better food, if, say, they include areas where insects are abundant; some might offer greater protection from predators because they have many strong, high reeds where a nest can be built safely out of reach of marauding mink, weasels or water snakes. A female could be more fit as a fifth or sixth wife than as a single mate, provided the harem master offered her a territory with reproductive advantages sufficient to compensate for the loss of his exclusive services. As far as natural selection is concerned, impoverished monogamy takes a back seat to plush polygyny.

Since females are selected to behave in ways that maximize their fitness, a major component of their mate-selection strategy should be "What's in it for me?" From the female viewpoint, there are three major concerns in choosing a mate: (1) mating with the best possible male (that is, choosing the best possible genes to combine with her own, thereby maximizing the chances of her own genes' success); (2) gaining access to the best possible combination of environmental resources (that is, the best possible combination of food, defense against predators and so on); and (3) acquiring a male whose behavior will contribute directly to her reproductive success, perhaps by helping to provide food for her offspring, to defend them against predators and so forth. The red-winged blackbirds seem especially to exemplify concern number 2—resource-based mating systems. It might be helpful to look at each of these systems in turn. There are useful animal examples for each. Obviously, in many cases, several of these considerations operate simultaneously. The "best possible male" (the one with the best genes) is likely to be the one who was victorious in competing for the best resources, and may also be the one with the most helpful behavior.

What does this have to do with *Homo sapiens?* Probably a great deal. It may well be that in varying degrees all three of these considerations operate in human mate selection: genetic quality, access to resources and behavioral tendencies of the ideal mate.

•

Let's look first at the genetic quality of the prospective mate. In some species, the male does not provide any resources to the female, neither assistance in rearing her young nor even a territory in which she may do so herself. In such cases, males often compete among themselves, performing elaborate courtships at communal display sites. Females come to these arenas, pick out the dominant males, and mate with them.

For example, among prairie chickens and sage grouse, members of the pheasant family, males stake out display arenas (called "leks") that are often adjacent to each other. The best leks, generally at the center, are most commonly won in competition by the best males. When the females arrive, pandemonium breaks loose, the males prancing, booming, hooting or drumming (depending on their species). Males generally remain within their own leks, however, and the final reproductive decision is the females'. Significantly, the great majority of females mate with a very small number of males, who enjoy the reproductive privileges of a harem, but sequentially rather than simultaneously.

This pattern is not limited to birds; it holds for many mammals and even for certain insects. What does the female gain by choosing the best dancers, prancers, or other performers? Why does she bother to choose at all? There are probably two reasons. First, by selecting only the best males, females are likely to acquire only the best male genes to pair with their own. Second, once females of a species show a preference for a certain male trait—whatever its original utility—the trait can develop further reproductive utility of its own. For example, if large male feathers "turn on" female peacocks (peahens), females who prefer males with elaborate plumes will be more fit than those who don't. The gain of fitness becomes obvious in the next generation: the sons of an appropriately turned-on peahen will tend to have desirable plumes and will therefore be more attractive to the next generation of females. The net effect is to provide more grandchildren to the initial chooser. The implication is that certain characteristic male traits—in many species, perhaps even our own—may be little more than the rather absurd result of "sexual selection" by females.

Females need not simply be passive bystanders to male-male competition. In many cases, they exert real influence by deciding which male is to be successful. They hold the reproductive cards, and it is reasonable that this be so, because the greater parental investment is surely theirs. In some species, females actually incite males to compete. Such provocation benefits the females by helping them choose the best competers. Although the females' action seems like unfair exploitation, it is as value free as anything else about evolution. A female mallard duck engages in a peculiar behavior early in pair formation, swimming toward a strange male, then retreating to her betrothed, turning her head from him to the stranger. Thus incited, the prospective mate often attacks the stranger. Presumably, this process gives the female a little extra information about her potential mate before she finally says, "I do."

Imagine, if you can, that you are a subordinate but ambitious male elephant seal. You have just mounted the damsel of your dreams, but much to your chagrin, she begins to scream loudly, bringing all the other males who happen to be around running (or rather, lurching, flopping and rolling) over to her. A free-for-all ensues, with the dominant bull displacing you and everyone else, then copulating with the female. The female's screams effectively activated the male dominance hierarchy, with the result that she was inseminated by the dominant male. A feminist friend to whom I described this process remarked angrily, "That bitch!" But the fact is, it is a wise bitch that looks after her own fitness.

For human beings, conscious concern about the genetic characteristics of prospective mates has a rather unappetizing air to it, conjuring up noxious images of eugenics, Naziesque breeding farms and so forth. But, unconsciously, our genes may well perform such calculations for their own benefit. There may well be a real evolutionary wisdom in what "turns us on" about someone else. Is it really surprising that regular features, good physique and a certain level of intelligence are considered desirable? And would it be simply coincidental if such traits were heritable and ultimately fitness-enhancing for those who could latch onto them in others?

The ideals of male and female beauty have varied greatly through human history and across different cultures, but there may well be biological sense underlying it all. The full-bodied Earth Mother Goddess of antiquity may have been a durable mate and a successful mother who could give birth and nourish her child with relative ease. The European ideal of later centuries, an ivory-white complexion, indicated exemption from outdoor work and, hence, good financial resources. In the last third of the twentieth century, a sufficient number of people work indoors so that a tanned skin indicates a level of wealth needed to afford an outdoor vacation. And Earth Mother has been replaced by Twiggy, now that modern obstetrics allows narrow-hipped women to bear children that otherwise might kill them.

Robert Browning wrote that our reach should exceed our grasp ... "Or what's a heaven for?" In our choice of the best possible mate, we may reach for a heavenly partner, but we grasp at what we can, and what is good for us and our genes.

•

In resource-based mating systems, males are selected to compete with other males for control of the best resources, and females are selected to mate preferentially with the winners for use of those resources. As the saying goes, "Those that have, get." The orange-rumped honeyguide is a brilliant-colored bird that lives in Nepal and loves to eat beeswax. Beehives are, therefore, highly valued and are defended energetically by males. To obtain beeswax, a female must copulate with the proprietor male, and, as an indication of the importance of the resource, only males defending hives do any copulating. While females find non-beehive-owning males totally resistible, one particularly "wealthy" male was observed to mate forty-six times with at least eighteen different females during one breeding season! Females probably gain twofold in this system. By copulating with proprietor males they gain access to a valued food; furthermore, by mating only with proprietors, they insure that they will be inseminated by the best males, those selected to compete for control of the hives. Those that win are likely to be the *best;* by winning, they have proven themselves.

A similar case has been described by Syracuse University biologist

Larry Wolf for purple-throated Carib hummingbirds on the island of Dominica. In this instance, the valued resource is certain trees that have an abundance of flowers. Hummingbirds are particularly fond of these blooms, and the males defend territories containing as many flowering trees as possible, aggressively driving off other males that attempt to feed there. Interestingly, they drive off females as well, unless the females copulate with them. Males, then, give food in exchange for sex. Wolf reported his observations in a scientific paper he entitled "Prostitution Behavior in a Tropical Hummingbird," and his use of this term is probably correct, since what is human prostitution if not the exchange of sexual favors for resources? In human prostitution the male client may not be trying to impregnate his companion, and she is almost certainly not trying to become pregnant by him. However, it is still consistent with biology that males seek sex and are willing to pay for it, and that females have something that males desire for which they demand payment.

The relevant point for human sociobiology is that we almost certainly base much of our mating on resources, although perhaps less directly than do red-winged blackbirds, tropical hummingbirds or Himalayan honeyguides. Certainly we have modified, sometimes even redirected, the internal whisperings of fitness maximization that control so much of animal behavior. With our remarkable ability to be subtle and complex, we encrust our biological impulses with culture, learning and psychological satisfactions that are often several steps removed from our biology. When we are sexually excited, reproducing our genes may be the last thing on our minds, but natural selection is under no obligation to let us in on its designs. It is probably no accident that when it comes to reproduction men are nearly always treated as "success objects," which is how beeswax may be very much like a Ferrari—and vice versa.

The connection between resources and human mating is particularly apparent in polygynous societies, where, not surprisingly, the standard pattern is for a man to acquire wives as he acquires resources. He may acquire his first wife at age twenty to twenty-five, his second at thirty-five to forty, his third at forty-five to fifty, and so on. There appears to be a strong connection between polygyny and gerontocracy, with older men having more wives. It may not be coincidental that older men also have more resources. In addition, senior members of a society have often proved themselves in hunting, war or other activities valued by the group. The practice of trophy hunting and collecting is nearly universal; it may well have evolved as a technique for males to display their competence to attentive females. Among Muslims, who may have up to four wives, the number, appropriately, is controlled rather strictly by the man's wealth.

To consider such societies as exploiting women is to be both nearsighted and culture bound. A woman may be far better off, in terms of both personal amenities and reproductive success, as the third wife of a wealthy sheik than as the only wife of a pauper.

Among many Australian aboriginals,

> The women tended to aggregate themselves in collectives of co-wives around the men at the peak of their productive capacity, and this tendency reached its maximum when the women had their greatest child-rearing burdens. It will be immediately noted that in this explanation it was the women and not the men who took the active role to establish polygynous units, and that this type of family provided the optimum conditions for the rearing of the younger generation inside the collectives of co-wives of the polygynous families.

Note that men are at the "peak of their productive capacity" when they are in their mid-forties—that is, when they are most able to provide resources for their families, and not when they are at their sexual peak, which occurs in the teens. Sperm are produced in such amounts, even in middle age, that potency takes a back seat to other considerations.

Throughout the world, "May-December" marriages are common, almost always with the man December and woman May. It is fascinating that shortly after taking the Senate floor to denounce the "immorality" of former United States Supreme Court Justice William O. Douglas for taking a wife less than half his age, South Carolina's Senator Strom Thurmond did the same thing, marrying a woman young enough to be his granddaughter! Although tongues may occasionally wag at such behavior, it is not generally regarded as discrediting, perhaps because of grudging, if unconscious, recognition that the people involved are maximizing their fitness, or at least behaving in ways consistent with evolutionary strategies of resources and mate selection. But consider the scandal when an older woman associates with a much younger man! This relationship is somehow "against nature." Given the sociobiology of mate selection, the movie *Harold and Maude,* which told the story of a sexual liaison between a seven-teen-year-old-boy and an eighty-year-old woman, had no alternative but to be tragicomic.

Hypergamy (literally, "marrying up") is widespread among humans. Predictably, it is especially a strategy of women. It is much more common for women to be influenced by the accomplishments of potential husbands than for men to be concerned with similar traits in their wives. Which situation seems more incongruous, a male doctor, college professor or business executive whose wife has only a high-school education, or a female doctor, college professor or business executive whose husband hasn't gone to college? This tendency to hypergamy places successful females in our own society in a difficult position. They are much more limited in their choices of suitable mates than are equally successful males. Men can find mates from the entire spectrum of female population, while women tend to be uncomfortable with men who are "beneath" them. Although in fairy tales there is always the princess who runs off with the gypsy, it requires a man with an especially strong ego to accept a mate who is more successful than he is.

The tendency for female animals to select males that provide resources that contribute most to their fitness and the corresponding tendency of males to oblige them has had some bizarre results. Males of many different species of birds and insects present their females with food as part of courtship. In certain cases, the male even gives his female the ultimate gift: himself. The female dines on the male during or after, or, in some cases, before copulating with him. This behavior can be seen as the gruesome result of a female's selection of males who provide her with additional food, that is, males who will contribute to her fitness. A male concerned with his own fitness has no alternative but to accede.

Courtship in the natural world often involves gift giving and receiving, and because males and females are constituted differently, they almost never go "Dutch treat."

Among the small carnivorous insects known as empid flies, females are larger than males, and, not uncommonly, an unlucky male finds himself being a meal rather than a mate. This is fine with the females, so long as they are eventually fertilized by an occasional "lucky" male. In certain empid species, males avoid this fate by first securing a ritual offering, generally a smaller fly of another species, and presenting this juicy morsel to their chosen female. While she feeds happily, he may copulate unmolested. Males of other empid fly species first adorn their gifts with silk, perhaps in order to make them more conspicuous to the female. This decoration may also ensure that it takes longer for the female to open the package, thereby giving the male more time to copulate. Males of yet another species suck the prey dry themselves—and wrap it in an especially large amount of silk. Presumably, once the deception is discovered by their paramours it is too late. Other empids dispense with the prey altogether and simply take a twig or piece of leaf, making certain only to wrap it well. And in one species the males don't even bother with the contents; they go a-courtin' with an elaborate silken balloon containing . . . nothing whatever!

•

> He floats through the air with the greatest of ease,
> The daring young man on the flying trapeze.
> His movements are graceful, all girls he does please
> . . . And my love he has taken away!

Why does the daring young man please the girls? In answering this question, we are considering the third case of mate selection—desirable behavior on the part of the prospective partner. Once again, real sociobiological wisdom is operative here, bound up tightly with the advantage females gain by mating with males who will maximize their fitness. For their part, males are not above deceit in impressing females. After all, the stakes are high.

Damselfish live among teeming coral reefs in the warm, clear water off the coast of Hawaii. Females swim about in large schools with other females, while at various locations below them individual males defend small territories. When a female school swims directly over one of these territories, the resident male swims up and begins various courtship movements. A female who is sufficiently moved responds to the male's gyrations and swims down to his territory to spawn. After a few minutes, with her eggs deposited and fertilized by the proprietor male, the spawned female returns to her school, leaving the eggs to be tended and guarded by the male. Each new prospective father has a great deal of work to do, because the reef abounds with other fish, many of which would love a meal of fish eggs. If an egg batch is left unguarded for more than a few minutes, it is invariably eaten by a predator. The male must remain constantly on guard, driving away the intruders who threaten his reproductive investment, sometimes darting at them several times per minute.

Now, let's look at a female. What excites her? To whom will she entrust her precious batch of eggs? Damselfish have no flying trapezes, so what sort of male behavior will please the girls? A female damselfish should be especially susceptible to any male who somehow indicates that he would contribute significantly to her fitness. Certainly his ability and inclination to defend the female's eggs would be a major factor, since predators are ever-present and those females who deposit their eggs with reliable defenders leave more successful offspring. Consequently, any genetically influenced tendency to prefer such males should be strongly selected. I tested this prediction by spending more than one hundred hours scuba diving off the coast of Maui, observing courtship among the damselfishes. It was actually quite easy to compare the different males as territory defenders. I simply observed how each responded when a potential egg eater intruded on his newly established territory. Some males were vigorous in defending their territories, aggressively attacking all trespassers. Others were more lethargic. What of the females? It appeared that they were making the same comparison that I was, and their preference was for active, defending males. They consistently deposited their eggs with these rather than with the lazier males.

Since females swoon over males who assertively defend their territories against potential predators, we would expect males to exaggerate their aggressive, fishy "manliness" when females are nearby. This proves to be the case. Males are significantly fiercer in chasing away potential egg eaters when a school of females is directly overhead than when they are not being watched. It's no use flexing your muscles when no one is around. Male damselfish normally allow wrasses (one of the egg-eating species) to approach to within about four feet of their nests before driving them away. However, I once saw a territory-owning male chase off a very surprised wrasse that was innocently lounging more than ten feet away; not unexpectedly, there happened to be some female damselfish watching.

With the female damselfish selected to prefer aggressive males and the males therefore selected to appear as aggressive as they can, the system seems to be ripe for deceit. What is there to stop a male from exaggerating his aggressiveness? Why not pretend to be more aggressive than he really is? Should that happen, one possible defense of the female would be to discount a certain proportion of male aggressiveness as mere show, feigned simply to impress the ladies. But this distrust would penalize the "honest" males, if there were any, and would in fact require that all become liars if any were to have a chance at successful reproduction. This false aggression may have actually come about, although more research is needed if we are to know for certain.

I once spent almost an hour watching a spectacular aerial display: two sparrow hawks were courting, flying in elaborate loops alternating with power dives. They had a small mouse which one of them had caught, and at different points in the exhibition, one of the birds would drop its prize and the other would gracefully swoop down and snatch it in mid-air. It was an impressive demonstration, and it occurred to me only afterward that I was probably not the only one who was impressed. Certainly I was not the one for whom it was intended.

Imagine that you are a sparrow hawk. It is spring and your hawky hormones tell you it's time to find a mate. What sort of mate are you going to seek out? The partner of your dreams would of course have to be another sparrow hawk, one of the opposite sex and one who is interested in breeding. But that's only the beginning. Sparrow hawks hunt for their food, and it takes great effort on the part of both parents to catch enough small insects and mice to satisfy the ravenous appetites of their little ones. Furthermore, hunting is not easy, and as a hawk you will be well advised (read here, "most fit") if you choose a mate who is a good hunter. You certainly do not wish to make a reproductive commitment to a bird that is clumsy, slow, crippled or in any way inadequate. One good strategy, therefore, would be to engage your prospective partner in a prolonged bout of aerial maneuvering in order to assess its competence. I never saw a sparrow hawk drop its mouse, but if I had, I would not have been surprised had the other flown away in disdain.

It appears that courtship may have a real function in testing competence, and we might expect that such tests would be especially prolonged in monogamous species, and those in which mated partners must rely heavily on each other. Monogamous species do in fact often form prolonged "betrothals" during which male and female associate with each other before actually mating. This period gives ample opportunity for each to assess the other. Promiscuous species, however, in which the mating partners want only each other's sperm or eggs, associate only briefly. Another aspect of competence is being genetically "available," and one sure way to fail a betrothal test is to reveal that you have another partner, or, worse yet (if you are a female), that you are already inseminated. Long betrothals provide for just this contingency. With time, the truth will out, whether it involves a pregnancy, fertilized eggs, or simply the fact of a boy or girl friend hiding in the bushes.

Female ring doves perform a vigorous "nest soliciting" display when they meet a male. In a laboratory experiment, Duke University psychologists Carl Erickson and P. Zenone presented male ring doves with two types of females: one group had previously been exposed to males and were therefore already "nest soliciting," while the second had not been exposed and therefore did not perform the display. Predictably, the males showed less courtship behavior and more aggression toward the already-courted females than toward the "virgins." By definition, a virgin's reproductive investment is not yet committed to another male, and so she represents a fitness-enhancing prospect for the would-be suitor.

The ring dove's rejection of already-inseminated females has a strong parallel in the frequent human insistence on virgin brides.* The bride, of course, need not beware a pregnant groom, and there is relatively little concern from her side of the family that he be sexually "pure." There is a widespread assumption that the desirable marital combination is a sexually experienced man and a virgin woman. Often, this obsessive concern with bridal virginity is made quite explicit. A young Zulu suitor pays a special price to insure that his future wife couldn't possibly be carrying someone else's genes, while among the African Buhaya people, the would-be blushing bride must be physically examined by a select deputation of the groom's relatives, who will then vouch for her virginity.

*Anyone prepared to argue for the role of cultural factors here—women as property, "macho" men who are also subconsciously afraid of sexually-experienced women, etc.—should bear in mind that culture and biology are not mutually exclusive. On the contrary, they are often mutually reinforcing, as seems to be true in this case.

In some societies, however, people have recently been discovering how to get around the telltale evolutionary warning of a ruptured hymen—Japanese physicians have a booming business creating virgins by plastic surgery.

Since reproduction is the cornerstone of evolutionary success, and individuals of monogamous species rely so heavily on their partners, we might also expect evolution to select for them to change partners when they have information that such a change—divorce—would benefit their fitness. Such a practice has even been observed among the gulls known as kittiwakes, a European species that nest on sheer cliffs. Most of these birds retain their mates of the previous season. Such old married couples generally begin breeding earlier than "newlyweds," because they seem to benefit from the increased coordination that comes with mutual familiarity. There is a definite cost in leaving an old mate and starting over with a new one. But selection of new mates does sometimes occur, and here is the rationale: pairs that failed to hatch any young the previous year are three times as likely to change partners as are those that bred successfully.

The human implications? Certainly failure to consummate a marriage is often sufficient grounds for annulment, and impotence and infertility are frequent causes of marital breakup. It would also be interesting to determine whether divorce is more likely following death of a child. Prolonged betrothals are obviously characteristic of humans, and although I know of no data available, it's a fair guess that monogamous societies encourage longer betrothals than polygynous ones, and, furthermore, that such betrothals are more prominent in societies in which expectations of fidelity are high and the opportunities for divorce are few. In other words, the more a husband or wife stakes his or her evolutionary future on the behavior of the other, the fussier you can expect him or her to be. Certainly, one could not expect that an engaged couple would have enhanced potential for domestic bliss if the woman became pregnant . . . by another man.

Defending damselfish and soaring sparrow hawks. There is no precise human parallel here, but I suspect we all recognize the more general nuance. In some societies, males dance impressively and seek glory in war, hunting or feats of endurance. They may strive to impress via their sense of humor, or by their ability to sing, to tell stories, to drink beer, to spend money or to knock down another man on a football field. Or they may slay dragons, hunt the Holy Grail or swim the Hellespont. A male damselfish courts female damselfish by showing what a good defending father he can be. A male sparrow hawk exhibits his value as a domestic partner. But the fish are unusual in that the males are responsible for all of the parenting, and sparrow hawks are unusual in that the female needs a swift-flying, sharp-hunting mate. For mammals such as ourselves, males do less as fathers, but they nonetheless may do a great deal as males. Males everywhere seek to impress the ladies. Deep inside them is the ultimate motivation any different from that of the male damselfish or the male sparrow hawk? And are the females deeply different either?

•

Lions are among the sexiest animals on earth. A lioness may copulate one hundred times a day with the same male, maintaining this level of activity for as long as six or seven days. Leopards and cougars lag not far behind. What's going on here?

We may admire the passion of the lioness and the endurance of the male, but such behavior also presents us with a puzzle. Given that animals copulate in order to reproduce, couldn't they be more efficient about it? Surely it shouldn't require quite that many couplings to achieve fertilization. Ethologist Randall Eaton of the University of Washington, an expert on felids—the cat family—has suggested an explanation for their extraordinary sexuality. Lionesses may be competing with each other for the attention of the male. If a lioness were sexually receptive only when she was about to conceive, then she would probably attract the male's attention for only a brief time, after which he could become available to mate with other females. And, if food were scarce, the female might be less successful in rearing offspring (that is, less fit) if there were too many other litters competing with her own for a share of the kill. So a lioness is most fit when she has an enormous sexual appetite. By remaining in heat for a long period, she deceives the male as to when she is most likely to conceive, thus forcing him to attend her to the exclusion of other females. And, by demanding sex almost constantly, the lioness may keep the male so exhausted that he is unlikely to look twice at another female.

We don't copulate with the frequency of lions, but in the long run we are even sexier than they. For all their lasciviousness, lions restrict their coupling to a limited period, in which the females are ovulating, while humans enjoy sex throughout the year without regard to season and almost independently of a woman's reproductive state. We may be unique among animals in our regular enjoyment of non-reproductive sex.* Humans have achieved liberation from reproduction's tyranny over sex.

By the standards of any other animal, the frequency of human sex is amazing. It is ironic that religious prohibitions on contraception are often based on the notion that to deprive sex of its reproductive function would be somehow "animalizing." The truth is exactly the opposite: non-reproductive sex is a human specialty, an expression of our humanity.

What is the evolutionary significance of human sexuality? Why are we sexier than lions? The generally accepted explanation is, curiously, that we are preoccupied with sex because of our larger brains and our ability to walk upright on two legs. The argument is interesting. Our insistence on an upright posture forced some rearrangement of our mammalian pelvis, so that women now have uncomfortably small birth canal openings. Combine this fact of anatomy with the very large head of a newborn infant, and we have problems. It is likely that excessively large-headed offspring and small-pelvised women have, in fact, been selected against. No animal has as much difficulty giving birth as *Homo sapiens.* In addition, our infants, because of the upper limit on head size at birth, have a great deal of growing and learning to do, and this requires an incredibly long period of dependence on adults. During this time, the chances of a mother successfully rearing her child increase greatly if she has another committed adult available to help her obtain food, chase away enemies, and so on. According to this argument, non-reproductive sex evolved as a lure to keep the man nearby. This dependency may explain our unique liberation of sex from procreation to recreation.

*There has been at least one intriguing suggestion of the possibility of non-reproductive sex in animals. Oxford zoologist John MacKinnon reports that on Sumatra orang-utans copulate without much regard to reproduction. A special condition on Sumatra is that both predatory leopards and siamangs, another ape species that compete with orangs, live there. It is in the female orang-utan's interest to keep the large, strong male nearby, and her sexual availability may be one way of accomplishing that. On nearby Borneo, where there are also orang-utans but no siamangs and few leopards, female orang-utans copulate only when fertilization is likely. Otherwise, they apparently can't be bothered. As might be expected, male orangs on Borneo show none of the attentiveness characteristic of their Sumatran cousins.

This argument is at least plausible, although clearly difficult, if not impossible, to prove. And it does raise some puzzling questions. For example, as with all female mammals, women are biologically competent to care for their offspring, and in many hunter-gatherer societies, they actually provide a good portion of the calories. Also, if we were, as suggested earlier, polygynous in early times, a small number of males probably associated with a larger number of females in any case. And if male assistance was so important for the success of offspring, why weren't males selected for doing their share of the parenting, regardless of the sexual rewards (as is true of most birds, for example)?

My guess is that male parenting in human beings, as in virtually all mammals, is not nearly as innate as modern sexual egalitarians might wish it to be. The really "natural" human bond is that between mother and young—not that of male and female—and significantly, most human groups have created elaborate rules to keep couples together. Betrothal and marriage are often accompanied by a great deal of ritual and public rigmarole, perhaps indicating the importance of bonding between man and woman in our species. Certainly, anything related to reproduction is likely to be considered as important. On the other hand, our preoccupation with marriage and man-woman bonding may also reveal just how precarious this bond really is. Why otherwise should we be so insistent on making such a fuss about it?

Finally, what about the female orgasm, another uniquely human trait? Any comprehensive theory of human sexuality must account for this factor. According to British zoologist Desmond Morris, the female orgasm may have evolved as a way of keeping women lying down following intercourse. Because we walk upright, there is a possibility that semen could leak out of the vagina. So, goes Morris's theory, anything that keeps a woman horizontal, even if for a few extra minutes, could be selected for. Another explanation for its existence is that we may not be all that different from lions or Sumatran orang-utans. Non-reproductive sex could represent an evolutionary strategy for keeping the male nearby, but not simply as an appeal to pleasure (recall why it is that sugar is sweet). Female sexual receptivity throughout the reproductive cycle may actually be a loving form of deceit, as is true in the lions. If women enjoy making love and are motivated to do so (enter: the female orgasm), men might not want to stay away too long. They will remain nearby and look after their genetic investment. Other species have clearly discovered the economic potential of sex. Female chimpanzees have been observed to present their sexually-swollen rumps to males who are eating bananas or other desirable food. When the male puts the food down to mount the female, she picks it up and casually eats it while he is otherwise engaged.

This discussion reminds me of a friend's observation of "girlie" magazines. Rather than berate them for their exploitation of women, she admires them . . . for showing how easy it is for women to exploit the weakness of men.

•

We have offered here a powerful mix of theory and animal data, all pointing toward several general behavior patterns: (1) Male aggressiveness, along with insistent and relatively undiscriminating sexuality, as opposed to female docility and sexual fussiness; (2) male-male competition; (3) a widespread tendency toward polygyny (harem formation); (4) a major role for female choice, acting through preference for mates with "good genes," access to important resources, and/or appropriate—that is, fitness maximizing—behavior.

When it comes to the human species, the situation is obviously more fuzzy. We are very special animals, since we are also linguistic and cultural creatures with much behavior that seems arbitrary, symbolic and stylistic. At this point, it is only possible to point out the similarity between the predictions of natural selection, confirmed time and again in all other species, and the reality of human behavior. We may then decide simply to marvel at the coincidence. Or we may deny it as altogether irrelevant, misleading or perhaps even dangerous. Or finally we may consider it suggestive enough to warrant some very careful examination. This last choice points toward the establishment of the new field of human sociobiology, and it is on that choice that I am betting.

This is, in many ways, a troublesome chapter. I hope, of course, that it will not incur the wrath of feminists, but more than that, I worry that it will be misinterpreted and used as support for the continued oppression of women. My intent has been only to explore the evolutionary biology of male-female differences, not to espouse any particular social, political or ethical philosophy. Evolution simply is—or, better yet, evolution *does*. It says nothing whatever about what ought to be. It does have its share of imperatives, of course, but they're not moral imperatives. If females appear to be scheming and yet basically passive, males are nasty and aggressive, sometimes ridiculous and, given modern weaponry, very, very dangerous. There is probably a risk that the sociobiological understanding of male-female differences will be used to justify sexist attitudes, to defend the view that it is only "natural" for men to be aggressive and for women to be more passive, and all the rest. But, as we've said before, what is natural is not necessarily what is good. Furthermore, the inclinations predicted by sociobiology are just that: inclinations. They are not certainties.

It will be a gross abuse of science if evolution's insights are used to support the culturally mediated exaggeration of sex differences in behavior. Modern society continues to exploit women intolerably and to deprive them of their rights to an extent that demands redress. We owe it to ourselves both to evaluate the differences in the treatment of males and females and to understand the differences that do exist. A just society demands objective, unbiased facts. We need far more information in order to understand the real nature of men and women. The Jeffersonian principle is that all people are created equal, not that they are identical (which would be the case only if we were all born from one single egg). If society has an obligation to provide all of its members with the fullest realization of their potential, we had better explore that potential and give up being intellectual ostriches.

To my thinking, sexism occurs when society differentially values one sex above another, providing extra opportunities for one (usually the males) and denying equal opportunities for the other (usually the females). As such, it has nothing to do with sociobiology. On the other hand, sexism is also sometimes applied to the simple identification of male-female differences, and on this count, sociobiology is, I suppose, sexist. No one would think it awful to state that a man has a penis and a woman, a vagina. Or that a man produces sperm and a woman, eggs. But when we begin exploring the behavioral implications of these facts somebody is sure to cry "Foul." If male-female differences are sexist, we should put the blame where it really belongs, on the greatest sexist of all: "Mother" Nature!

4

Parenting: Murderous Monkeys, Paternal Marmots and Sexism (Continued)

What could make more sociobiological sense than having children? Kids may be a pain in the neck, but they're good for our fitness. At this point, more than one harried parent might remark sourly, "Thank God they're good for something," but the fact is, in addition to their long-range evolutionary significance, children also provide a whole universe of immediate rewards. "We had a lot of kids, trouble and pain, but oh Lord, we'd do it again," goes the folk song. As with sugar, there is much about children that "tastes sweet"—and for similar genetic reasons. Sociobiology not only suggests *why* we need to satisfy our parental sweet tooth, it also offers some remarkable insights into how we go about doing so.

Evolutionary theory suggests that all living things devote themselves totally to the propagation of their genes, or, to put it the other way around, the *raison d'être* of genes is purely self-propagation. One of our leading evolutionary biologists, Richard Alexander of the University of Michigan, suggests that the function of each cell in every living thing is to "commit suicide according to a particularly evolved pattern which enhances the survival potential of its genes." Of course, the fitness of each gene is greatest when it is appropriately combined with genes from a member of the opposite sex and then suitably nurtured. The care and feeding of children is the nurture of our own fitness.

Whether we recognize it or not, much of the way we live is devoted to promoting the success of our genes. The most direct means of achieving this success is to have children. But, even before we can do that, we must support our basic body "housekeeping" functions—eating, eliminating, sleeping, breathing, maintaining our heartbeats—which, while taken for granted, are all performed in support of our fitness. More closely related to our consciousness but no less vital for our fitness is our social behavior: mate selection, competition with others of the same sex, courting, defending territories, avoiding predators and rearing young. This sort of behavior, as it bears on fitness, is the core of sociobiology's interest.

How much should parents invest in reproduction? The answer, easy in theory, extremely complex in practice, is that they should invest as much as possible, consistent with maximizing their lifetime fitness. Human beings have many concerns but, if we examine these closely, we often find a particular obsession with fitness, usually as represented by our children. This anxiety is poignantly demonstrated by the pervasive, living nightmare of the gentle mountain Arapesh of New Guinea, who were studied by Margaret Mead. These people live a marginal existence, fighting a never-ending battle to keep themselves fed on the meager calories available. Often there is no food at all, and the most heart-rending task of Arapesh parents is to ignore the hungry cries of their children. The Arapesh do not doubt that they must invest all they have in reproduction. But often their sacrifices are not sufficient, and they live in constant fear that, in each generation, the children whom they labor so hard to feed, the children who are so important to them even though they know nothing of evolution or fitness—those children may become smaller and smaller.

•

On the other hand, how can we explain the Ik? These African people, displaced from their traditional hunting grounds by the creation of a national park in Uganda, are starving. Nearly devoid of a social system, they almost seem to have lost their humanity as well. They appear, for example, to lack parental love. They laughed, reports anthropologist Colin Turnbull, when an infant was badly burned after crawling into a campfire and, on another occasion, they expressed no regret when a child was eaten by a leopard. This last incident seems only to have provided quiet satisfaction: everyone was now certain the leopard would remain nearby, sleeping off its meal, and would therefore be easy prey to be caught and eaten in turn. In view of the overwhelming biological importance of children, it is not strange that our revulsion is especially aroused at the indifference of Ik parents to their children. But remember that the Ik are literally starving to death, and it apparently required such dire straits to make them so "inhuman." What is interesting is that when emergency food supplies were provided to the Ik, Turnbull reports, they kept this food from the elderly, with a spokesman claiming that "they are going to die anyway and they are useless; they cannot even give us any more children." They also chose to let the very young starve, but a glint of fitness maximization was still visible: "In any case, we can always get more children if we need them, so we [the breeding group] are the ones who should have the food and stay alive."

●

We can't have it both ways. We can either produce a large number of children, and invest relatively little in each, or have a smaller number and take better care of each of them. Ecologists refer to these two strategies as "r-selection" and "K-selection." In this case, "r" refers to the natural rate of increase in a population, sometimes called the "Malthusian parameter." Individuals who are r-selected maximize their fitness by maximizing the number of their offspring. The term "K" as used in "K-selection" is the ecologist's notation for "carrying capacity" of a habitat, the number of individuals who can successfully live and reproduce in a given place. When a population (perhaps initially r-selected) reaches a size that approaches its carrying capacity, K-selection takes over and evolution favors the production of quality offspring over quantity. In crowded situations, competition begins to become a factor, and simple fecundity takes a back seat to size, prowess and a good start in life.

A female codfish may produce more than a hundred thousand eggs at a single spawning—she is r-selected. A mouse may have a litter of ten as often as three times in one year—she is K-selected compared to a codfish, but r-selected compared to us. Human beings are among the most K-selected animals. We strive for quality rather than quantity.

In E. B. White's great children's story *Charlotte's Web*, the spider-heroine Charlotte dies after producing her batch of eggs. She never meets her children but, although White did not express it in quite this way, through them she insures her evolutionary success and so dies serene. Unlike a spider or a codfish, a human cannot satisfy its obligation to its children simply by depositing fertilized eggs. For us, reproduction is a two-way street. In caring for our children, we care for a very important part of ourselves. Just as we depend on them for our evolutionary future, they depend on us. Children need a great deal of time to grow and mature. In addition to the more obvious biological requirements, such as food, rest and protection, they have an enormous amount to learn.

Most of us readily provide our children what they need. Why do we do so? Because we love them, of course. But why do we love them? Here we are back in the realm of evolutionary events, where human inclinations are so often revealed as the handmaidens of fitness. We love our children "because" it is adaptive for us to do so. Love of parent for child is an evolutionary stratagem insuring that parents will invest in the child in a manner that maximizes each parent's fitness. The child, of course, is equally motivated to love its parents, "because" such an attachment to appropriate adults enhances its own chances of ultimate evolutionary success. In other words, parental and filial love, solicitude and care are ultimately selfish.

As with love between adults, the love of parent for child is so strong that our emotions may easily blind us and prevent us from examining it as a biological fact. It may therefore help to consider some animal examples. Not very long ago, a commercial fox-raising farm was put out of business when an airport began operations nearby. Although the vixens continued to give birth normally, they had begun to eat their own pups. Of course, many animals will cannibalize their young, as quite a few mouse and hamster owners have observed to their horror. Why such behavior? Not because these animals don't "love" their offspring; a female fox or hamster may be quite fierce in defense of her young, even willing to risk death. The paradox is resolved if we look to evolutionary strategies. When mice are kept in overcrowded cages, perhaps with inadequate food, or, similarly, when foxes that have just given birth are subjected to sudden stress (such as the roar of airplanes overhead) they are following an adaptive strategy if they relinquish their bad investment. To the agitated mouse or the decibel-battered vixen things seem so bad that her offspring appear unlikely to survive. To provide further nourishment for them would just be throwing good calories after bad. She may as well get a good meal out of it, and try again —in better times.

Human parents may be similarly "inhuman" to their offspring, exhibiting behaviors that, while seemingly devoid of love, in fact highlight the true significance of love as an evolutionary device. In an article entitled "The Evolution of Social Behavior," Richard Alexander points out that in more than half of 160 human societies for which such information is available, infanticide is (or was) practiced on one or both offspring when twins are born. If the demands on the mother are simply too great, the ruthless solution is probably fitness enhancing in the long run. Closely-spaced babies may also be killed. One Yanomamo mother tearfully told a visiting anthropologist that she killed her newborn because it would have taken milk away from her still-nursing son. Many human societies prohibit intercourse while a mother is nursing, a rule that reduces the chances of another conception's following too closely on the heels of the previous one. Our own physiology works toward the same end. To some extent, lactation tends to inhibit ovulation, thereby reducing the need for abortion or infanticide.

In Australia, aboriginal babies were killed regularly during drought, and sometimes even fed to their brothers and sisters. Anthropologist Marvin Harris has pointed out that, in societies that engage in frequent warfare, infanticide is often directed particularly at girl babies, thus producing more male warriors as well as preventing overpopulation. Although the details vary, the generality is nonetheless clear: parents, even human parents, use their children to enhance their own evolutionary fitness.

•

Many animals have glands for growing larger, for becoming sexually mature, for balancing salts and for digesting sugars. But would you believe there exists a gland for dropping dead? Incredible as it seems, at least one animal—the octopus—appears to have a kind of self-destruct mechanism, the optic gland, built into its already peculiar anatomy. A female octopus normally dies about one month after laying her eggs. She loses her appetite, spends all her time guarding her new brood, and then dies. However, if her optic gland is removed, she will regain her appetite, ignore her brood and may even become interested in male octopuses again. In a recent experiment, females that had their optic lobes removed lived an average of almost six months after laying eggs (compared to an average of one month for those whose glands were not interfered with; one octopine Methuselah survived for nine months after egg laying). What is this gland all about? Were the female octopus to go out after its own food, she would have to wander away from her eggs, thereby exposing them to someone else looking for food. So she in effect forgoes eating —forgoes living—in order to ensure success for her brood.

What makes the octopus's optic gland especially interesting is that the mechanism appears so clear-cut, with one particular organ assigned to do the job. Many other species are less obviously programmed to self-destruct, although reproduction and dying often do go hand in hand. For example, Pacific salmon, like female octopuses, have only a single chance at reproduction, which they do all at once in what biologists irreverently call a "Big Bang." Reproduction is an all-out effort, and the adults die, just as surely as if their little fry had eaten them alive. True, they are exhausted and virtually beaten to death by their upstream journey to spawn. However, sad but true, reproduction is the ultimate, evolutionary reason for their death.

Bear in mind, this suicidal behavior is not necessarily equivalent to "mother love," at least not as it is expressed in the sentimental terms of a children's story. Rather, it is the cold-blooded, calculating strategy of genes, which will not hesitate to sacrifice the adult body in which they reside in order to ensure the future success of copies of themselves in many hopeful new bodies, all of which will follow exactly the same plan when their time comes.

Of course, even parental self-sacrifice has its limits, set by each parent's selfishly maximizing its own fitness. For example, consider two subspecies of white-crowned sparrow found near Seattle, Washington. The southern subspecies, adapted to a long Oregon and California breeding season, normally lays two or three clutches of eggs each year. Should it lose a nestful of eggs to a predator, it will lay more eggs to replace them. The northern subspecies, which breeds as far north as Alaska, is adapted to short breeding seasons and produces only one clutch of eggs per year. If these eggs are somehow lost, they cannot be replaced, since the season is simply too short.

Now, small birds such as these may be remarkably brave at times. They are commonly seen to "mob" predators, diving at the much larger intruders while calling loudly. It's a risky behavior, but one that often pays off. Many predators appear quite discomfited when attacked in this manner, and often beat a retreat, looking like large bombers pursued by a cloud of angry fighter planes.*

Knowing the differences in breeding patterns of northern and southern white-crowned sparrows, I was curious about their relative "bravery" and designed an experiment to test this. I placed a clothesline pulley near nests of members of the two subspecies and attached a formidable-looking plastic model of a great horned owl to the cord running through the pulley. I then slowly brought the owl model closer and closer to the nest, noting the behavior of the parents. Although the common response of the sparrow parents was to mob the owl, there was a significant difference in the intensity of the assaults of the northern and southern subspecies. The northerners were very daring and persistent in their attacks on the false owl, but the southerners were much less so. In general, the northerners seemed quite determined to drive off the owl, or die trying, while the southerners tended to put on a half-hearted show, then to fly away.

Since the northerners cannot breed more than once a year, they have literally placed all their eggs in one basket. When that basket is threatened, it is not surprising that they respond as strongly as they do. But for the southerners, who can breed again and replace their losses, it doesn't "pay" to sacrifice their lives in defense of their eggs. Genes that influence southern parents to yield to an invader without risking their lives probably produce more long-range success than do "bravery" genes. For southern white-crowned sparrows, he who fights and runs away lives to breed another day.

Humans are not subject to the same restrictions in parenting as salmon, octopuses, or white-crowned sparrows. Because we breed more than once, our genes do not program us for kamikaze-style parenthood. Our longer life span and our ability to breed many times grant us the foresight and the capacity to think ahead, to plan beyond the moment. In most cases, our parenting behavior conforms rather closely to what is "best" for our genes, and when children are concerned, the whispering within us often rises to a shout.

Humans, fortunately, have few occasions when the alternatives

*I have seen crows mob an owl, and shortly thereafter, starlings mob a crow, then English sparrows mob a starling—a progression reminiscent of Jonathan Swift's observation that "a flea / Hath smaller fleas that on him prey; / And these have smaller still to bite / 'em; and so proceed *ad infinitum.*"

are as stark as those facing the white-crowned sparrows: save one's children or save oneself. Certainly most parenting involves some short-term cost for the parent, compensated by gain for the offspring, but in the long run the parent gains as well, through the success of its offspring. Whether it be awakening in the middle of the night to change a dirty diaper or moonlighting in order to pay college tuition, modern parents are constantly acting to benefit their children, at some immediate cost to themselves.

It would be interesting to compare the behavior of an eighteen-year-old woman with that of a thirty-four-year-old, each mothering a first-born child. The eighteen-year-old is, in some respects, like the southern white-crowned sparrow: she has a good, long potential reproductive career ahead of her. The thirty-four-year-old, on the other hand, is more like the northern subspecies. She may have little or no opportunity to reproduce again. We might therefore predict that the younger mother would not be as self-sacrificing a parent. A particularly productive study might contrast the relative inclinations of these women to have abortions, or even more to the point, the response of each if faced with the decision to save herself or save her children. It is interesting to note that most American hospitals are especially solicitous whenever a newborn is the first child of an older mother. Such children may well be singled out for particularly heroic life-saving measures, if necessary.

We can also predict that parents in general will be more "parental" toward older children, since loss of an older child would be a greater casualty (in evolutionary terms) than the loss of a younger. Because a young child is more easily replaced, it represents a smaller evolutionary investment and should accordingly be valued less. If we project this analysis back to a just-fertilized egg, it may be noted that even the most ardent opponents of abortion generally have less objection to terminating the life of a fertilized egg than to aborting a seven-month fetus. The older the offspring, the greater will be the parents' defense. This observation holds true for many different animal species, for good evolutionary reasons, and there is every reason to expect that it holds true for us as well. While killing or abandoning a newborn child is even more difficult to countenance than abortion, it is easier to bear than the abandonment of a three-year-old. The older child, who has successfully weathered the hazards of infancy, represents a better bet for evolutionary success than does the newborn.

In most cultures, there is less grief over the death of an infant than there is for the passing of an older child. Significantly, psychiatrists have observed that the greatest emotional pain experienced by parents (at least in the United States) upon death of a child occurs when that child had been an adolescent. This loss is the classic, pathetic situation that so often induces bereaved parents to mummify the lost child's room, possessions and clothing, as though expecting its eventual return. It may not be coincidental that adolescence is the period in which children have the greatest potential to produce successful offspring themselves. Loss of a child who has reached (in the technical argot) its "highest reproductive value" is the greatest evolutionary loss that parents can sustain, and in their grief we may be hearing the wail of frustrated genes. *199072*

To many readers, this discussion of human parenting may seem to have ignored an obvious point: perhaps love for a child and grief over its death have nothing at all to do with adaptive strategies and fitness maximization. It should not be surprising that a mother finds it more difficult to kill a newborn than a just-fertilized egg. After all, she has felt the infant grow and develop, thought about it and planned for it. Similarly, we suffer more at the death of a three-year-old than that of a newborn because we have grown to love the young child, while we hardly knew the infant. And, despite the vicissitudes of adolescence, we will have come to be more attached to the children we knew more fully.

But why *do* we grow to love a child? Perhaps because the older it is, the more clearly it represents our evolutionary future. As with love between parents, love of parent for child is highly adaptive. Genes that decide to invest preferentially in the right offspring in the right ways and at the right times will ultimately produce more successful offspring than will those which follow less adaptive strategies. As a result, those successful genes and their bodies will be more fit, and eventually the majority of the population will have these traits. We already have a name for the mechanism that ensures appropriate parental investment; it is a universal behavioral means to a biological end, and we call it love.

Let us consider abortion once again: not consciously induced abortion, but those natural miscarriages that modern medicine describes as "spontaneous." No events are truly "spontaneous," of course. We must assume that all effects have causes, and "spontaneous" means, simply, that we do not know the cause. If the bodies of pregnant women are carrying out instructions that lead to maximum replication of their genes, at least some "spontaneous" abortions may represent an adaptive strategy. In particular, if the embryos in question are bad evolutionary investments, women carrying them would be most fit if they aborted early in development before any more time and energy were wasted. The mother's body must have access to infinitely more information concerning the well-being of its developing fetus than does the obstetrician with a stethoscope. We may, in fact, be the masters of our reproductive fate and the captains of our embryos to an extent previously unappreciated by physicians.

During the Dutch famine of 1944–45, there was a dramatic reduction in the number of conceptions that were carried to term. In a period of severe food shortage, the optimum genetic strategy is to delay reproducing, especially since, unlike the salmon, octopus or northern white-crowned sparrow, we can almost always try again at some later point. Several University of Washington researchers recently conducted a study of 268 female prison inmates. Approximately one-fourth of these women were addicted to some drug, one-fourth were prostitutes, one-fourth were both addicts and prostitutes, and one-fourth had committed other offenses. Of this group, 136—just over half—had experienced at least one unusual termination of pregnancy. The rates of still birth and "spontaneous" abortion were far above those in the rest of the population. But a further, really striking statistic exists. These women had 373 live children, and, given the United States average, we would expect that 27 of those offspring had been born with birth defects. In this case, none of the children showed such defects. This finding does not mean that prison inmates on the whole produce healthier children than noninmates. Rather, it suggests that when a pregnant woman experiences a stressful life, "spontaneous" abortion is more likely, and when these abortions occur, they will tend to discriminate against less competent fetuses, that is, those carrying birth defects.

In such cases, we can imagine that the mother may be able to force her "will" on the fetus. She may deny it continued nourishment, or simply expel it prematurely. However, there is also reason to believe that the fetus may "altruistically" cooperate in its own abortion, so long as this action contributes to the fitness of the mother. We will return to this point later on.

•

If we care for children because they represent our best hope of evolutionary success, we should care only for those who are truly *our* offspring. In most cases, there is no genetic pay-off in helping to rear someone else's children. There may actually be a real advantage in harming the offspring of others, a fact that leads to some of the most gruesome incidents in the whole panoply of life.

Have you ever wondered why stepparents are invariably represented as unpleasant characters? From Cinderella through Hansel and Gretel to Snow White, it is almost always the evil stepmother who tries to harm the heroine, often to benefit her own children. Since the stepparent and the child are not biologically related, they share no genes, and the stepparent has no evolutionary investment in the child. Such fairy tales seem especially unpleasant in view of our current high divorce rate and the frequent stepparenting, day-care and other forms of "alternative parenting" so often required by single-parent families. We do not like to consider the proposition that caring for children may be influenced by biological factors, but it may well be that our nursery stories have long been sending us an important message about our nurturing behavior.

An innovative experiment recently conducted by Rutgers University biologist Harry Power has transferred Cinderella from the story books to reality. In this study, however, the cruel stepmother was replaced with a stepfather, and the fairytale characters with mountain bluebirds. After the experimenter had set out nest boxes which male and female mountain bluebirds found ideal for rearing young, the males were removed. Had they been left undisturbed, these fathers would almost certainly have followed the normal behavior pattern of gathering food, alarm calling when predators approached, and so on. In their places, however, came new males, apparent strangers who had not fathered the young, but who now moved in with the widow and her brood. What happened then? As predicted, these bluebird "stepfathers" did virtually nothing to assist their new mates in rearing the offspring. Only one out of twenty-five helped feed the nestlings, and none gave alarm calls, as the real father would have done.

In behaving as they did, these stepparent males were simply looking out for themselves, or rather, for the replication of their own genes. They probably consorted with the females only because of a general shortage of good nest sites. To a male bluebird concerned mainly with the success of his own genes, a widow may not be as good a choice of mate as a virginal bride, and a widow with offspring may be of even less value. However, a widow with a good nest site is better than nothing at all. Because of their attractive nest boxes, these female bluebirds appeared to be wealthy widows, and by consorting with them the males were, in effect, gambling on the possibility that they would be fathers in the next mating season. They were behaving selfishly, as always for good evolutionary reasons. One might argue that the males were acting somewhat altruistically by not killing the nestlings, but my guess is that even in this case they were selfish. It is possible that, were the females to discover such infanticide, they would not allow the males to breed with them later on. The price of breeding is tolerance, but this tolerance stops far short of "love."

If these bluebird fortune hunters seem reprehensible, what can be said of lions and langur monkeys? While the bluebirds allowed their adopted young to survive, some of our mammalian cousins are nastier stepparents. Consider the langurs, monkeys that live in India and Ceylon (now Sri Lanka). These animals normally travel about in harems presided over by a single dominant male who mates with his many females. He fathers the young of his troop and is the very model of langur paternal behavior. However, as discussed in the previous chapter, success of one male in a harem-making species generally occurs at the expense of others, who are forced into bachelorhood. Such unmated males travel in loosely organized bachelor bands, ever eager to displace the ruling male of the troop. Eventually, of course, they succeed. After this victory, squabbling breaks out among the bachelors until one finally emerges as the new harem keeper. He drives away his former colleagues and, as victor, assumes control of the spoils: the females and their young.

The females, naturally, are valuable to the newly ascendant male as potential mates, but the infants are quite another story. They were fathered by the deposed male; they are *his* ticket to evolutionary success. To the new harem master, the infants are at best an inconvenience, and at worst a hindrance to his evolutionary success. This is true because female primates are not likely to ovulate while they are nursing (which is part of their own adaptive strategy). The new harem master therefore embarks on a bloody and ruthless course of fitness maximization. Methodically, remorselessly, he pursues the suckling infants and kills them. Sometimes the slaughter is quick, sometimes it takes days or even weeks as the helpless infant monkeys gradually succumb to a combination of trauma, blood loss and infection from their repeated woundings. The whole grisly process has been described and photographed in great detail by Harvard anthropologist Sarah Hrdy.

The male's atrocious behavior brings him a double evolutionary reward. Not only have competing mouths been eliminated, but the bereaved mothers soon come into heat, whereupon they copulate with him. Why does the female langur "reward" the murderer in this way? Why doesn't she refuse to mate with him, thereby holding him to at least a minimum standard of conduct, as was suggested might be the case for female mountain bluebirds? The female bluebird probably has an advantage over the female langur; because of the frequent shortage of nest sites, a female bluebird can usually breed with another male if she denies herself to the killer of her offspring. However, langur social structure is such that only one male is present in a troop at a given time. Once her infant is dead, the best choice a female can make for her fitness is to become pregnant again—as quickly as possible. So she copulates with her infant's murderer. In the hard-headed calculus of evolution, there is no room for sentimental morality that does not provide concrete returns.

In their violent society, langur mothers may find themselves in a cruel evolutionary bind. Given that males are most fit when they commit infanticide, females would be most fit only if their male offspring also became infant killers when they reached maturity (so long as they didn't kill their own brothers or sisters, of course). What better way to insure the appearance of a genetic trait in your offspring than by mating with an adult who exhibits that trait? In the face of such savagery, however, females are not entirely helpless. One of their more ingenious strategies is played out when a female is pregnant at the time her troop is taken over by a new, potentially murderous male. We might expect that when she gave birth to her infant it would be killed by the new male, who was not its father. However, female langurs do an extraordinary thing: when a male conquers the troop, the pregnant females often come into a "false estrus." They develop the sexual swellings of a non-pregnant female in heat, and copulate with the new harem master. When the child is born (fathered, of course, by the previous harem master), it is tolerated by the leader, who apparently treats it as his own.

Infanticide is by no means unique to langur monkeys. It has, for example, been well documented in lions, when newly arrived males make short work of cubs sired by a deposed patriarch. We also now have reports that even the normally peaceful chimpanzees and gorillas are occasionally murderous. We can confidently predict that such behavior will occur whenever adults can enhance their own fitness by disposing of others, especially if these others are relatively helpless infants, unrelated to themselves. It's not pretty, but it's a reality. Even humans are not above similar behavior. There is abundant historical evidence that infant killing as a form of "evil stepparenting" has occurred for thousands of years. The Bible, for example, contains numerous references to the slaughter of children. Significantly, it is most often the male children that are put "to the edge of the sword." In Numbers 31, verses 17 and 18, Moses directs his people to kill all of the adult men among their enemy, and then to "kill every male among the little ones, and kill every woman that hath known man by lying with him. But all the women children and those that have not known a man by lying with him, keep alive for yourselves."

•

If human parental behavior is influenced by actual genetic relatedness to the children in question, we would expect real differences between parents and stepparents in such behavior. Psychologists Martin Daly and Margo Wilson have examined statistics compiled at the National Center for Child Abuse, in Denver, Colorado. They find that children in families containing at least one stepparent are significantly more likely to be abused or neglected than are children living with both biological parents.

Psychologists have given considerable attention to the difficulties faced by a child in adjusting to loss of a parent or in accepting a new one. Virtually no one has considered the adjustment required of a stepparent. In nearly all cases, the stepparent who joins a single parent and child(ren) does so because of his or her relationship with that parent, and not with the children. I certainly would not expect the stepparent to act as drastically as a langur monkey or a male lion, yet I'm not at all surprised to find something of the expediency of the mountain bluebird in his or her behavior.

Does this mean that only biological parents can be good parents? Not at all. Although it may at first seem to contradict evolutionary principles, human beings are quite capable of adopting children successfully, and, having done so, can develop as much love as biological parents feel toward their genetically related offspring.

To understand our own species in this regard, it may help to look at animals once again. Some species that recognize their young will reject strangers and may even kill such intruders. Others will readily adopt strangers and treat them as part of their own brood. Not surprisingly, species that are likely to misplace their young, or whose offspring may wander away and mix with strangers, must often have the ability to distinguish their young from those belonging to another.

Herring gulls, for example, breed on open beaches, often constructing their nests only a few yards apart. About a week after hatching, the gull chicks begin wandering about. To achieve maximum fitness the adults should invest only in their own chicks, and it is clear that they recognize their own young and reject strangers. Similarly with the wildebeest (or gnus) of the African plains, which often travel in herds of several hundred or even thousand. Wildebeest mothers will nurse only their own youngsters, and all strangers will be rejected. A similar pattern holds for many other hoofed mammals; a nanny goat must smell her kid within a few minutes of its birth or she will refuse to nurse it. In all these cases, it is maladaptive for parents to invest in youngsters that do not carry their genes, so the danger of such errors selects for avoiding them. Herring gulls and wildebeest are neither good stepparents nor good adopters.

The kittiwake, another species of gull, which nests on sheer cliffs, is an interesting contrast. The ledges where these birds make their homes may be only a few inches wide, and, as might be expected, kittiwake chicks don't wander from the nest very often. Genes inclining their bodies to go for a stroll along the cliff edge will find themselves at the base of the cliff in bodies no longer able to reproduce. Unlike herring gulls, kittiwake parents have no worry that a strange chick will appear unbidden at their nest to take advantage of their parental generosity. As a result, they have no need to recognize their young and lack the ability to do so.

Similarly, the infants of many other species, such as rats or mice, are utterly helpless for quite some time after birth. In such cases, there is also little likelihood that mother will find herself nursing a strange youngster who just happened to crawl into her den before it could be weaned. We can add strange young to a female's litter in many of these species without evoking the slightest protest. They therefore make good adopters.

It should be obvious into which of these groups humans fit. A human baby is helpless at birth. There is simply no way for it to wander off and be replaced, accidentally, by another child. We almost certainly do not possess the automatic, lock-and-key recognition of our young that is found among herring gulls. Admittedly, with their large, impersonal hospitals, modern, technological *Homo sapiens* do occasionally go home with someone else's child, but switches of this sort must have been rare among the small bands that characterized the social structure of our species during the millions of years of our evolution. The fact that such mistakes do now sometimes occur and that we can be fooled confirms that we don't automatically identify our own young and reject others. Our evolution leaves us with a rather "open program" that enables us to adopt children comfortably.

This helps explain why human beings are capable of adopting but not necessarily why they actually do so. Anthropologists are agreed that in our long "adolescence" as proto-humans we must have lived in small bands, probably numbering fewer than fifty individuals. All members of the group were, therefore, almost certainly closely interrelated. If a child was orphaned, it could be adopted by another adult or pair of adults in the band, at least one of whom was likely to be an uncle, aunt, cousin or other relative. For most of our evolutionary history, then, adoption may well have been an adaptive mechanism, maximizing an individual's fitness by caring for his or her genes in other, related individuals.

On the other hand, adoption is rarely as smooth and trouble free as many would think, or wish. If we take a hard, unromanticized look at adoption in Western culture two significant facts stand out. First, despite a great deal of social approval, adoption is overwhelmingly a second choice for parents. Given the option, most people prefer to produce their own children. Although extended-family members—grandparents, aunts and uncles, cousins—may sincerely attempt not to treat the adopted child differently, it is notable that such effort is required at all. A second fact about adoption is that our society subjects would-be adoptive parents to intensive scrutiny, while extending virtually none to would-be biological parents. It is remarkable that we require a license to drive an automobile but none to carry out the much more difficult task of having and raising a child.

There are probably two reasons why we treat potential adoptive and biological parents so differently, both of which are consistent with the process of natural selection. For one, we accept reproduction as a fundamental human right. Why? Ask evolution. For another, there seems to be a universal, often unspoken presupposition that biological parents will "naturally" care for their children, while adoptive parents must prove their willingness and ability to do so. In fact, there is probably real wisdom involved in this assumption; in scrutinizing the motives and suitability of would-be adopters, child welfare agencies may be good sociobiologists without being aware of it.

Given that our internal whisperings are especially forceful where reproduction is concerned, it is not surprising that adoption is a natural and much-desired choice, particularly for childless couples. Saccharine does an impressive job of mimicking the sweetness of sugar, taking chemical advantage of our sweet receptors, which we evolved for recognizing the real thing. The existence of adoption shows why saccharine also tastes sweet.

If reproduction is the very essence of our fitness, what can we conclude about intentional childlessness? As with adoption, the conscious decision not to reproduce is another sociobiological puzzle, one less easily explained. It must certainly be something of an evolutionary novelty. Primitive efforts at contraception were either so dangerous to the mother or so inadequate that they apparently had little real effect. Natural selection, therefore, may have been able to tolerate occasional parental deviation, so long as it had no major effect on fitness. Women may have been less than wildly enthusiastic about spending a large percentage of their adult lives either pregnant or nursing, yet as long as they ultimately became pregnant, such feelings had no real evolutionary consequences.

In this regard, the pill, coil, condom, spermicidal jelly and other contraceptives may be precipitating a revolution in evolution. For

the first time in their history, women are being offered the opportunity to act on whatever ambivalence they may feel toward childbearing. Intentional childlessness is one of the hopes for alleviating the
increasing over-population of our world, but for it to be effective it
must prevail against several billion years of evolution. It will be
interesting to study the long-term personal consequences of not
becoming a parent, the emotional costs as well as the benefits. Also
to be considered are the long-term genetic consequences. Because,
by definition, selection will favor those people who wish to have
children, and any genetically influenced tendency for lesser reproduction will eventually disappear, leaving us with a population of
even more eager breeders.

•

There is no human society, historically or in recent times, in which
women have not borne the primary responsibility for child care.
Parenting is a largely sex-linked occupation. In all societies, men do
men things and women are left holding the babies. But why does this
occur? Since one-half of the genes making up every individual have
been contributed by each parent, then each parent should have the
same interest in each child. Right? Wrong.

There are several explanations for the fact that men appear inevitably less parental than women. One relates directly to the male-
female differences in parental investment, which we have already
explored in some detail. Recall the argument: a child is the product
of an equal genetic contribution by each parent, but while it constitutes a large proportion of the mother's total reproductive potential
and a huge investment of her time and energy, it represents but a
small cost for the father. It is no surprise that a mother is heavily
committed to her child's success.

Another factor that has a bearing on disproportionate parental
responsibility is the biologically dictated difference between faith
and knowledge: while males may have faith that "their" children are
in fact genetically theirs, only females know with certainty that their
genes have been successfully passed on. Females are, therefore, guaranteed that all their investment in their offspring will ultimately be
to their own evolutionary benefit and not to that of someone else.
The genes within a man simply cannot have such a guarantee.
Throughout their evolutionary history, males have generally been ill
advised to devote themselves too strongly to the care of children,

since the undertaking might turn out to be a wasted effort.

Among many non-Western peoples, a husband may put on a great show while his wife is giving birth. With much ceremony, he takes to his bed, moans and groans, and pretends to be undergoing labor and childbirth. Meanwhile, his wife is someplace out of the way, doing the real thing. This male performance, known as "couvade," serves to emphasize a connection between the mother's husband and the child—a connection that is otherwise not particularly apparent. And, despite the ceremony, the connection still need not be very real, in a genetic sense.

Even with their common biology, human beings show a wide diversity of sexual styles and behaviors. They also exhibit an extensive range of male child-care patterns, running from doting fatherhood to indifference to outright antagonism. It would be fascinating to determine whether males in more highly promiscuous societies are less "paternal" than those in monogamous societies in which paternity is more assured. Even within a single society, of course, a "father's" solicitude for his child might vary with his confidence that the child was in fact his. Parents and their relatives delight in pointing out family resemblances ("He has his father's chin"), and it would not be surprising were such attention observed to be greater from the father's side than from the mother's.

There are, in fact, a few mammal species in which males are responsible for a great deal of the child care. Such cases are very instructive. For example, male siamangs—monogamous great apes of Southeast Asia—spend a great deal of time with their offspring. A siamang father is the primary parent during the day, carrying the juvenile and generally being an attentive nanny, returning it to its mother only at night for nursing. Significantly, siamangs are highly territorial, so that a male is very likely to be the father of the child he is caring for. Baboons, macaques and chimpanzees, by contrast, show little paternal care. There are many males in a single troop, and a single male has much less reason for confidence in his paternity. In other words, males who are less sure of their fatherhood are not as likely to be "good fathers."*

Let us propose an odd but a fair question: why don't men lactate?

*In these species, a male commonly forms a "consortship" with a particular estrus female. It would be interesting to discover whether he is more solicitous of her offspring at a later point. Preliminary findings by Hank Klein, a psychologist at the University of Washington, indicate this may be the case.

Such an ability might seem to make sense. After all, the woman has just completed a lengthy pregnancy, during which she has had to nourish the developing child, and she is now exhausted from childbirth. Why doesn't her mate step in and help out? Natural selection again suggests that women are simply more "interested" in the well-being of their children. Not producing milk is neither laziness nor thoughtlessness on the man's part. It is simply further confirmation of the woman's greater parental investment and her greater confidence that the child is in fact hers. Of course, this issue is somewhat more complicated. Once females are selected to nourish their newborn young, as they are among all mammals, males are then freed from such responsibilities. Female parenting is thus a positive feedback loop: more mothering leads to less contribution from the male, for the more care she provides, the less he has to. His lack of involvement, in turn, necessitates even greater nurturance by the female. Of course, among modern technological *Homo sapiens,* modern child care provides women with some relief, but more of this later.

If male mammals are generally less involved than their mates in caring for offspring, what *do* they do? Bear in mind that the ultimate goal of all living things is to maximize fitness, to project as many of their genes as possible into the future. Although both sexes are equally interested in accomplishing this, each carries it out differently. Males tend to achieve fitness by making themselves as attractive as possible to females, then rely largely on the females to take it from there. Often they compete with other males, either for direct access to mates or for access to resources, which help them acquire mates. However, we occasionally find even in mammals, among the least paternal of all creatures, some—but not very much—direct concern for offspring.

A few animal examples should help clarify the human situation. Biology is certainly less coercive on human behavior than on the behavior of animals, but its influence is not different in kind. Hoary marmots, so named for their grizzled, whitish fur, are large ground squirrels closely related to woodchucks. Marmots, however, live in social groups, while woodchucks are basically solitary. As with most mammals, hoary marmot mothers do virtually all the parenting. What does the father do? In large hoary marmot colonies, he busies himself with the other adults. He is ever-vigilant, chasing away neighboring males who constantly attempt to intrude into his colony and copulate with his females. He may also be found—not surprisingly—attempting to copulate with his neighbors' females, probably being driven off in turn.

Hoary marmots also occasionally live in much smaller groups, consisting of only an adult male, a female and their offspring. In such instances, when there are no other adults with whom he can interact, the male emerges as a doting parent, spending much more time with his children than do the fathers in larger colonies. Of course, these parental marmots have greater confidence of paternity, since there are no other males present to threaten such assurance. And since the males are liberated from the rat race of male-male and male-female interactions, they are free to maximize their fitness in the next-best way—by helping to care for their offspring.

A consistent pattern exists among mammals. For females, child care is virtually obligatory; for males, it may or may not occur, depending on what other options are available. Males may do some of the parenting, but almost invariably they do so only when they cannot enhance their fitness more directly, usually by making themselves attractive to females and/or competing with other males.

Another good example of this pattern might be the orang-utan, the original "wild man of Borneo." On Borneo, male orangs defend territories within which females and their offspring travel freely. The males compete with other males rather than care for their own young. On the island of Sumatra, however, males associate closely with the females and their young. Why are Sumatra orangs "better fathers"? It seems that more predators and other competing primates, such as gibbons, live on Sumatra. A father may be maximizing his fitness by remaining with his family and helping them out of tough scrapes. We might say that Sumatra male orang-utans "love" their children more than do their Borneo counterparts. Similarly, male hoary marmots in isolated family sites "love" their children more than males do in large colonies. In both cases, however, theirs is a love born out of evolutionary selfishness.

Marsh wrens are small birds which, not surprisingly, breed in marshes. Male marsh wrens are polygynous. Early in the breeding season, they do not assist their mates in feeding their young, but rather occupy themselves in courting additional females. Later in the season, when all available females have been claimed and it has become too late to start new broods, the males switch roles and become model fathers, helping to feed the nestlings within their territory. Their parenting behavior is flexible, and adaptively so, like that of marmots and orang-utans . . . and human beings?

Actually, responsibility for child care may be quite flexible, even among animals, and such care is not necessarily limited to the biological parents. Once again, a significant pattern emerges, differing for male and female. Birth of a new baby is an exciting event for many species of monkeys. Certain members of the troop gather around the infant with great interest, trying to touch the recent arrival. Almost invariably, these "aunts" are females, and they are often adolescents. They may well profit from these short babysitting episodes by learning about child care, an education that benefits their own fitness when they become mothers themselves. Significantly, there is no comparable "uncling" by males. A male primate's involvement with infants is much more selfish and less oriented toward the welfare of the baby. One classic behavior that has been observed occurs when a male is in danger of attack from others in the troop. He may pick up an infant and hold it in front of him, almost like a hostage. It seems to be the primate equivalent of the warning not to hit a man wearing glasses.

Things are almost never as simple as they first appear. This axiom may be especially true of human sociobiology. We simplify in hopes of clarifying but sometimes mislead in the process. As we have seen, throughout the natural world females tend to be the doting parents, not the males. Females are more likely to be genetically related to the offspring over whom they dote and they necessarily invest more in them. This much is pure biology. Males have been selected more for competitiveness than for parenting, since the winners of a struggle enhance their fitness at the expense of the losers by gaining more access to these doting and hence highly sought-after females. This also is pure biology. But biology doesn't stop there. The nature of maleness and femaleness does not necessarily restrict all living things to this pattern. Other considerations may even reverse it.

For example, among sea horses, instead of the male's depositing sperm inside the female, she places her eggs inside him in a special brood pouch. Sea-horse fathers then grow a placenta and nourish their young. Mothers have no further parental role; not surprisingly, since males of this species invest more and have confidence of genetic relatedness to their offspring, the *females* are the highly competitive sex. Male sea horses are shy, coy and sexually fussy; females are larger, more self-assertive, and are the sexual aggressors.

Even among mammals, there are many species in which females are larger than the males, although I know of no cases in which females aggressively compete for male attention. Depending on the ecology of the species in question, female fitness may sometimes be maximized by growing to a large size. In these cases, bigger mothers are proved to be better mothers, regardless of how large the father may be. For example, in many species of bats, females are larger than males. The crucial fact here is that bats are flying creatures and that a female bat often has to carry her nursing infants with her. A bat large enough and strong enough to carry the extra weight is clearly a fit bat.

These apparent exceptions to the rule of relative sizes of the sexes are of course no less biological than is the general rule for male-female differences in parenting. They simply emphasize the fact that natural selection takes all factors into account before arriving at the bottom line of the evolutionary ledger: the pattern that maximizes the fitness of each individual. Production of eggs and possession of a uterus do not necessarily relegate all female mammals to the nursery, to non-competitiveness, and to reduced size. But, for human beings, the fact remains that neither the biology of physical investment and certainty of genetic relatedness (as in sea horses) nor the biology of larger females (as in bats) applies to us. In our reproductive biology we are rather average mammals. Yet the same is true of marmots and orang-utans, which show a great deal of adaptive flexibility. I would like to think that we have it in us to be equally flexible, even though our biology may well incline men to be significantly less paternal than women are maternal. If we wish to behave in a manner that belies our basic biology, we must learn to do so by exploiting whatever marmot and orang-like flexibility we have, because not much is going to happen naturally.

•

Although a man can't be a wet nurse, he can still be a good father. In fact, more and more fathers are now demanding—and receiving —custody of their children following divorce. This development offers strong testimony for the flexibility of our parenting. But, as sociologist Alice Rossi has pointed out, the vast majority of women can still choose to have ex-husbands much more readily than ex-children. It is probably unlikely that most fathers will even want their children—or, stated more precisely, most will not want them as badly as will the mothers.

Biology suggests a straightforward explanation for the consistent finding that men are generally more involved in job-related activities, while women tend to concentrate on domestic and child-rearing concerns. Such a disparity may be due to early experience and social learning, when little girls are rewarded for acting like "little mothers" and little boys are expected to be "just like daddy." But this interpretation is unlikely to provide the whole answer, for it fails to explain the worldwide prevalence of these tendencies. In Israeli kibbutzim, for example, child care and other "domestic" duties tend to fall most heavily on women, despite the fact that these mini-societies have consciously organized themselves to be non-sexist. It seems that male *Homo sapiens* generally follow the pattern of male hoary marmots in large colonies. They become occupied in interactions with other adults, "making their fortune" in the world outside the domestic sphere (although the procedure for humans may not be quite as explicit as chasing strange males and soliciting strange females). Because men maximize their fitness differently from women, it is perfectly good biology that business and profession taste sweeter to them, while home and child care taste sweeter to women.

One magic phrase of recent days has been "alternative lifestyles." Young people especially are fascinated by such experiments and often yearn to explore them. All too often, however, they provide alternatives to our biology. Frequently at issue are child-care practices, and predictably there is a cost in disregarding biology. Communal child rearing, for example, often strives to "liberate" the biological parents, particularly the mother, from the social responsibility of child care. The father may be liberated by necessity, since often he cannot be identified. Ironically, parental liberation of this sort often places enormous emotional stress on parents, particularly on the mothers, who frequently become more and more dissatisfied and eventually seek to regain control of their children. All this occurs despite the fact that such selfish exclusivity is often expressly forbidden by the rules of the commune. Non-parents simply tend not to "care" enough to suit the parent(s), who find it very difficult to relinquish responsibility for their offspring to others.

Of course, biology doesn't always win. While it may be true that it's "not nice to fool Mother Nature," it can be done. Biology's whispers can be denied, but in most cases at a real cost. For example, Rothchild and Wolf's recent study, *Children of the Counterculture*, paints a grim picture: children are often neglected, deprived, emotionally disturbed, often incapable of prolonged attention spans or of retaining friends. Although women who participate in such a system may be attracted by the promise of "liberation," they are in fact simply adopting a male strategy while denying their own. Evolution has designed male parenting to be on-again, off-again, depending on the benefit to fitness in each case. Cavalier female parenting is maladaptive for all mammals; for humans, it may be a socially instituted trap that is harmful to everyone concerned.

In most human societies, there is an explicit folk recognition of the female contribution to fertility and nurturing. The ancient figures of earth mother goddesses are an example. Even today, in much of Africa, women retain control over rituals influencing fertility, including that of the land. Colin Turnbull reports that among the Tswana it is felt that no rain will fall unless "young maidens fill the sacred pots with water and carry them ceremonially throughout the land, sprinkling the ground to bring fertility as well as rain."

Throughout the world, women are seen as the nurturers, and until very recently women who have refused that role have been seen as unnatural, as witches. Margaret Mead, once again:

> The witch figure, which recurs with dreadful monotony over the entire world, among the civilized and the uncivilized, in the far reaches of the jungle and at the crossroads of Europe, is a woman who has ridden away on a broomstick or a peeled wand leaving her empty skin by her husband's side to deceive him into believing that she is still there. It is not without significance that we have no such recurrent monotonous image of the male who does evil magically. Sorcerers, witch-doctors, and black magicians appear and disappear through history and in different cultures. The witch remains as a symbol so deep that she seems to resist dethronement by even the most vigorous cultural imagination. . . . The figure of the witch who kills living things, who strokes the throats of children till they die, whose very glance causes cows to lose their calves and fresh milk to curdle as it stands, is a statement of human fear of what can be done by the woman who denies or is forced to deny child-bearing, child-cherishing.

Does all this mean that men must not care for children or that women must do nothing else? Not at all. Through our cultures, we are constantly redefining ourselves. Whatever redefinition we choose, however, will be circumscribed by and consistent with our biological foundations.

If men are ever to be at peace, ever certain that their lives have been lived as they were meant to be, they must have, in addition to paternity, culturally elaborated forms of expression that are lasting and sure. Each culture—in its own way—has developed forms that will make men satisfied in their constructive activities without distorting their sure sense of their masculinity. Fewer cultures have yet found ways to give women a divine discontent that will demand other satisfactions than those of childbearing.

If we honestly look inside ourselves, we will probably know quite well what, deep down, we wish to be doing. This desire differs from individual to individual, from culture to culture, and it seems almost certainly to differ between men and women. Denying these differences is likely to generate discontent.

The differentiation of the sexes is, by no means, something that necessarily ought to be nor is it the way they have to be. But it is the way they are, and it is important that we understand why. Although society has exaggerated these differences, it certainly did not create them. Rousseau was right when he said that "man is born free, and everywhere he is in chains," and now we are beginning to understand some things about freedom and restraint that Rousseau could never have guessed. Still, one person's freedom is another's tyranny, and thus far our species has not been particularly successful at designing environments that liberate rather than enslave us. It may be that now sociobiology will at last bring us face to face with ourselves.

•

As we look from one society to another, we see a great deal of variety in human family structures. This diversity provides some good opportunities to explore evolutionary principles. Although it may seem "obvious" to Americans that the "natural" family consists of a man, woman and their children, this so-called nuclear family may well be a rather recent human invention.

As one alternative to the nuclear family structure, we might consider the Nayar people of India. Some time before they have reached puberty, all daughters of an extended group of female relatives are married simultaneously to the same one man, who is not related to them. But this man never has intercourse with his wives. Three days later he is divorced, given appropriate presents and bidden farewell, not to be seen again. Later, when the child brides become mature, they may have sexual intercourse with other Nayar men. However, these new mates are never considered husbands, since Hindu law limits a woman to one marriage during her lifetime. The male lovers have no economic obligations to their women, and although they are clearly the biological fathers of any children produced, they have no status in the home and no authority over their biological children. Actual authority rests in the mother's brother (or nearest male relative, if there is no brother). The "legal" father is the man the mother married while she was a child, although it is impossible that he could be the progenitor.

The Nayar is one of many systems of kinship employing what anthropologists call the "avunculate" (Latin *avunculus* = *uncle*). Placing parental responsibility on an uncle is remarkably common among non-Western peoples and, while the details vary from culture to culture, one general pattern is consistent: the mother's brother functions as the father figure. He has authority over the children and responsibility to care for them. Often they live in his house, and not in that of their real father.

A human male has two strategies in reckoning his children: he can identify as offspring those born to his wife (or wives), or those born to his sister (or sisters). Given that the bond between brother and sister is much older than that between husband and wife, it is perhaps not unreasonable that much of humanity traces descendants through a sister's children rather than through a wife's. However, an avuncular system does seem to go "against" biology in one very important respect: the children of a mother's brother aren't really a man's biological children; rather, they are his nieces and nephews. In many societes the biological father is well known and easily identified. He is nevertheless expected to relinquish paternal influence to his brother-in-law and to value his nieces and nephews above his own biological children, with whom he shares more genes. This kinship agreement seems to contradict the expectations of natural selection, and its prevalence demands that we examine it further.

As it happens, the avunculate actually supports the sociobiological rule. Avuncular societies tend to trace descent in the female line rather than in that of the male. Most societies can be classified as either patrilineal (male-line) or matrilineal (female-line), although some have characteristics of both. While there have been many examples of societies changing from matrilineal to patrilineal kinship reckoning, there have been none going in the other direction. In other words, avuncular systems seem to be unstable, with much of the instability apparently deriving from the fact that in such systems fathers are expected to value their sisters' offspring over their own. The result is a difficult, conflict-ridden situation. Anthropologists have noted many instances of fathers sneaking benefits to their "real" offspring, over the objection of their culturally defined children.

There is, however, one way in which avuncular systems could actually be stable—if they were to become consistent with evolution. Until this point we have accepted the assumption that men are more closely related to their children than to their nieces and nephews, but this need not be the case. As should be clear by now, a man is guaranteed nothing simply by virtue of marrying a woman. He may have no genes carried in her children, if those children are conceived by another man. Brothers and sisters, on the other hand, are guaranteed to share genes, and, since every mother is also guaranteed to share genes with her children, her brother is assured some relatedness to them as well. The relatedness may be somewhat less than ideal, since in a promiscuous society brother and sister might be only half-siblings, if each were fathered by a different man. Nonetheless, brother and sister are at least assured of having had the same mother, and the certainty of at least some genetic connection may outweigh a substantial genetic connection that is less certain.

Our proposition is, then, that if adult males have sufficiently little confidence in their paternity they may be more fit if they invest in the offspring of their sisters, in whom they are guaranteed a degree of relatedness. And, sure enough, Pennsylvania State University anthropologist Jeffrey Kurland has pointed out a correlation between avuncular family structure and low confidence of paternity in a substantial list of societies, including the Ashanti, Bemba, Dobu, Mayombe, Plateau Tonga, Trobrianders and Yao—not to mention the Nayar, in which the husband's paternity is guaranteed to be zero.

The Dobu claim that "virtue in marriage is the dullness of a fool," and casual "bush encounters" are so common in this society that many husbands are in the habit of mentally timing a wife who goes into the forest to relieve herself. In the Trobriand Islands, men often return home after a year or more at sea to find that their wives have one or two new children. According to Bronislaw Malinowski, the famous Polish-born anthropologist who studied and wrote about the Trobrianders, these additional offspring are cheerfully accepted as further proof that intercourse has nothing to do with producing children! Nevertheless, Trobriand males surrender paternal responsibilities to the mother's brother, rather than insisting on their presumed biological prerogatives. Given that they often have no real biological interest in their wives' offspring, while they are guaranteed an interest in the offspring of their sisters, this accommodation makes perfectly good biological sense.

In another kinship arrangement existing in many human societies, men are able to "buy" wives, a practice that also makes evolutionary sense. Actually, the usual procedure is for the groom to buy his wife's *children*—in advance. After she has borne her husband's children, the bride is then usually free to return to her own family; however, if the family retains the bride wealth, all the woman's children are expected to remain with her husband's family. Payment is returned if the woman is revealed to be barren. Accordingly, bride wealth should more properly be called "child wealth." A point of interest is that an especially large bride-wealth payment may be used in avuncular societies to ensure that the children of the bride will be sired by her husband. Men in such societies are, in effect, not purchasing a wife but making a deposit on evolutionary success. It would be instructive to learn whether large bride-wealth payments correlate with a relaxation of avuncular control, that is, whether a man's greater confidence in his paternity inclines him to be less willing to surrender his children to his brother-in-law.

Once again, from animals to *Homo sapiens,* we've come a long way in looking at parental behavior. It is interesting that most people accept the fact that animals are dominated by their biology but many fewer can acknowledge that, in our complex social behavior, we are influenced—even remotely—by ours. To my knowledge, no animal species exhibits the avunculate or makes bride-wealth payments; these are human specialties. Might such instructions, as complex and as symbol-laden as they are, possibly be independent of our biology? It seems not. It seems they may be yet further examples of the wonderfully varied ways in which we respond to the subtle but insistent whisperings that come from within.

●

Menopause is another uniquely human characteristic, but unlike the avunculate, it appears to be wholly a product of our biology, and a curious one at that. Since the evolutionary process is so closely related to reproduction, why should women rather abruptly lose the ability to reproduce when they still have thirty or more years of life remaining ahead of them? And why doesn't the same process affect men? (Despite current interest in the so-called "male menopause," men are not really subject to any physical change equivalent to that gone through by women, and most men remain biologically capable of reproducing all their lives.) What's going on here?

Once again, evolutionary biology offers a good plausible explanation. Pregnancy is a demanding experience. Since the human body becomes weaker with age, women eventually reach a point where continued childbearing would endanger their lives. Men, on the other hand, do not face any greater risks by reproducing at a middle age or later. Since the costs and dangers of childbearing do not fall on him, there is no evolutionary pressure for a man to stop reproducing. Older women are also more likely to produce eggs that are genetically defective. Not only is a fifty-year-old woman more likely to die during pregnancy or childbirth, but, even if she were successful, her child might not be.

This explanation sounds reasonable, but it's not yet complete. Although the risks of reproduction are higher for older women and the return may be lower, they still should be selected, as are men, to die trying. The genes carried by older women who average just one additional child because of some Herculean, possibly suicidal, reproductive effort should still surpass statistically the genes carried by other women who elected instead to enjoy a peaceful, unencumbered but unproductive old age. Unless, of course, the non-reproducing older women had an even better way of enhancing their fitness. And, it turns out, older women *do* have an alternative means of fitness enhancement. By the time reproduction has become dangerous for them, many women have children who are young adults and who are likely to have reproduced themselves. As grandmothers, middle-aged women can provide for their fitness by caring for their children's children, instead of bearing more themselves. It is probably adaptive for women to cease reproducing at a certain age because, as the personal risks for them are increasing, so are the opportunities for aiding their own genes, which are now also carried by their grandchildren.*

Grandparenting is a worldwide human activity. Its fitness-maximizing role is not usually as loudly trumpeted as that of parenting; but its ultimate effect is as real. Among the Pondo of South Africa, every ambitious mother wants her sons to marry as early and as often as possible, since her daughters-in-law become essentially her domestic slaves, both aiding her and adding to her prestige in the village. Of course, they also provide her with grandchildren, lending her "evolutionary prestige" as well. In many Polynesian societies, it is common for grandparents, especially grandmothers, to assume the full burden of rearing their grandchildren, particularly when the parents are in their teens or early twenties. The grandparents' rationale is that young people should be free to enjoy themselves while they are young; the grandparents, of course, are enhancing their own fitness. Significantly, a mother's parents are more likely to care for their grandchildren than are a father's parents. This is, once again, consistent with the calculus of evolution, since a mother's parents have more confidence of genetic relatedness to their grandchildren than do the parents of her husband. Again, faith challenges knowledge, with the contest now one generation removed.

What can we conclude about menopause and grandparenting in Western society? Clearly, not all post-menopausal women are grandparents, and those that are may have little opportunity to engage in grandparenting. In some cases, their children are childless, and, in any event, there is an expectation that one's children will leave home at marriage, so that young couples who have children often live great distances from their parents. Also, many grandparents feel they must maintain an emotional distance in response to a general social proscription against grandparental "meddling."

*A lengthy post-reproductive lifespan is rare among animals, most of which reproduce up to the time they die. It is notable that we share the ability to live beyond the period of reproductive capacity with baboons, chimps and possibly elephants and whales—all species in which aged individuals can assist their grandchildren.

Frustrated grandparents who must content themselves with occasional long-distance telephone calls and eagerly awaited Christmas visits may well be frustrated in fulfilling a major biological satisfaction as well. Maiden aunts and bachelor uncles may be similarly deprived, but what is more interesting is that, in a system such as ours, characterized by isolated nuclear families, even parents too may be laboring under stresses that are antithetical to their biology.

It is possible that the family organization of modern Western society is an aberration in terms of the biological history of our species. Contrast the nuclear family with the usual familial pattern of non-industrialized peoples, in which children tend to settle near their parents, and their children in turn are brought up in an extended family of grandparents, uncles, aunts, cousins and other relatives. Although life was certainly difficult for our remote ancestors, they evolved in close social networks, and probably received a great deal of aid in child rearing from their relatives, especially from their parents. Everyone profited. The dependent children almost certainly gained by the attention. The parents gained by diffusing the responsibility of child rearing in a biologically appropriate manner, thus freeing themselves for other activities. And the grandparents (particularly grandmothers), who were likely to be skilled at child care since they were experienced at it, undoubtedly found it to be "sweet."

In our society, such options for an extended family unit rarely exist at present. Probably to their loss, grandparents and other relatives are effectively shut out of child rearing, while parents assume responsibility for such care, probably to their detriment as well. Of course, our self-generated domestic strains can be eased somewhat by other arrangements that we make: babysitters, day-care centers, and, possibly, communal living arrangements. But for grandparent and parent alike, our turning from biology may have robbed child rearing of much of the serenity it once possessed.

•

None of this is to say that if only we made peace with our biology everything would be smooth sailing. The sociobiology of parenting involves many built-in tensions and conflicts, some of which may be worth looking at.

Until recently, the Mundugumor of New Guinea were headhunters and cannibals. Adult male Mundugumor use their daughters to buy more wives for themselves. However, they have to act quickly, while their sons are still too young to object, for as these sons grow older, they will compete with their fathers, wanting to exchange those same girls (their sisters) to obtain wives for themselves. Freudians may see in this struggle fresh evidence for the universality of the Oedipal conflict, with sons eternally arrayed against their fathers. And there may be some truth in such a view, but not quite in the orthodox fashion. The reality is that fathers and sons are genetically different, just as are mothers and sons, fathers and daughters, and mothers and daughters. Because they share only one-half their genes, they have different interests when it comes to maximizing fitness. Remember, each individual is more interested in his or her own fitness than that of another.

Because of the biology of maleness, fathers and sons are in fact quite likely to compete, but I seriously doubt that primordial love for the mother has a great deal to do with this competition. More basically, fathers and sons are both males and both therefore best maximize their fitness by mating with females. In the process, any female taken by one becomes unavailable to the other. Father-son conflict may simply be a special case of male-male conflict, made conspicuous by the closeness of the participants.

Conflict of this sort isn't limited to parent and offspring. It may be even stronger between husband and wife. Returning to the example of the Mundugumor, competition between husband and wife is at least as real as that between father and son. Mothers wish to use their daughters to buy wives for their sons, rather than allowing their husbands to obtain additional wives for themselves. Again, the evolutionary rationale should be clear. A wife gains nothing when her husband takes another wife. He clearly will be enhancing his own fitness, but that will do nothing whatever for hers. Her stake is with her own sons, and she can maximize her fitness by trying to make the best possible deal for them, which in polygynous societies means helping them to acquire as many wives as possible. Evolutionary imperatives generate competition and conflict, even within families.

Since their interest in each other is essentially selfish, husbands and wives are especially likely to be in conflict. A mate is important in evolution only insofar as he or she contributes to one's own fitness. Then, husbands and wives are joint shareholders in any offspring produced, and in this sense they represent a true partnership, each simultaneously attempting to maximize his or her fitness. But, just as a business partner is unlikely to be enthusiastic about profits that another partner makes through personal moonlighting, we might expect husband and wife to disagree about any fitness-enhancing activities by one that does not equally benefit the other. Not only is reproductive moonlighting unlikely to enhance the marriage partner's fitness, it may reduce it, for it represents an expenditure of time and energy for someone else's benefit.

When sex is both procreative and recreative, it is important to have confidence in one's partner. In a sense, the principle of sexual fidelity may come to function in a system of mutual restraint, with each partner implicitly threatening to be unfaithful as a means of keeping the other honest. Certainly, when a husband or wife learns that the other has been having an affair, a not uncommon response is to go out and do likewise. Israeli sociobiologist Amotz Zahavi has gone so far as to suggest that much of the behavior between mated pairs—in animals as well as people—involves testing the degree of the partner's commitment. Arabian babblers, a species of small birds, lean against each other during courtship, until one member of the couple literally can no longer "stand" it. Don't humans also demand constant affirmation of their mates' devotion? American couples are encouraged to remember birthdays, anniversaries, Valentine's Day, Mother's Day, Father's Day, and to provide each other with almost daily proof of their continued commitment. As with Arabian babblers, we often lean rather forcefully against each other. And, of course, we test a lot: "If you *really* loved me . . ."

Perhaps one of the most persistent disagreements built into human parental behavior involves in-laws. The mother-in-law joke may well be the oldest joke in the world, and for what should now be obvious reasons. Conflicts between a young adult and the parents of his or her spouse are virtually guaranteed by biology: parents are interested in the success of their own child and not that of the person he or she married. They will therefore be selected to evaluate their child's spouse by one important criterion—how much the spouse contributes to the fitness of their son or daughter (and hence to their own fitness). Parents of the bride are especially concerned with their son-in-law's competence as a provider and as a "good family man." The groom's parents will be especially concerned with their daughter-in-law's competence as a mother, and are, of course, particularly infuriated by any infidelity on her part. The bride and groom themselves are concerned only with their own fitness, regardless of how it is achieved. They might well resent meddling in-laws, particularly since from the perspective of the son- or daughter-in-law, fathers- and mothers-in-law are intolerably narrow-minded, and worry only about contributions made to their offspring, while neglecting the wider options available to whoever has "married into" the family. Our reproductive reach often exceeds our grasp, if for no other reason than that others are always reaching in a slightly different direction.

●

Truly new and exciting ideas come along only rarely, even in science. I was privileged to be at the public unveiling of one of these ideas. It was December, 1972, and the occasion was the annual meeting of the American Association for the Advancement of Science in Washington, D.C. The featured symposium on the "ecology and evolution of social behavior" was nearly completed when Harvard sociobiologist Robert Trivers began speaking. He used no notes, seeming to figure it all out as he went along, but I'm sure he wasn't doing anything of the sort. In any event, it was arresting—and brilliant. When the young Huxley first read Darwin, he is said to have exclaimed, "How stupid of me not to have thought of this!" The ideas Bob Trivers presented that day had much the same appeal as Darwin's work—simple, elegant, important and almost incontrovertibly true. Because of the vicissitudes of professional publication, his ideas didn't appear in print until two years later, but long before that evolutionary biologists were buzzing with excitement.

Trivers's theory describes the nature of conflict between parents and their offspring. We might expect, at first glance, that parents and children ought never to disagree, since parents are interested in maximizing their fitness and, of course, the principal method for accomplishing this is through the success of their children, the primary carriers of their genes. The children are likewise interested in their own success, so the stage should be set for a heart-warming story in which the generations work together with love and cooperation. The truth is otherwise. Love is a motivating factor, but cooperation only exists insofar as it benefits each cooperator, who is primarily concerned with his or her own selfish evolutionary ends. Since parents and children are genetically different, their interests are different as well.

We can begin with an explanation of Trivers's theory of parent-offspring conflict, which can be explained with barely any mathematics. Because each parent has one-half of its genes reproduced in each child, it should have an equal interest in the success of each.* When a parent assures a child that there is enough love to go around and that all are loved equally, he or she probably speaks with more than an ounce of truth. However, the children are not likely to think favorably of this sort of democracy, for each is evolutionarily more interested in itself than in a sibling. It is 100 percent related to itself but it shares only 50 percent of its genes with its brothers or sisters. In other words, each child can expect to project 50 percent of its genes into the future when it reproduces, while no more than 25 percent of its genes will be passed on when a brother or sister reproduces. Each child will therefore be twice as concerned about itself as about any other sibling. This computation is pure, unadulterated biology.

Let's take a practical case. Two adults have a child. They care for it, protect it and give it food. Initially, there is little conflict between parents and child. The parents want to invest in it, and it welcomes their investment. At a certain point, they will probably want to have a second child, and we can expect them to be as interested in it as they already are in the first. However, we can also expect that the first child will see things rather differently. It would prefer that its parents continue investing in it, rather than in the brother or sister that they intend to produce. A period of conflict ensues, with the parents wanting to reduce their investment, while the child wants the parents to preserve it. Finally, the conflict ceases, checked by several factors. First, the child may have grown sufficiently so that it no longer needs whatever the parents are providing, or at least it may not need as much as it did previously. Second, although each child's genes should value their own body more than that of a brother or sister, this does not mean that siblings are totally worthless: they're merely worth half as much as the child itself. Eventually, a point is

*For now, we'll omit such complications as boys versus girls, or the favoring of one child over another depending on which one is likely to bring the largest genetic return to the parents. These are important, but not to the present discussion.

reached at which the first child benefits more by having a sibling than by greedily demanding all parental care for itself. At this point relative harmony should descend once again.

Using a similar argument, it can be shown that, in addition to disputes over the duration of parental assistance, parents and offspring should also disagree over the amount of investment provided at any one time. This second struggle develops because while parents are seeking to give the most they can to their offspring at the least cost to themselves, each offspring is only one-half as concerned about the parents' welfare as are the parents. This disparity is due, of course, to the fact that parents and offspring share only one-half their genes. Children are, therefore, more likely to demand more resources from the parents than the parents wish to give. This conflict should be familiar to us all, in activities ranging from nursing to gift giving.

Parent-offspring conflict theory has striking implications. For example, we can expect parents and children to disagree over the behavior of children toward one another. Since parents are equally related to each child, they will encourage one to assist another whenever the cost incurred by the altruist is less than the benefit received by the beneficiary. In such an instance, the sum total of benefit to the family is increased, so the parents' fitness is increased. However, we can expect the potentially altruistic child to appraise the situation differently. Since it is only one-half related to the child benefiting from the act in question, it should resist its parents' exhortations, unless the sibling benefits more than twice as much as the altruist suffers. Again, we encounter an example of conflict between parent and child. How often do parents badger their children to "play nicely with your brother (or sister)"? How many times have we all implored our own children to share? And how stubbornly have they refused!

Parents of more than one child are invariably struck by the degree of sensitivity each has to just how much the other gets, whether the benefit is food, toys, parental attention, or simply staying up late. The competition may remind us of the squealing of suckling piglets, each jostling for its mother's best nipple.

In addition to helping us understand sibling rivalry and the generation gap, parent-offspring conflict theory sheds new light on the "first child syndrome"—the general tendency of the oldest child in a family to be the highest achiever. Psychoanalytic theory has long speculated that weaning involves a crisis of trust for the young child, based largely on a fear that it will no longer be nourished. Resolution of this early personal crisis presumably determines much of future personality. If trust is retained, the child develops optimism, hope, a "sunny" disposition toward itself and the world. If trust is not established, the personality is characterized by anxiety, mistrust, and an overpowering sense of doom. The greater need for achievement shown by oldest children may also reflect their attempt to compensate for the potential loss in fitness they suffered when their parents reproduced a second time.

Familial conflict doesn't end within the nuclear unit. Parents and their children are not equally related to members of the extended family, and accordingly we can expect their inclinations toward their relatives to be unequal. For example, parents share ¼ of their genes with nieces and nephews (since they share ½ with their own siblings, they share half of that ½ with the offspring of their siblings). Cousins, however, share only ⅛ of their genes, so that we can expect them to be only one-half as kind to each other as their parents would like them to be (⅛ versus ¼). An instructive study would determine whether friendship between cousins tends to decrease after their parents have died. The degree of genetic connection between the cousins would not change, of course, but the parents would no longer be present to manipulate the relationship for their own benefit.

Many other interesting predictions come to mind through the application of Trivers's theory. A child's altruism toward a sibling should vary to some extent with its genetic relatedness to that sibling. To this point, we have been assuming that siblings share one-half their genes, that is, that they are full siblings. This is only true if they have the same father as well as the same mother. In families or societies in which children are full siblings, we can expect less parent-offspring conflict over the duration and amount of parental investment than when different, unrelated males successively father the offspring. Similarly, we can predict that half siblings would be less kind to each other than full siblings would be. I suspect that a study of children in harem societies would show that the offspring of different wives compete more vigorously with each other than do the offspring of the same woman.

We might also expect that older parents would experience less parent-offspring conflict than would younger parents. Older parents have less potential to produce additional children in the future, and should therefore be less inclined to hold back their investment. There is good evidence that the youngest child in a large family is "babied"; parents often feel closer to it and vice versa. In addition, older parents will have had more experience in dealing with feisty, selfish offspring and might therefore be more likely to win any conflicts that do arise. Trivers points out that infants cannot fling their mothers to the ground and nurse at will. So they can be expected to employ psychological rather than physical tactics to get their way—that is, to exact more parental investment than would be in the best interests of the parents to give.

The infant has an important method of making demands on its parents: it can cry. It cries when it is hungry, or cold, or wet, or frightened, or when it is hurting and simply wants to be held. Of course, it is in the parents' interests (that is, the interests of their genes) to be sensitive to these messages from the child. The child knows better than the parent when it needs help or when it is hungry. On the other hand, we can expect the child to take advantage of its leverage, perhaps by crying for more investment than it really needs, simply because it can obtain it. This exploitation would then place a premium on the parents' ability to distinguish a real need from a feigned one. It is an interesting battle, and it is far from clear just who wins!

How else can offspring secure investment from otherwise reluctant parents? They might pretend that they really need parental care, a pattern that could carry well beyond infancy. Since they are likely to be most convincing when they really believe their own story, and since there is no particular evolutionary reason why they should see through the designs of natural selection, children might honestly think that their needs are as pressing as they claim. Parents, on the other hand, should be inclined to invest not only in children who need it but also in those most likely to profit greatly from it. We can therefore expect children to brag and advertise their achievements, to make themselves appear to be good investments. But children should be selected to avoid going too far, either in bewailing their neediness or in trumpeting their accomplishments. Parents may be disinclined, at one extreme, to invest in a lost cause, or, at the other, they may withhold investment from a child who shows he doesn't need it. In summary, we can expect children to exaggerate either their needs or their competence, and we can expect parents to have some skill in seeing through their ruses.

This view of parent-offspring conflict is quite different from the manner in which developmental psychologists and psychiatrists have tended to understand early socialization and child rearing. It is true that their explanation may be more emotionally appealing, but I believe ours is more accurate. Typically, anthropologists and sociologists see "early socialization of the child" as a process of enculturation, during which the youngsters are simply introduced to the details of their parents' culture for the benefit of all. Psychiatrists and psychologists emphasize the close "symbiotic" fit between parent and child. But, as Trivers explains, given the conflicting evolutionary strategies of parents and children, parents will attempt to get their children to behave differently from the way the children would like to behave. The parents do hold a big edge, though. They have many of the things that children need. Furthermore, considering that the parents have survived at least to reproduce, the existing adult culture must have at least some minimal adaptive value, regardless of what its youthful critics may believe. Because of their greater experience, parents almost certainly have much that is worthwhile to impart to their children. Children should, consequently, be selected for susceptibility to adult teaching. But, once again, the situation isn't that simple. Parents might be expected to take advantage of such a vulnerability on the part of their children by exaggerating the significance and importance of their teaching, while using such teaching to further their own manipulation of their offspring. As Trivers points out, it is not surprising that the prevalent view of child rearing and socialization, in which children are pictured ideally as passive recipients of parental beneficence, is one that is enthusiastically supported by adults.

Parents commonly exhort their children to do all sorts of things that the children don't want to do: go to bed early, do your chores at home, study hard at school, don't fight with your siblings, don't gamble or drink, and please share. Perhaps we shouldn't be surprised that children disagree with these parental prescriptions and consider them unpleasant, unnecessary, and generally "a drag." Perhaps our children are possessed of more enlightened self-interest than we normally realize or would like to acknowledge. Perhaps their stubborn insistence on doing their own thing rather than ours simply reflects their unconscious, adaptive perception that "our things" maximize our fitness rather than theirs. An appeal to their own selfish interests just might work wonders in producing cooperative children.

•

The world of reproducing beings seems ridden with selfishness and conflict. It is a world of individualists, each wanting only to get ahead. It is a world in which everyone is set apart—mate from mate, brother from brother, parents from children. It is a world in which even love is a strategy and each of us is very, very much alone. But, like it or not, it is our world, created by the same genes that created us and all the rest of life. If we differ from other living things, it is largely in our ability to look at ourselves and our world, to rue them or rejoice in them as we see fit.

Francis Bacon once wrote: "He that hath wife and children hath given hostages to fortune; for they are impediments to great enterprises, either of virtue or mischief." What Bacon didn't say is that children are also our passports to life's most pressing enterprise— maximizing our fitness. Whatever the variety of our social forms, we are all hostages to natural selection.

5

Altruism: Kin, Karma and Kamikazes

A stranger arrives at a settlement of Australian aboriginals. He waits outside, dusty and nervous in the hot sun, while an old man, well versed in genealogies, comes out to interrogate him. If the stranger is found to be related to anyone in the camp, he is accepted inside. If not, he is killed. When the Tiv of Nigeria seek to expand their territory, they invariably select for attack the adjoining group to which they are most *distantly* related. A small band of Kalahari bushmen are traveling from one water hole to another: they carry enough water to make the trip, which may be two or three days but no more. Anyone who is injured or is taken seriously ill during these treks, so that he or she is unable to keep up, is left, almost certainly to die. No arguments—or hardly any. A male baboon detaches himself from his troop and dies defending it against a leopard. A honeybee worker gathers pollen, tends the developing grubs and finally dies while stinging a bear who is raiding her hive. And in New York a successful business executive finds a nice vice-president's job for his nephew.

What do these cases have in common? They are all examples of something very important—the remarkable interest that genes have in themselves. Much of the social behavior shown by all animals, including human beings, involves parents and their young. Less obvious, but no less true, is the pervasive concern that living things show for their relatives. We may be unique in writing down our genealogies and counting our kin, but, in doing so, we may simply be answering our whisperings within. And in that we are not unique. Blood is thicker than water for all living things—not just human beings; and natural selection has a great deal to say about why.

The ultimate task of all genes is to manipulate the bodies within which they find themselves, so as to make as many copies of themselves as they possibly can. They do so by choosing mates that will contribute as much as possible to their success (which we discussed in chapter three), in particular by producing offspring (which we discussed in chapter four). However, our genes are copied not only in our offspring; they also occur in our relatives. The closer the relative, the more genes we share. So, when we look out for a relative, our genes are actually looking out for themselves, or rather copies of themselves enclosed within the body of another.

According to traditional Christian belief, our souls leave our bodies when we die, floating away to heaven or hell. According to Hindus, they are reincarnated into other living beings. Our concern is with genes, of course, but we might find it useful to picture every individual as composed of many of these "little souls," some of which leave our bodies in our eggs or sperm whenever we make children, and some of which we already share with others through inheritance from our common ancestors. These others—our relatives—are very special to us, because they each carry a little part of ourselves.

When a parent rushes into the street to snatch his child from an oncoming car, he is endangering himself and, hence, his genes. On the other hand, he is saving a portion of his "soul"—one-half to be precise. Perhaps in doing so he seems to be "altruistic," since he is helping someone else at real risk to himself. Now, given the fundamental selfishness of evolution, true altruism should never occur, since any genes producing altruism should be less fit than genes that produce selfishness. So is the rescuing parent an evolutionary anomaly? Not at all. In fact, he is not really an altruist, since his genes are doing neither more nor less than saving some of themselves. The same can be said of any behavior by one individual toward another, so long as the two have some genes in common. Caring for our own children or for others with whom we share genes, is, then, just a special case of those genes selfishly promoting themselves by watching out for others in whom they also reside.

Genes selfishly looking out for themselves while appearing to be altruistic: it all seems so obvious now, but as little as fifteen years ago, it wasn't. The apparent altruism seen in nature was much more of a paradox before a brilliant insight by British biologist W.

D. Hamilton, who worried about why worker bees are sterile and who wound up ushering in a new era in evolutionary biology and perhaps in the study of human behavior as well. The basic problem tackled by Hamilton was simple enough. If natural selection rewards only individuals and genes that contribute to their own reproduction, then how can it have produced altruistic behavior? If we take natural selection at its hard-headed best, then individuals should always be selected to maximize their own fitness. Hamilton's insight was, simply, the realization that altruism by an individual may be consistent with selfishness by his genes, so long as those genes are helping themselves in another body. But that other body must be the body of a relative—one's kin—and the process of aiding oneself through aiding one's relatives has come now to be known as kin selection.

Among the social insects—wasps, bees and ants—which Hamilton studied, only the queens and certain males reproduce. The vast majority of hive members are females, genetically similar to the queen but non-reproductive. These worker bees are insect kamikazes, since their abdomens may be ripped apart when they sting an enemy. Obviously this is bad for their fitness. And the fact that they are sterile seems even worse for their fitness. What is going on? The fitness of worker bees comes, of course, from the fact that they labor ceaselessly for the reproductive success of the queen. They tend her offspring, gather nectar and defend the hive. Their penchant for suicide is clear enough, since their inability to breed gives them little reason for not dying. (In genetic terms, the death of a sterile worker is no more serious than is "death" of one of our fingernail clippings.)

Nonetheless, a puzzle exists: why are the workers sterile in the first place? Why should worker genes help queen genes to reproduce? Wouldn't natural selection favor those who selfishly reproduce themselves instead of altruistically helping another? Hamilton's answer, in part, is that worker bees are usually daughters of the queen (even though they act more like chambermaids than princesses). Because of the peculiar genetic system of bees (males have only one set of chromosomes instead of the usual two), each worker shares ¾ of its genes with its sisters. By contrast, were it to produce its own offspring, it would share only ½ of its genes with them. So worker bees share more genes with their sisters than they would with their own offspring. As a result, they actually contribute more to their fitness by staying home and helping rear their sisters than by going out and starting families of their own.

Everyone has heard the expression "lazy as a drone." Male bees —drones—are, in fact, notoriously lazy, contributing next to nothing to the welfare of the hive, especially as compared with their diligent sisters. Since the apparent altruism of workers seems attributable to the fact that they share many genes with those they are helping, it seems reasonable that "laziness" among drones should result from sharing fewer genes with the other hive members. This happens to be the case. Because of their genetic system, drones share only ¼ of their genes with their sisters (whereas sisters share ¾ with each other). So it is not surprising that the males are much less concerned about the welfare of their sisters.

The "altruism" principle goes beyond any particular behavior in any particular species. The central question for all living things is how genes can influence their carriers to behave in a way that reduces individual success while increasing the success of other individuals. The answer is that they can do so provided that in the process they actually increase themselves. In other words, altruistic behaviors will be selected so long as they are not truly altruistic. Real, honest-to-God altruism simply doesn't occur in nature.

How about people? It is probably no coincidence that human beings everywhere organize their behavior around their kin. And nepotism—favoritism toward relatives—is a universal human trait. The Carnegie Medal for bravery is a peacetime equivalent of the Congressional Medal of Honor, and its bestowers unconsciously recognize the sociobiology of altruism by not giving the medal for bravery in saving the life of a relative. Helping a relative in distress is apparently expected. What is unexpected, and therefore worthy of a medal, is encountering danger to help a non-relative.

•

A number of years ago, the great biologist J. B. S. Haldane was asked one day in a pub if he would give up his life for his brother. No, said Haldane, he wouldn't do that, but he would sacrifice himself for *three* brothers or, failing that, nine cousins. His reasoning: humans share one-half their genes with brothers (or sisters), one-quarter with half-siblings, one-eighth their genes with cousins, and so forth. Therefore, any gene that influenced its carrier to risk its body in order to save three brothers (or nine cousins) would result in making more copies of itself than would be lost, even if the individual died in the attempt. Each of us is likely to have more copies of our own genes in the bodies of three siblings or nine cousins than we have within ourselves. In most cases, of course, the choices are not nearly so stark as life and death. But, any time a behavior involves a cost in terms of fitness, we are justified in looking for a benefit in terms of fitness. (Both costs and benefits are measured in the same way, in units of fitness—numbers of genes projected into future generations.)

Actually, relatedness between two individuals is not the only factor determining whether one will be altruistic toward the other. There are two other important considerations: the cost to the altruist in performing the act and the benefit derived by the recipient. Kin selection is a rather complex equation. If we could eavesdrop on a gene's advice to its body, it would go something like this: "You should be more inclined to help someone the more closely related to him you are. At the same time, you should be more inclined to help him if he really will benefit from it and less inclined if the risk to you is high." Expressing it quantitatively, we can say that for altruism to evolve via kin selection, the benefit gained by the recipient multiplied by the proportion of genes shared by the would-be altruist and recipient must exceed the cost in fitness suffered by the altruist. This, in a nutshell, was Hamilton's great insight. Living things tend to maximize their *inclusive fitness:* the total of their reproductive success through their offspring *plus* that of their relatives. Of course, in maximizing its inclusive fitness, each living thing is expected to devalue relatives proportionately as they are more distantly related— that is, as they share fewer genes with the would-be altruist. A brother or child "counts" one-half as much as one's self, a cousin one-eighth, and so on.

Does this mean that genes must be good at elementary algebra? Absolutely not. The fact is that evolution has done the arithmetic during the many long generations of every species' history. In the course of time, some genes have directed their bodies to make bad choices, that is, they made errors in solving the critical equation that includes costs, benefits and relatedness. These error-prone genes have left fewer descendants than those whose calculations were more accurate. The result is that we and everything else that lives might not get A's in arithmetic, but we behave as though we are mathematical geniuses. We are selected to do the right things although we may not know why. We are very calculating creatures: How do I love thee? Let me count thy genes.

Before considering ourselves in some detail, let us look at a few more animal examples of genetically selfish altruism. Imagine you are a prairie dog peacefully nibbling at the edge of your colony. There are other prairie dogs nearby, similarly occupied. Suddenly you see a hawk: what do you do? The safest thing, of course, is to hightail it for the nearest burrow, and, indeed, that is what most prairie dogs do. In addition, however, they often give an alarm call that alerts the others. By doing so, they have conferred a benefit on these others, who now have a greater chance of escaping. However, in alerting the other prairie dogs, the alarmists have suffered a personal cost, since they made themselves more conspicuous to the predator and used time calling that might have been time spent running away.

Imagine two prairie dogs: a caller and a non-caller. The altruistic caller stands a better chance of dying (and therefore not reproducing) than the non-caller, who selfishly keeps quiet and therefore is more likely to survive and reproduce. Doesn't that suggest that calling is therefore selected against? Wouldn't there be fewer callers in succeeding generations? Yet, alarm calling in small rodents is very common. When would we expect natural selection to favor the evolution of such apparent altruism? Clearly, when the benefit is high, the cost is low, and the relatedness between alarmer and hearers is high enough to make the equation give a positive fitness benefit to alarmist genes. We have every reason to believe that this is exactly what happens, and although not all hearers and callers are necessarily related, enough are to permit the system to evolve. In point of fact, though, calling is generally reserved for situations in which relatives are nearby.

Round-tailed ground squirrels are rodents similar in many ways to prairie dogs. The males wander quite a bit, especially in the spring, and if we look at a colony of these animals in the spring, we'll find that the males are likely to be unrelated to their neighbors. What happens when a predator appears? You guessed it: Christopher Dunford of the University of Arizona observed twenty-five alarm-calling episodes, between January and April: of these, twenty-three were performed by females. There is a further test. The young are born later in the year, and by summer those juveniles remaining near their mothers are surrounded by close kin. At this point, more than coincidentally, males are as likely as females to give alarms. Zoologist Paul Sherman of the University of California, Berkeley, has found similar results in an intensive study of another species of ground squirrel. Reproducing females do more alarm calling than those without off-spring nearby; those with living relatives nearby do more than those without; residents do more than transients; and females generally do more than males. As you might expect, males in this species live far from their relatives (male animals are often less likely to associate with relatives, probably because males tend to be the more competitive sex), whereas females live nearby.

Take another example: white-tailed deer snort when they see a predator, thereby warning their colleagues. Females, who travel in groups of kin, do more of this altruistic snorting than males, who form bachelor groups of unrelated members. If we observe deer during the breeding season, we are likely to find a buck with a herd of females. But he doesn't "lead" the herd, and indeed he shows little altruism toward its members. When a mountain lion appears, for example, the does and fawns all follow the eldest female, who is related to many of them. The buck? He bounds away, as quickly as he can.

This sort of male-female difference may be rather widespread. Geneticist Glayde Whitney of Florida State University has suggested that female mammals are generally more predisposed to altruism than are males because of the genetics of maleness and femaleness. Females share more genes with other females, since all females have two X chromosomes whereas males have one X and one Y.* This is an interesting notion, especially since it predicts the opposite tendency among birds, in which males are XX and females are XY. Significantly (perhaps), this is what we observe: male birds are more likely to show altruism toward their "brothers," leaving the "sisterhoods" to mammals.

Remember the murderous male langurs who killed infants they

*In a sense, the genetic relationship between two female mammals is therefore similar to that between sister bees, if we consider only the sex chromosomes. However, this analysis may be open to dispute, because there may well be substantial, although unappreciated, genes on the Y chromosome as well. It is a thought-provoking idea, nonetheless.

had not sired? It is interesting that, despite the risk of injury at the
hands of the bigger, more powerful males, older adult females often
helped defend the victimized infants. We do not know whether
these protective, altruistic females were related to the beneficiaries
of their act, but that seems likely. Among Japanese monkeys, an
attack against an infant brings retaliation by its mother, sisters, aunts,
grandmothers—the whole enraged female side of the family. Is it any
surprise that adult male Japanese monkeys are very tolerant of infants? They have even been seen to run away when infants approach.
Anthropologist Jeffrey Kurland of Pennsylvania State University
found that Japanese monkeys who were attacked were often defended by other members of the monkey troop, and that more than
80 percent of these altruistic defenses occurred within the "matri-
line"—the group of female relatives.

In its most extreme form, the converse of altruism is probably
antagonism, resulting in a reduction in the fitness of the victim.
Japanese monkeys don't usually hurt each other seriously. But it is
significant that, when they do, the aggressor is usually a non-resi-
dent and non-relative. Closer to home, pre-industrial human societies are often at war—not the organized full-scale wars of conquest
that we practice in our "advanced" societies, but rather a continuing pattern of feuds and skirmishes. And, no less than among Japanese monkeys, kinship counts. These human hostilities are especially difficult to halt, since they often seek to avenge "blood debts"
incurred in the past. A killing requires revenge, and all relatives on
each side must help. Of course, successful revenge demands further
revenge from the most recently injured party, and so it continues.
Although this system of kin avenging kin is somewhat hard on its
victims, it does serve as a damper to massively destructive antago-
nisms, since everyone concerned knows that injustice visited upon
someone else will be a cause for retaliation. Each individual is in a
sense protected by his or her own network of relatives. For this
reason particularly, young women of many tropical Amazonian
tribes are terrified of being married to a man in a distant village—
among strangers, they will have no relatives to defend them from
their husband's likely brutality.

We all live within a very real and personalized fabric of relatedness, most densely woven near ourselves and progressively thinner

as we move away. Accordingly, we expect—and find—the greatest altruism within our immediate family, less among those to whom we are less closely related, and finally perhaps, outright antagonism toward (and from) strangers. We can all recognize this pattern in our daily lives. We *give* Christmas presents to those that are close to us, without reckoning what we get in return; we *exchange* cards with those we know but don't "love"; and as for a total stranger such as a merchant, we may have little compunction about cheating him— or he us—when either party can get away with it. We are hardly alone in this pattern. University of Michigan anthropologist Marshall Sahlins has shown that among non-industrialized societies, something close to selfless altruism prevails within a household and to a lesser extent among more distant relatives; tit-for-tat holds within the village or the larger ethnic group; and interactions between villages or tribes may be frankly exploitative. The close fit between the expectations of sociobiology and the facts of human social behavior is especially striking when we consider that Sahlins's description was not developed with evolutionary considerations in mind. When American university professors, Amazonian maidens, and honeybees independently conclude that two plus two equals four, it somehow makes us more confident that they are right.

When feuds break out within a village, there is a real danger that the very social fabric will be disrupted. Strong pressures develop, therefore, for such disputes to be settled peacefully, through arbitration. Usually this is accomplished by impartial individuals who, significantly, are unrelated to any of the antagonists or, more likely, related to both. However, when the opponents are more distant—for example, residents of different villages or altogether different tribes—fewer participants feel any need to seek arbitration.

The Nuer of the southern Sudan have no formal government. As with most non-industrialized peoples, their social relations are organized mainly by kinship. As recently as several decades ago, they were almost constantly at war with each other, except when they united to raid another tribe, the Dinka, who, of course, were not their relatives. There is an old Arab proverb: "Me against my brother; me and my brother against our cousins; me, my brother and my cousins against our non-relatives; me, my brother, cousins and friends against our enemies in the village; all of these and the whole village against the next village . . ." and so it has ever been, and—if our genes have their way—so might it ever be.

•

So the sharing of genes appears to be crucial for certain aspects of social behavior. Although groups of living things can reside together without sharing genes, they are unlikely in such cases to show much in the way of altruistic behavior. On the other hand, when genetic relatedness is high, altruism is to be expected.

My dictionary defines nepotism as "favoritism shown towards a relative, on the basis of relationship." Webster and his associates were not sociobiologists and neither are most people, but we are all carriers of genes that have scored well on their evolutionary cost-benefit calculations. This is, in part, probably why nepotism is a virtually universal human trait. Kinship is a basic organizing principle in all human cultures. It is the backbone that supports *Homo sapiens* society, and sociobiology provides a coherent explanation for why: we maximize our inclusive fitness when we treat relatives differently from strangers. Obviously, not every peculiar detail of human social life is determined by the requirements of our inclusive fitness, but biology does provide the underlying matrix—the cake—on top of which human cultural diversity lavishes the icing. What could be more natural?

Among the Fulani herders of Africa, large communal camps are formed during the wet season. Camp members regard themselves as members of one clan, identifying common ancestors, often many generations back, to unite them. During the dry season when the population must disperse to individual watering places, smaller groups are formed, each of these tracing itself to a much more recent ancestor, often only a grandfather, or sometimes even a father. Here, as anywhere that *Homo sapiens* is found, a person without relatives would be quite lost.

Although our species is unique in its passion for identifying blood lines, many other animals organize their social life around kinship—their genes are no less intelligent than ours. For example, so far as I know, there is only one case of full-time wife sharing among animals —the strange case of the Tasmanian native hen. Here, eternal triangles are often formed, consisting of two males and one female. These trios are more successful in rearing offspring than are simple male-female duos, apparently because the extra male helps in guarding the young, finding food, and so forth. However, any one male runs the risk of not getting to father the chicks, so how does this system "pay," insofar as male-carried genes are concerned? As it happens, the males are brothers, so any male who does not end up being a father is at least guaranteed to be an uncle, thereby profiting via his inclusive fitness. In this way, kinship influences social organization of these animals.

For another example, consider the North American wild turkeys, from which our Thanksgiving turkeys are descended. The males parade around in pairs, established earlier when two brothers met and struggled for dominance. When mating time arrives, each brotherhood duo struts and displays in competition with other such duos. Then, when a female is ready, subordinate brotherhoods yield to the dominant one, and within this pair, the subordinate yields to his dominant sibling. In one case, for example, out of 170 males at one arena, only 6 cocks ended up doing all the mating. Here again, the subordinate brothers profit (via kin selection) even when they are "altruistically" celibate, so long as their dominant brother is reproductively successful. It pays a turkey to be its brother's helper, if not its keeper.

Of course, polyandry (one female mated to many males) is very rare in nature, probably because of the biology of maleness and femaleness, which inclines males to compete with other males, rather than share females with them. Not unexpectedly, it is also rare among humans. In one survey of 565 human societies, only four practiced polyandry, and then it was often combined with polygyny. Wealthy, successful men at the top of society had several wives, while the least successful, at the bottom of the system, shared a wife. Even half a wife was apparently better than none.

We might predict, further, that where polyandry occurs there should be a preference for "fraternal" polyandry—that is, wife sharing among brothers, as among the Tasmanian native hens and wild turkeys. Such an arrangement would mean that each man would have in his inclusive fitness both nieces and nephews (relatedness equals one-quarter), if his brother sired any children by their shared wife, and his own children (relatedness equals one-half) if he fathered any. Fraternal polyandry, it turns out, is the dominant form. It occurred among the Todas of South India and has been reported for the

Tupi-Kawahib of tropical Brazil. Wife sharing among brothers is also common among certain Himalayan peoples, where a man may be away for months at a time, on salt-trading treks. While he is gone, his brother stays home to mind the store and, apparently, to look after his wife as well, thereby keeping everything "in the family."

Among the Tre-ba people of Tibet there was only one marriage in each generation for each family. Sons joined together to share a common wife, all remaining in the same household. The Tre-ba owned a great deal of land, and although the sons might have preferred to have their own private wives, polyandry was accepted because it avoided dividing up the family landholdings.

Among some of the Pahari-speaking people of north India, brothers pool their resources and buy themselves a wife, who is sexually shared by all of them. When they can afford it, they buy another, and then perhaps another after that, and so on. The result is the only known instance in which several adult males cohabit with several adult females, with no special bonding between any one man and any one woman.

There are several interesting points about the Tre-ba and Pahari cases. First, once again we see polyandry linked to wife sharing among *brothers*, rather than unrelated men. Second, in both cases, the typical pattern of male-female sexual politics still holds. Although a family may consist of several men and just one woman, it is the men who obtain the woman and not the other way around. Furthermore, the men are not equivalent to harem wives; they dominate their wife, who must defer to each of her husbands. And, if she fails to produce children for them, they return her for another wife. Once again, it seems, different people are telling us that two plus two equals four.

Genetic relatedness and human social behavior clearly have more than a little influence on each other. The situation in some instances can get truly complex, and kinship arrangements among the Australian aborigines have kept an army of anthropologists befuddled for generations. It turns out, though, that there is good sociobiological logic behind much of what goes on. Reflect, for example, on the selfish evolutionary wisdom of the "generous" Yanomamo headman who gives excess wives to his brothers. Among African cattle herders such as the Masai, Zulu and Swazi, obtaining a wife requires "bride payments" that may range from ten to twenty head of cattle. The number of wives available to one man is obviously limited by his cattle supply, and since cattle ownership in these societies is in the male line, fathers and sons must compete, since they draw from the same herds in order to get wives. Oedipus again? Perhaps, but I suspect the reality is much more practical. Fathers should want to produce children since each would share one-half of their genes. In fact, they should prefer this to producing grandchildren, which is what they get when their sons become fathers. This follows because an adult shares one-half its genes with his children, but this relatedness is diluted by one-half in each succeeding generation. Accordingly, a grandfather shares only one-quarter of his genes with his grandchildren. So every male should prefer a wife for himself over one for his son.

For the sons, things are exactly reversed: they would prefer children ($\frac{1}{2}$) over half siblings ($\frac{1}{4}$). There is a prediction here that screams out to be tested: fathers should benefit more if their sons acquired three wives to their one, since $3 \times \frac{1}{4} = \frac{3}{4}$, which is greater than $\frac{1}{2}$. Therefore, considerations of kin selection suggest that very few Masai or Zulu fathers would choose to get one additional wife for themselves if the same bride-wealth payment could obtain three wives for their sons. Of course, in a full-scale calculation, the possibility that either father or son would be cuckolded should also be included, as well as such factors as the economic and social capacity of both father and son for rearing successful offspring. The simple fitness reckonings of evolution become rather difficult in practice.

Nonetheless, we humans seem, in general, to be doing a very good job of adhering to biology. For example, 80 percent of all human societies have patrilocality as the dominant form of residence, that is, married couples live with the husband's family. It is possible that this is simply another example of male domination over women, but the sociobiologist may fairly ask: Why should people choose such a system in the first place? One evolutionary result of patrilocal residence is that the family of the groom can oversee its evolutionary investment. The bride's parents are already secure. They know that, wherever she lives and whoever is the father, their daughter will bear her own children, who in turn are guaranteed to carry at least $\frac{1}{2}$ of her and $\frac{1}{4}$ of their genes. The bride's family can afford to "give her away." The groom's family, however, is more inclined to keep tabs on their new daughter-in-law. They want to make sure that she bears their son's offspring. It would be interesting to learn whether, in general, husbands' families are more intolerant of wifely infidelity than wives' families are of infidelity by husbands.

In addition to allowing the husband's family to oversee their genetic investment, this "patrilocal" system also facilitates polygyny, the marriage of one man to several women. Clearly, if the husband moved in with the wife's family, his further matrimonial options would be limited to other female relatives also living there, perhaps the sisters of his first wife. But if he stays put, then a theoretically unlimited number of women (related or not) can come and join his harem.

This arrangement may, of course, be less than idyllic. Even if the wives are related to each other, they are still more closely related to their own offspring than they are to each other's children. We can, therefore, predict a great deal of jealousy and backbiting, with each wife resenting the attention given to another and striving to maximize the success of her offspring, if necessary at the expense of anyone else's.

A similar recipe for conflict was part of traditional Chinese family life. Here, the ideal household consisted of the aged parents, their unmarried daughters, their sons, and the wives and children of their married sons. However, as anthropologist Marjorie Wolf points out,

> This ideal is occasionally achieved by the wealthy, but among the poor, *two married brothers rarely maintain a joint household after the death of their father.* The wife of one is too sure that the wife of the other feeds her children more when it is her turn to cook, or that she shirks her share of the housework. While the brothers' mother is still living and active, she can control or at least mediate disputes in the kitchen, but the loser of any dispute is sure to whisper to her husband about the favoritism his parents are showing to the other brother's children. . . .

It is a familiar pattern. The grandmother is equally related to all the grandchildren and, as expected, she equalizes any potential favoritism within the family. But the wives are unrelated to each other or to each other's offspring; and with their mother-in-law's death, kin-selected biology rears its head. Finally, the young husbands, it is interesting, are apparently less jealous than their wives; they are, after all, related to each other's offspring, as biological uncles.

As a general rule, marriage and legitimacy are of much greater concern to societies having patrilineal descent, that is, those that trace relatedness through the male line. This too is appropriate, since there is a greater "need" to protect the genetic interests of males. Compare the African Nuer, among whom large bride-wealth payments are the rule, with the Indian Nayar (whom we discussed earlier), who use the avunculate and regard marriage as trivial. Since biological fathers don't really count for much among the Nayar, and they often can't even be assured of their paternity, it is entirely appropriate that Nayar husbands don't pay very much to obtain their wives. Nuer men, by contrast, "get" fatherhood and so they must pay for it, by exchanging cattle for wives—and fitness.

Another common marriage pattern is the "levirate," found among the ancient Hebrews (for a reference, see Deuteronomy 25, verses 5–6) and still practiced by the Bedouins of Arabia and North Africa, among others. In this system, when a married man dies, his widow is taken over by his brother, or even sometimes his son, so long as it is a son by another wife. The result is that the genes are kept within the family, or to be more accurate, the family is extended to encompass the genes. Most anthropologists distinguish the levirate from "widow inheritance," in which the widow actually becomes the spouse of her dead husband's brother or son, and any children produced are considered as belonging to the new husband. In the levirate the widow doesn't remarry, so that socially the dead husband remains the "father" of any subsequent children. Biologically, of course, he is an uncle (or grandfather).

The Nuer of the Sudan carry this pattern of widow inheritance even further and practice "ghost marriage." If a man dies before he has married and had sons, his brother is expected to marry a wife in the dead man's name. Any children they produce are considered to "belong" to the dead brother, rather than to the actual father. The genetic consequences, whether those involved are aware of them or not, are that a man is assured that he will leave some genetic mark behind, even if he dies early. This is no less than a system of evolutionary life insurance. It pays a man's genes to take out a policy, even though society's explanation may be that it is all being done merely to perpetuate his name.

There is a similar evolutionary appropriateness to "sororal polygyny," in which sisters marry the same man. The effect is to make the children of co-wives each others' cousins as well as half-siblings. Thus, when co-wives aid each other's children, they are also helping perpetuate their own genes.

One more case. Although most human societies prohibit extramarital sex by women, those that do permit it nearly always limit their approval to such in-law liaisons as a wife with her brother-in-law. Perhaps a man is simply less likely to be sexually jealous of his brother than he is of a stranger. But it is also true that since brothers share one-half their genes they have less to be jealous about, whether or not they know anything about genetics.

As far as evolution is concerned, the effect of the behavior is what counts, not the explanations that people attach to it. As with the bees that help rear sisters or the Eskimos who design perfect igloos without knowing thermodynamics, we may do a great deal that is adaptive without actually knowing why.

●

We may soon be able to conduct a made-to-order experiment in kin selection: cloning. In this process, the genetic material of an egg is removed and replaced by a nucleus taken from someone else. If that egg then develops normally, it produces an individual who is genetically identical to the donor. Cloning has already been carried out successfully on plants and even frogs, and the time seems not far off when we will be able to clone human beings as well. We need only enucleate a woman's egg, replace the nucleus with someone else's genetic material, and then implant the egg cell in her uterus or in a test tube. Wait nine months and then, presto, a perfect Xerox copy of a human being.

I am not necessarily advocating the process, but if it ever does happen—and I find it hard to believe that it won't someday soon—let's watch it very closely. Certainly the extraordinary interest cloning has already generated may in itself say something important. Can it be that the notion of copying ourselves is profoundly stimulating because it involves perfect replication of our own genes? In any event, the obvious thing to look for will be extreme altruism between cloned individuals, since they are genetically identical to each other. But would this necessarily be the case? As with identical twins (a natural, but rare event), cloned people would emerge without the benefit of a prolonged evolutionary history during which such altruistic tendencies would have been strongly favored by selection. A gene that instructed its body to "be nice to your clone" probably was not very strongly favored by natural selection during our evolutionary history. So I'm not at all sure that extraordinary altruism should actually be expected between a person and his or her clone.

●

The sociobiological rule that genetic relatedness breeds altruism may go a long way toward explaining the way different parts of the same body "behave" toward each other. The human body is composed of literally millions of cells, cooperating to make a healthy, successful person. And it may well be that the main reason they get along so well is that they are all, in fact, genetically identical. The cells that make up our skin, brain, kidneys and gonads are all produced from the same fertilized egg, and the differences between them are due entirely to differences in the chemical and physical environments of these cells during embryonic development. It is very much in the selfish interest of each cell to do its job for the good of the body as a whole. This may be a novel way of viewing our bodies, but it is consistent with our understanding of how evolution works.

Consider what happens in the case of cancer, for example. Certain cells go out of control, reproducing themselves excessively (forming tumors), to the ultimate detriment of the individual concerned. It may be no coincidence that cancer cells often carry mutations. Unlike normal body cells, they are not genetically identical to the rest of the body and hence they are less "concerned" with its fate.

A similar interpretation might apply to aging. As each of us gets older, the cells that make up our bodies tend to become more different from each other, since individual mutations that occur during the life of each cell are passed on to its daughter cells. No wonder they are more sluggish and less responsive to the needs of the body as a whole. Significantly, biologists have already found that older people produce more antibodies to their own tissue than do younger people. The body of an elderly person treats parts of his or her own body as somehow different from other parts, and this auto-immune reaction may be at least partly responsible for the general decline in vigor that we associate with aging. Perhaps there will be an even newer science in the future—the sociobiology of individual bodies.

●

We are masters at deceiving ourselves. This makes perfectly good sense when we consider that we are so often called upon by our selfish genes to deceive others. The best liars are those who believe their own untruths, since they cannot betray themselves. Since kinship is so potent a force for promoting solidarity and altruism, it is not at all surprising that we make use of it even when it is biologically inaccurate, so long as it has ultimate, fitness-enhancing value. It is hard to resist appeals to the "brotherhood" of all men, and counter-culture language is filled with pseudo-sibling references. In Kurt Vonnegut's novel *Slapstick,* disorganized post-nuclear-war Americans were given a new lease on life when computers gave everyone a new middle name, thereby providing instant family for all. All "daffodil-11s" felt instant solidarity with each other, and not only that, they competed antagonistically with "raspberry-13s."

Once, an orphaned Yanomamo teenager joined a village in which he had no kin. He called the headman "father," quickly picked up all the genealogies, and immediately assumed all that man's kin patterns, such as refraining from wooing his new "sisters." The pygmies of Zaïre call Premier Mobutu their "father." Kinship, even if fictional, is a powerful whisper within us.

Similarly, we might have a brief look at peasant societies, rural people living close to towns or other urban centers, in which they may trade their farm produce for industrial products. To such people, kinship is still important, although generally less so than among tribal peoples. Here we see the development of some fairly elaborate social fictions, such as the *compadrazgo* system of Latin America. Here, two otherwise unconnected sets of parents are linked as *compadres,* since one set is made godparents for the other's child. Similar patterns, although with different terminology, occur in the Mediterranean, in parts of Nepal, Tibet and India.

Carolyn Attneave at the University of Washington is one of our most innovative clinical psychologists. Drawing from her own Native American background, she recognized the importance of social networks—composed usually, but not exclusively, of kin—for the normal, healthy functioning of human beings. She has developed a gigantic form of "group therapy," resembling a town meeting rather than a personal therapy session. The emotionally-troubled patient must show up with around forty others who care about him or her —at least, they must care enough to be there. What had been an individual's problem then becomes a communal responsibility, to be handled by the artificial but effective "super-family" that the therapist has demanded. It works. None of us are so far removed from tribalism that we cannot benefit from the sort of emotional support and security that such an all-embracing network provides. Modern life does much to deprive us of such support, and the more it does so, the more anxiety-ridden we may become. Kin-selected altruism works both ways. Not only does it provide each of us with opportunities to maximize our inclusive fitnesses by benefiting our relatives, it also provides us with opportunities to profit from the kin-selected altruism of others.

Kurt Vonnegut has coined the terms "kavass" and "gran falloon." A kavass is a group of people who share a profound connection. To sociobiology, an individual and his or her close relatives are a kavass. A gran falloon is a group of people who proclaim affiliation but whose real connectedness is trivial. For example, Indiana residents— "Hoosiers"—are a gran falloon. So too are political parties, the class of '62, office parties, and the Benevolent and Protective Order of Elks. Our susceptibility to gran falloons may well be due to our biological fondness for network affiliations, which throughout most of our evolutionary history centered around kin groups, associations that were profoundly important. Not surprisingly, we seek to recreate them at nearly every turn. Adolescents do so most prominently, perhaps because they are detaching themselves from their nuclear-family kavass and have not yet created their own reproductive unit. In *West Side Story,* the kids sing, "When you're a Jet, you're a Jet all the way . . . you're never alone, you're never disconnected. . . ."

Humans are marvelously inventive when it comes to making connections, creating alliances and dedicating themselves to the group. Often they unite themselves with symbols—mascots, emblems, theme songs, or simply names. The American Legion, the Democratic party, the running bear clan, the mods and rockers, the People's Republic of China. These gran falloons are not only important to our mental health, they may have more obvious practical value as well. Threads of kinship tend to run vertically, from one generation to the next, but if a large number of committed young males is needed to defend the village, say, or the country, it helps to have affiliations running horizontally as well. This problem has been most clearly solved by the warlike people of East Africa, who need devoted warriors to defend and enlarge their precious cattle herds. Masai males are born into an "age set," a linkage of equal-aged men who retain their gran falloon unity throughout life. Of course, it is not all falloonery. When they are young, fierce and vigorous, they constitute the much-feared Moran—the guardians of the cattle. Falloons such as these were successful in defying modern British weaponry for many years.

It is a powerful thing if a gran falloon can be turned into a kavass, that is, if an artificial assemblage can be made into something with potent evolutionary consequences. It should be no surprise that human beings are masters at doing just this, and that, furthermore, we often do so by creating genetic bonds between people who were previously unconnected. We cannot make Siamese twins out of independent adults, but we do the next best thing, uniting groups by making them co-shareholders in the next generation. Throughout history, alliances have been forged by arranging marriages between the offspring of different social networks. It works, because much as we might bicker with our in-laws, we are disinclined to make war against them. This is perhaps the primary social significance of exogamy—the near-universal tendency to marry outside the circle of immediate relatives. It makes potential enemies into allies, if sometimes uncomfortable ones. Genesis 34:16 says it all: "Then will we give our daughters unto you, and we will take your daughters to us, and we will dwell with you, and we will become one people."

•

To the Mundurucu of Brazil, there are only two types of people: themselves and *pariwat,* all the others. This sort of ethnocentric myopia is hardly unique to them. On Java, for example, the same word is used for "human" and for belonging to one's own group. You're either with us or you're against us, either a friend or an enemy, either a Hatfield or a McCoy. Intolerance, antagonism and exploitation make up the other side of sociobiology's coin of altruism. If, as is being suggested here, we are selected to be nice to our kin, then we may have few inhibitions against taking advantage of non-kin. But how do we recognize our relatives? How do our genes recognize our relatives? How do our genes recognize themselves in another?

It's not all that difficult. Even animals can be fairly confident that neighbors are more closely related than strangers, and genes that say "Be nice to your neighbors and less nice to strangers" are probably spread by way of kin selection. By their niceness they contribute to the success of other niceness genes in their neighbors—many of them relatives—while they profit selfishly at the expense of strangers, who carry fewer if any of the same genes.

Good neighborliness is only one possible strategy. Another is to be more discriminating and to dispense altruism specifically to relatives. But this requires some way to recognize one's relatives. For parents and offspring, it should be easy. Equally for siblings—just look around at your litter mates if you're a mouse, at your nest mates if you're a robin, at whom your mother nurses next if you're a monkey or a human being.

There are other clues to genetic relatedness, some of them cultural, as well as biological. White-crowned sparrows living in different parts of the San Francisco Bay area "speak" differently, using distinct dialects in their songs, which can be recognized by expert ornithologists (and presumably by in-group birds as well). Among humans, language is a real barrier to exchange. Of course, it is also a unifier. We are likely to be more closely related to others that speak our language, and even within a single society secret codes and passwords serve to separate "us" from "them."

Another possibility for kin recognition is that animals may actually be able to identify their relatives directly, by subtle signals such as appearance, odor, behavior or factors still unknown. Recent studies by Warren Holmes and Hannah Wu, working at the Regional Primate Center in Seattle, separated infant pigtail monkeys from their mothers at birth. Some time later, Holmes and Wu presented the young monkeys (now ranging from several weeks to nine months of age) with two infants, one a half sibling, the other an unrelated infant of the same sex and age. The results were striking. The juveniles consistently preferred their own kin, even though they had never met before! Furthermore, the monkeys were related only through their fathers, whom they also had never met.

Holmes has pursued this work further, using ground squirrels, animals that will readily adopt strange young. He produced four types of infant pairs: biological siblings reared together, biological siblings reared apart, unrelated individuals reared together and unrelated individuals reared apart. He then put the various pairs together and compared their behavior toward each other. Again, the results were a dramatic confirmation of ability to recognize kin.

Biological siblings, whether reared together or apart, are "nicer" to each other than are sociological siblings. They showed less aggression and more huddling and mutual grooming. The ultimate benefit is clear enough: genes help themselves by being nice to themselves, even if they are enclosed in different bodies. And presumably they use some aspect of resemblance (sight? smell?) to tell them who their relatives are, that is, where copies of themselves are most likely to be found.

Experimenters working with schoolchildren have shown that they can quickly divide a classroom into distinct camps, with real affiliation within each group and antagonism between them, simply by focusing on some identifiable trait that separates some and unites others. For example, blue and green eyes on the one hand versus brown eyes on the other. Or the purely arbitrary division into teams at summer camp "color wars." We seem always distressingly eager to make use of such distinctions, even when we are very young, and whereas the discrimination that develops may seem "inhuman," kin selection and inclusive fitness theory suggests that such behavior is all too human. Indeed, it even suggests an evolutionary tendency for racism.

People of different races *are* different. Although we are all one species and quite capable of exchanging genes, the fact remains that members of any race seem likely to share more genes with each other than with individuals of a different race. Physical resemblance almost certainly has some correlation with genetic resemblance, and, accordingly, we can expect the principles of kin-selected altruism to operate on this fact. More to the point, we can expect the other side of the coin—antagonism—toward those who are different.

We still do not know why exactly the human races are as they are. There have been many explanations offered for gross racial differences—protection from excessive ultraviolet by black skins in the tropics, absorption of scarce ultraviolet by light skins in Scandinavia, heat conservation among the stocky Eskimo, and so forth. The crucial point, though, may not be how the differences arose, but rather that they arose at all and that they correlate to some degree with genetic differences.

The Dutch sociologist H. Hoetink has proposed that human race relations are strongly influenced by what he calls "somatic norm images." These are the often unconscious stereotypes of physical appearance accepted by each society—skin, hair or eye color, body build and so on. Certainly these somatic norm images are not always very consistent (how many Germans noticed that Hitler was hardly the blond, blue-eyed "Aryan" whose virtues he extolled?). Nonetheless, these stereotypes persist, and Hoetink suggests that racial antagonism is greatest between human groups whose somatic norms are most different from the image that each race carries of itself. His theory has been applied especially to race relations in the Caribbean. It is interesting that Hoetink himself was unaware of the remarkable convergence of his observations with the principles of kin selection. Once again, someone is telling us that two plus two equals four. This time, however, the equation has a distinctly unpleasant sound.

Actually, the use of obvious physical features as an indicator of genetic relatedness is probably limited to situations in which dramatically different racial groups come into contact, perhaps following warfare or mass migrations. Among more sedentary peoples and in more recent times, it may well be that primarily cultural traits have been used to distinguish kin groups from non-kin. Such externals as dialects, clothing or hair style help provide precise differentiation between adjoining groups whose genetic distinctiveness might be real, but not especially salient. Ironically, our customs might often provide a more convenient handle on biology than does biology itself.

In *South Pacific,* a young Caucasian lieutenant falls in love with the lovely daughter of Bloody Mary, a Polynesian. Encountering resistance from a racist society, he sings angrily, "You've got to be taught, before it's too late, before you are six or seven or eight, to hate all the people your relatives hate. You've got to be carefully taught, you've got to be carefully taught." He may be right, but what do we have to be taught? If sociobiology is correct, we've got to be carefully taught *not* to hate others who are different from ourselves, because it may be our biological predisposition to do so.

If evolution does incline us to a degree of racial bigotry, that certainly does not mean that such inclinations are justified. What may have been adaptive under the conditions of our early evolution, when groups rarely met and were likely to be strongly competing when they did, is today not only dangerous and stupid and socially reprehensible but woefully maladaptive. We could, of course, wait for evolution to catch up and select against such racist tendencies, but this would probably take a few hundred generations. Perhaps one lesson to be gained from sociobiology is that we must demand that our cultural institutions, such as education and child rearing, make sure that we are "carefully taught" to love one another. Because, sad but true, we seem unlikely to do so by ourselves.

•

The sturdy Chukchee people of Siberia used to travel great distances with their reindeer herds. As with the proverbial seaman who had a woman in every port, adult Chukchee males could count on finding one at every encampment on their journeys. But such an arrangement could not be left to chance; the harsh arctic environment would not permit it. The northland places a very great premium on cooperation, and so Chukchee men made reciprocal wife-lending contracts with other men in distant parts of their range. Each man entered into a wife-sharing agreement with several others, each of whom lived in a region normally traversed by him. It was basically "you scratch my back, I'll scratch yours," only for the Chukchee the guarantee was that someone else would be provided to do the back scratching.

The men making these arrangements did not have to be related at all. And, in fact, they were not really altruistic at all. They profited from their "generosity" by the guarantee that they would receive equivalent benefits when they were out on the trail. The Chukchee case exemplifies another important aspect of the biology of altruism, second only perhaps to kin selection and the concept of inclusive fitness: reciprocity. The linking of reciprocity and fitness is the brainchild of Harvard sociobiologist Robert Trivers, who pointed out that under certain conditions apparent altruism can be adaptive even between individuals who are totally unrelated. The primary requirement is that the giver will be the getter at some later time. This being so, genes for such behavior could be spread by natural selection, since the ultimate effect of entering into a mutually-beneficial system is that each participant profits and increases his or her fitness.

So reciprocity—sometimes misnamed "reciprocal altruism"—is not altruism at all. It is selfishness, pure and simple, since it takes place in the expectation that the personal rewards will exceed the costs. Kin selection, by contrast, promotes behavior for which the individual altruist does not receive an overriding personal benefit.

The kin-selected altruist, as we have seen, is not truly altruistic either, in that there is an eventual payoff in the form of genes surviving in the body of a relative. Nonetheless, both kin-selected altruism and reciprocity differ from such obvious selfishness as hogging food and otherwise "looking out for number one," in that, with altruism and reciprocity, genetically selfish ends are achieved by behavior which, on the surface, appears to be self-sacrificing.

The interesting thing about all this is that there may well be a biological basis for something like the Golden Rule: "Do unto others as you would have others do unto you." The evolutionary modification makes it a bit more selfish: "Do unto others if you have reason to believe that they will do the same unto you; if they won't, and if you are not related, then to hell with them."

Reciprocity even occurs among baboons. If a male baboon, call him A, sees male B consorting with a female, he may enlist the aid of a confederate, male C. This seemingly altruistic individual then helps male A by cooperating with him in threatening the one with the female. This is often successful and when it is male A—the original recruiter—gets the girl. What's in it for male C? He risked a fight with B, only to assist male A, to whom he is not even related. The answer comes some time later, when male C is attracted to a female who is already taken. You guessed it, he goes right over to male A and apparently reminds him of his past debt. Significantly, adult male baboons do not respond when a juvenile seeks to enlist their aid. Presumably, this would not be a good bargain for the adult, since the juvenile does not carry enough social clout to fulfill his side of the reciprocal pact.

A workable system of reciprocity must involve individuals who recognize each other, who associate enough so that each can trust the other, and who are smart enough to drive a good bargain. Although some animals, such as baboons, are apparent reciprocators, reciprocity as a way of life may in fact be something of a human specialty.

Reciprocity is a powerful force in regulating human behavior. Barter and exchange are found nearly everywhere, and the concept of a fair trade often goes far beyond the exchange of material goods. If a Rwala Bedouin returns a greeting, he is obliged to help that individual in the future—a bond has been forged by the social exchange itself. In the Molucca Islands, headhunting could only occur from behind. After one had seen an opponent's face, to kill him would be murder. The parties would then have "exchanged" something, if only each other's visages. In most cases, the exchange is more concrete. Commonly, in Latin America, the statue of one village's patron saint will be brought to visit another village for an important festival, and that visit is reciprocated by the other's saint the following year. The need to reciprocate is very strong. Most of us feel guilty if we receive a Christmas card from somebody and realize that we didn't send one!

It is often a serious insult to refuse a gift, perhaps because along with the acceptance comes the expectation of a return. If we don't accept someone's offering, we need not pay it back. In the famous potlatches of the Kwakiutl Indians of the Pacific Northwest, the great chiefs vied with each other to give away the largest amount of goods. Huge quantities of food or blankets were given to guests at potlatch feasts, or perhaps even destroyed. The guests sullenly received their bounty, while the giver sang of his magnanimity and how he shamed his rivals and shows himself to be the "greatest chief of all." Of course, part of the reason for the glumness of the "getters" is the requirement that they reciprocate in kind, and the shame they know they will incur if they do not.

To a large extent, the amount of an offering in a reciprocal relationship indicates the depth of one's commitment, this fact being especially apparent in food sharing. Sociologist Saul Feinman points out that we offer coffee to our acquaintances, whereas friends stay for dinner. Food sharing is an extraordinarily powerful act, rare among primates, and often it is restricted to close kin. When calories are scarce, sharing is limited. Copper Eskimo men scramble for the best cuts of seal meat, all simultaneously attempting to cut preferred pieces for themselves, and of course, for their immediate families. It is even considered socially acceptable to cut off another's fingers in the process, and in fact, willingness to risk loss of a finger during the melee is considered a sign of manhood. The usually-amiable pygmies of Central Africa share meat only with considerable argument and distrust, although here too it is given to close relatives and, significantly, there may be a special obligation to share meat with pregnant women.

The reciprocal sharing of food almost universally relieves tensions. To share food with another is to treat him as kin—and kin are generally treated well. But there may be a further bond created, one based ultimately on a deep-seated expectation of reciprocity. An anthropologist once related how a rather casual nibble on a ginger root, in the company of a native Papuan, ultimately saved his life. Some time later, when he found out that his companion was a head-hunter and cannibal, he asked him whether his life had been in danger. He was reassured that, since they had eaten together, he had been safe. In much of Polynesia, infanticide has always been an accepted part of life, but it is permitted only if the child has not begun nursing. Speaking of his native Russia, Prince Kropotkin writes: "Even today (1903) when feuds are ended in the Caucasus the guilty party touches the breast of the eldest woman in the tribe with his lips and becomes the 'milk brother' of all men in the injured family."

The reciprocal patterns that occur in most human societies serve to keep us biologically honest, or at least true to the maximization of our own fitness. Our inclination to behave altruistically to younger individuals may well have something to do with the likelihood that they will be able to pay us back in the future. Altruism toward the aged is probably more truly altruistic, in that the benefited individual may die before having the chance to reciprocate, and when that happens, the altruist has suffered an evolutionary loss. Might our woeful neglect of the elderly stem from this? It is no accident that the societies which are more humane toward the aged are those in which the elderly retain useful roles. It is probably also no accident that in the United States many more physicians go into pediatrics than into geriatrics, or that the poster used to stimulate aid for starv-ing peoples almost always features a starving child, not an adult.

We should conclude this introduction to reciprocity and altruism by going back to basics: our selfish genes. We have already seen how genes can promote their own replication through behavior that might even sacrifice their host body, so long as other bodies carrying copies of those genes are sufficiently benefited in the process. This is kin selection, and its result is the maximization of inclusive fitness. Reciprocity theory explains how genes can promote their replication by self-sacrificial behavior, even toward unrelated individuals, so long as the recipients are likely to pay these genes back in the future.

A system of this sort is vulnerable, as any good con man knows. Why not take the altruism from another, then refuse to pay it back? If this happens, genes for altruism are at a disadvantage, since they incur a cost but no benefit. And cheaters gain doubly, since they profit once from the others' altruism and again by never incurring the cost of repayment. Perhaps crime does pay.

Of course, the evolutionary process can be as calculating as the cheater, maybe more so. If selfish individuals are cheating in a reciprocal system, selection would favor those altruists who could discriminate true reciprocators from those who had cheated the last time around. It could become a never-ending spiral: greater care by would-be reciprocators selects for greater slyness on the part of the cheaters, which in turn selects for greater discrimination by the altruists, and so on. Where does it all lead? Just look around.

●

No human behavior comes entirely from our genes. We must always remember that our behavior is the result of interaction between our genetic makeup and our learning, all in some specific ecological context. The interplay is complex and, at this point in our knowledge, all but impossible to sort out. American anthropologists Ted and Nancy Graves, working out of New Zealand, have been conducting fascinating work in the gray area between psychology and traditional anthropology. Some of their findings are reported in a study titled "The Impact of Modernization on the Personality of a Polynesian People, or How to Make an Up-tight, Rivalrous Westerner out of an Easy-going, Generous Pacific Islander."

The Graveses studied the people of the Cook Islands, a Tahiti-like paradise whose inhabitants are warm and generous, and contrasted them with New Zealanders, who typify Westerners in their relatively aggressive approach to life. In one test, Cook Island children and New Zealand children played a game that provided them a variety of choices. The rule was that each time a child made a choice, he or she would get a certain number of pennies and another child would get either more pennies, fewer pennies, or the same number, depending on the choice made by the first child. Thus, a child might get to choose between getting two pennies for himself while someone else got only one; getting one for himself while the other simultaneously got two; and so forth. The children were then classified on the type of decisions they made: "self-maximizing" (always taking the most for themselves, regardless of what this meant for the other), "altruistic" (maximizing the other's return rather than their own), or "rivalrous" (spiteful, minimizing the other's return, even if this meant a lesser payoff for themselves).

The results were dramatic. Self-maximizers were about equally common in both cultures (around 30 to 40 percent of the children), but 45 percent of the Cook Island children were altruistic as compared to just 18 percent of New Zealand children. New Zealand children were much more likely to be rivalrous than were Cook Islanders. Why this difference? The Graveses point to the fact that traditional Cook Island behavior is highly social and generous and that children are taught to be cooperative and giving. This pattern surely makes good biological sense. Small, isolated populations are likely to contain numerous relatives, so kin selection alone could increase the opportunities for altruism. But the opportunities for reciprocity are also great, and such behavior is highly adaptive. (I help thatch your house, you help thatch mine.) This is not to say that Cook Islanders are genetically predisposed to be more generous than New Zealanders, although they might be. Human behavior is flexible within an adaptive range, and while we all recognize the value of reciprocity, we also recognize that it is valuable only when it can work. It is much more likely to work in places like the Cook Islands than in New Zealand—or London, or New York.

There is every reason to believe that Cook Islanders can learn to be just as competitive as Western children, and the Graveses have strong evidence for this as well. Older children exposed to the competitive environment of Western-style schools brought onto the islands became as "rivalrous" as their New Zealand counterparts. The evidence is overwhelming that these people are learning to be "uptight" and more selfish than they ever were before.

It is fashionable these days to mourn the passing of traditional ways of life, especially when they seem to have been so idyllic. But Westernization is coming, inevitably, to the Cook Islands, and it may be that Western-style rivalry is adaptive for anyone who must live this new style of life. Unfortunately, such an adaptation by individuals may be hurtful to their societies. Western-style schooling, the Graveses point out, seems to lead to rivalry rather than to altruism, and "those children who are being trained most vigorously and successfully for future leadership roles are also the ones who will be the *least* likely to want to use their talents for the benefit of the community as a whole."

This sort of situation is not limited to the rapidly-changing paradise of the Cook Islands. Throughout history, societies and people have had to reach an accommodation between the selfish tendencies of each and the benefit of all. Genetic selfishness, we have seen, can be expressed directly, through behaviors that promote the individual and his or her offspring; or less directly, through kin selection and its concern for more distant relatives; or, least directly, through reciprocity, in which apparent altruism evolves by the exchange of favors between individuals who may not even be related. This last is where society comes in. Among the Nambikwara Indians of tropical South America, the tribe relies heavily on its chief. He gives his wisdom in the hunt, his courage in battle and his own material goods when there are shortages. And in return he gets . . . extra wives. He contributes to the fitness of the group and the group, in turn, contributes to his.

Complex nation-states are less direct in their reciprocal payments, but their needs are every bit as real as those of the Nambikwara. The garbage must be collected, wrongdoers deterred, governments run. How do these complex societies get individuals to behave altruistically toward the larger group? Essentially in the same fashion as the Nambikwara. Society gets by because those who work to benefit the larger group are no less motivated by selfish fitness maximization than is the Nambikwara chief. We pay society's benefactors well, often rewarding them with prestige and power as well. More than two hundred years ago, Adam Smith recognized the power of appeals to selfish motive: "It is not from the benevolence of the butcher, the brewer or the baker, that we expect our dinner, but from their regard to their own interest. We address ourselves, not to their humanity, but to their self-love, and never talk to them of our own necessities, but of their advantages." At another time, he wrote, "We are not ready to suspect any person of being defective in selfishness."

Not surprisingly, society recognizes the need to offer extra compensation to those individuals of whom it makes extra demands. Veterans' benefits might be an example, or the emotional public funerals for policemen killed in the line of duty. In most cases, the rewards are more subtle, but no less real or important.

●

Remember the Three Musketeers? "All for one and one for all!" How about that as a basis for the evolution of altruism? Couldn't natural selection favor altruistic behavior if such behavior served to enhance the success of the group? Certainly, if the group prospered because of the generosity of its members, each individual should profit as well. This notion has a great appeal, since it describes the way we would like people to behave, curbing their personal selfishness for the benefit of the group. As a species, we are preoccupied with teaching ourselves to "respect the rights of others." I even remember a place for this on my fourth-grade report card. To some extent, biologists have also found this idea appealing and have coined the phrase "group selection" to describe the evolutionary process in which individuals sublimate their personal fitness considerations for the ultimate benefit of their group. It is quite a different process from selection operating on individuals or their genes.

The problem is that, appealing as it may be, group selection founders on the shoals of selfishness. Altruists would always be at the mercy of those ornery creatures who got low grades in "respect the rights of others" but correspondingly high grades in their own fitness. It is true that groups containing altruists might do better than groups without them, but individual altruists within those groups would lose out to their selfish colleagues. Mathematically-inclined readers might recognize that group selection is still theoretically possible, if altruistic groups reproduce themselves fast enough to make up for the loss of altruists within each group. But this is very unlikely.

Sad but true, the selfishness of some often puts real strains on the altruism of others. For example, much of this book was written in California, which at the time was suffering from the most severe drought in its history. Water was being rationed, with each household restricted to its own monthly allotment. In a sense, California is a group,* and the group as a whole stood to benefit if water consumption was kept down. However, appeals to individual altruism proved not to be enough, and quotas had to be established. But selfish individuals could still obtain additional water, for example, by showering at a public facility, and in so doing they used the same amount of water as they would have in their homes. The group suffered as a result of their selfishness, but since the water consumption was not charged to the non-altruists' home meters, they got away with something, at the expense of everyone else in the group.

*A gran falloon, if ever there's been one!

In this case, of course, the benefits to selfish individuals and the costs to altruists were trivial. Few people die for want of a shower, although I suppose it is possible that their reproductive success might be diminished. But imagine if the behavior was more significant, such as not sharing food, or such as producing excessive numbers of offspring and thereby benefiting oneself (in evolutionary terms) but at some cost to others through overcrowding, competition for scarce resources, and so on. In such cases, the selfish individuals win and the altruists lose. The fact is that appeals to group benefit rarely overcome the potential lure of individual selfishness; or, to be more accurate, individuals who place the group above themselves will be at a disadvantage compared to others who selfishly insist on "doing their own thing." It therefore seems to be a good general rule that selection operating at the level of groups will not produce altruism.

It has also been suggested that altruism might possibly evolve as a result of manipulation of offspring by their parents. Imagine that a parent can force one of its offspring to sacrifice itself "altruistically" for the benefit of its brothers and sisters. Conceivably, the manipulated child may be losing fitness while the parent is gaining, since the parent profits through the benefits received by its other children. Selectively killing certain children and perhaps even feeding them to the others would be an extreme example of such manipulation.

This hypothesis can be tested and it has been. Among the social insects you may remember that the sterile workers share ¾ of their genes with other workers, and only ¼ with drones. By contrast, the queen is equally related to both workers and drones (½ in each case). Therefore, Her Majesty would prefer if equal amounts of food were given to both workers and drones, since she is equally related to both types. On the other hand, the workers are predicted to disagree, preferring to invest in proportion as they are related: three to one —¾ to workers, ¼ to drones. Testing this proposition, sociobiologists Bob Trivers and Hope Hare found, sure enough, that workers feed other workers three times as much as drones, not equally as the queen should prefer. The workers are winning the battle of the generations. In fact, this suggests that perhaps we should view the queen as a tyrannized and well-tended egg machine, rather than as a sovereign ruler, squeezing altruism from her manipulated workers.

Although parental manipulation seems unlikely to cause much altruism, parents may occasionally be able to manipulate their offspring, especially when the children are young and helpless. For instance, in infanticide, there is little an infant can do if an adult decides to kill it. Also, recall our discussion of "spontaneous" abortion. An adult female can enhance her fitness by discarding a fetus that would otherwise use up more resources than it is worth in terms of the adult's total reproductive success. We can expect that the fetus views the whole business somewhat differently. Nonetheless, the adult has more power and can probably get her way. Alternatively, however, the fetus in some cases might also "want" to be aborted. Remember, the fetus shares one-half of its genes with its mother and it will share one-half its genes with the next offspring the mother will produce (assuming the same father in both cases). If by giving up on itself the fetus is able to confer a twofold benefit on its mother's next reproductive attempt, then altruistic suicide would be selected. But this would be kin selection, not manipulation of the child by the parent, since the child would be maximizing *its own* inclusive fitness.

This example points up a real problem in evolutionary analyses of altruism: the various mechanisms of natural selection are often hard to separate from each other. For example, kin often live in groups, so if altruism takes place, it is difficult to know whether kin selection or group selection is responsible. If it is both, one could ask, how much of each? Or there's the fact that both kin and group members are often in a position to reciprocate at a later time, so reciprocity is difficult to rule out. Or there might be the possibility that an altruistic individual is acting that way only because it has been manipulated by its parents. Or, finally, there is the difficulty in knowing for certain that a particular behavior isn't really selfish after all, as reciprocity normally is.

When older female langur monkeys help defend an infant against a murderous male, they may be responding to the dictates of kin selection (since the defenders are likely to be aunts, cousins and so forth). On the other hand, they may be entering into a reciprocal defense pact ("I'll help defend your baby, you help defend mine"). Or perhaps group selection is operating (if groups with baby defenders do better than groups without them, even though within such groups defenders are more at risk than selfish bystanders who refuse to get involved). Or maybe even parental manipulation is at work (if grandparents somehow "insist" that their daughters help defend each other's babies).

The problems of identifying the causes of altruism apply to most altruistic behaviors. Take the interesting situation of "helpers at the nest" for example. Among certain birds, such as Florida scrub jays, sub-adult males commonly help adults rear additional young. This appears to be altruistic on their part, since adults with helpers rear more young than those without, and in the process of helping the adults, the young males are forgoing reproduction themselves. The best explanation for this behavior seems to be kin selection, since it turns out that the youngsters are generally helping their own parents rear a second brood. That is, they are helping to rear siblings, with whom they share one-half their genes, the same as if they had bred themselves. But it is also possible that they gain reciprocity from their parents; in return for their help with child care, the parents may well be allowing the sub-adults to remain in the vicinity of the home nest, an area that is safe and where food is available.

And there are still other possibilities. Groups of birds with helpers might do better than groups without, so group selection can't be ruled out for certain. Or maybe the helpers are somehow being "forced" by their parents to do their filial chores, for the ultimate benefit of the parents themselves (parental manipulation). Or young helpers gain experience while helping, and if there is competition for obtaining a nest or mate, they may be better off waiting a while before attempting to breed in any case; in other words, their helping might be pure selfishness. And, of course, there is no reason why several of these could not be working at the same time.

So, then, any of these factors could lead to the altruistic helping behavior in question. I promised, early on, that sociobiology would provide valuable insights and that it would also be fun, but I never said it would solve all our problems—or that it wouldn't be complicated!

•

"Our virtues are most frequently but vices in disguise."

"The gratitude of most men is merely a secret desire to receive greater benefits."

These sayings are attributed to the swashbuckling seventeenth-century French Duc de La Rochefoucauld—soldier, lover of famous women, and one of the best one-liners of all time. His rather crabbed view of human nature shares some thinking with sociobiology. Michael Ghiselin, historian, taxonomist and marine biologist, puts it this way:

> No hint of genuine charity ameliorates our vision of society, once sentimentalism has been laid aside. What passes for cooperation turns out to be a mixture of opportunism and exploitation. The impulses that lead one animal to sacrifice himself for another turn out to have their ultimate rationale in gaining advantage over a third; and acts "for the good" of one society turn out to be performed to the detriment of the rest. Where it is in his own interest, every organism may reasonably be expected to aid his fellows. Where he has no alternative, he submits to the yoke of communal servitude. Yet given a full chance to act in his own interest, nothing but expedience will restrain him from brutalizing, from maiming, from murdering—his brother, his mate, his parent, or his child. Scratch an "altruist," and watch a "hypocrite" bleed.

Sociobiologist Richard Alexander of the University of Michigan has suggested that the remarkable, explosive development of the human brain may have been brought about by warfare between bands of primitive humans, and there is, in fact, a great deal of fossil evidence suggesting that our ancestors did not exactly treat each other according to the Geneva Convention. Our most dangerous predator may well have been ourselves, and selection would have favored those individuals whose brains were large enough to permit them to enter into workable alliances and to coordinate defense— and aggression—against other groups.

Dartmouth political scientist Roger Masters uses sociobiology to propose a somewhat less bloodthirsty view of our evolutionary past. Our large brain is clearly adaptive for war, tool making or practically any other purpose. Of course, it also gets in our way sometimes, and literally so at the most crucial time in our life—when we are born. We've pointed out already that a human's large head has an uncomfortably tight squeeze getting through the mother's pelvis, especially because our upright posture has narrowed the birth canal. We are unique among animals in having a high rate of mothers dying in childbirth, and it seems reasonable that this would set a limit on possible brain size of the newborn. In addition, death in childbirth would almost certainly be higher when the mother is alone than when she is receiving assistance from others. You may already have the idea: according to Masters, altruistic behavior during childbirth among our ancient hominid ancestors may have contributed to the evolution of our own large brains. Kin selection would probably be the most likely mechanism, with relatives assisting each other during childbirth. Evolution would strongly favor any correlation between genes for larger brains and altruistic tendencies such as assisting a woman during labor and delivery. I rather like the idea that midwifery and obstetrics may literally be our oldest professions, or at least the ones that "gave birth" to our humanity. If so, their payment was in evolutionary currency—fitness. And genetic fee-splitting would have shared the profits among all the newborn's relatives.

Evolutionary biology is quite clear that "What's in it for me?" is an ancient refrain for all life, and there is no reason to exclude *Homo sapiens.* Charles Darwin once stated that if it were ever demonstrated that a single characteristic of a living thing existed for the sole benefit of another species, it would annihilate his theory of evolution by natural selection. A remarkably bold statement, this, and one that has withstood more than one hundred years of careful scrutiny.

To date, no plant or animal has been shown to display true altruism, a behavior whose sole effect is to profit another individual, even one belonging to the same species. It remains to be seen whether this includes *Homo sapiens* as well. We can probably all relate incidents —real or imaginary—in which someone performs what appears to be an act of selfless heroism on behalf of another: rescuing a drowning man, entering a burning house to save a trapped child, risking death to smuggle Jews out of Nazi Germany or blacks out of slavery. Perhaps this is true altruism. If so, our species is unique. On the other hand, such behavior may reflect the accumulated, continuing indoctrination of each person within just about every human society. Practically from birth we are taught that it is good to help others, and that in fact, it is somehow reprehensible to expect recompense. If we were "naturally" altruistic, then why all the exhortations? It may well be that true altruism really does not occur among humans, except when they are coerced by society.

Let us look at a possible exception, the kamikazes. Legend has it that fourteenth-century Japan was saved from Korean "barbarians" by a divine wind, the kamikaze that destroyed the Korean war fleet. During its death throes in the Second World War, Imperial Japan apparently breathed some of this wind into its pilots in an effort to wreak the same havoc on the American fleet. The effort didn't work, but can we possibly question the altruism involved? After all, those pilots made the greatest sacrifice—their lives. And, unlike worker bees, they were not related to most of those at home they hoped to save. It might be worth taking a closer look at the Japanese kamikazes.

For one thing, it turns out they were promised an "eternal life" if they died defending their Emperor. For another, their rewards weren't only in heaven. Kamikaze pilots were given national acclaim and privileges; if these included sexual privileges, kamikazes' fitness may have been preserved after all. (This is not to suggest that these pilots were directly motivated by the arithmetic of evolutionary fitness, but their "sweet receptors" did recognize a good deal when they saw it.) Their families also gained enhanced status, and it is interesting that before volunteering to be kamikazes these men were often of low prestige, both socioeconomically and in the ranks as pilots. So their cost-benefit equation would have favored altruism. If at the moment of truth they refused to fly, they were shot, and once airborne, they had no parachutes and only enough gasoline to make it to the American warships. It had to be a one-way trip. Perhaps there is a question here whether the bargain these men were making was a fully altruistic one.

So where have we gotten ourselves? Evolution has left us a mixed heritage, selfish genes in weak bodies, which need society for their success but are likely to walk all over society and the bodies of others if it helps them get their way. We are selfish altruists, paradoxical creatures whose divided loyalties are never truly reconciled. If our "human nature" impels us to behave more selfishly than society would like, it is not surprising that societies everywhere have developed techniques to bend us to their will. No human society is without its shoulds and should-nots, its moral injunctions that coax, cajole, warn, threaten and punish. Whether we approve or not, this makes good sense, for insofar as evolution has made us self-centered rather than other-centered, it is up to society to make us more tractable. Indeed, if we ever hope to attain real altruism in human behavior, unalloyed by selfish concerns, we had better look to society to drum it into us, because there seems to be no other way it can get there.

As social psychologist Donald Campbell has pointed out, there may be real wisdom to the Ten Commandments and other such moral codes—from society's viewpoint, if not from that of each citizen. Perhaps we have to be told not to steal, murder or covet our neighbor's wife because those are just the sorts of things our internal whisperings are telling us to do, if they profit us and if we can get away with them.

In fact, the egocentric outlook that is biology's gift to each of us may go a long way toward explaining one of humanity's most disturbing paradoxes. It is absolutely undeniable that much of the world is in terrible shape. Famine, pestilence, tyranny and outright savage murder abound. We are rapidly destroying the only planet we have, polluting it and using up its irreplaceable natural resources at an unconscionable rate. We continue to wobble on the brink of thermonuclear destruction. Yet virtually everyone, regardless of circumstance, spends virtually all his or her time and energy attending to intensely personal concerns, centered largely around self, immediate family and friends. In many ways, it is an utterly absurd situation. Sociobiological theory may at least help us understand what is going on, and why we are all Neros, fiddling with barbecues, college tuition and haircuts, while the world burns.

On the other hand, maybe the evolutionary mechanisms for altruism allow us enough generosity, kindness and breadth of spirit to let us make a start in becoming admirable creatures in our own right. Maybe someday we will be able to view all of humanity and all of life as part of our reciprocating group or, in the most profound sense of the word, as our kin. Much depends on it.

6

Competition: Fighting, Male Groups and War

Most people want to be assured of their place in the sun, their share of the pie, their measure of fitness. When they aren't achieving enough of these—or feel they aren't—they are likely to compete with neighbors, friends or even relatives. If conditions become bad enough, they may even fight and sometimes kill.

In the American South, whenever the price of cotton fell, the frequency of lynchings would rise. This ghastly correlation reveals a great deal about the sociobiology of competition and aggression: when resources become scarce (as when King Cotton gets a little shaky), most living things become more aggressive. Unpleasant as it may be, this response is simply their way of getting what they need. Clearly, aggression in modern *Homo sapiens* is often grossly maladaptive, yet because aggression is a part of all of us, we had better take a hard look at the evolutionary biology of our nastiness. We may not like what we see, but that is all the more reason to make sure we don't ignore it.

According to evolutionary theory, we expect individuals to compete whenever such competition enhances their fitness. In gene language, we would say that competitive behavior evolves whenever genes that produce this behavior leave more copies of themselves than do genes that influence their carriers to behave less competitively. We expect, in short, that when it works competition will be a successful evolutionary strategy. When it fails—that is, when it doesn't enhance fitness—we do not expect it to occur.

Of course, some living things simply can't do much to compete: there's not much that an oyster can do about another oyster that appropriates its resources. Trees, though, can contend with each other in a struggle to obtain sunlight; the losers are left to wither in the shade. And mobile animals are quite a different story. Leopards, bison, human beings can compete much more dramatically than by merely trying to outgrow their rivals.

For competition to be adaptive, an animal must have not only the ability to compete but a reason to compete. Competition will be selected only when its benefits outweigh its costs. Struggling with others expends both time and energy and, when push comes to shove, it may even be quite dangerous. Discretion is invariably the better part of valor, unless there are good—that is, fitness-enhancing —reasons to behave aggressively. There may, for example, be a critical shortage of some necessity, such as mates, nest sites or food. When this occurs, competition is inevitable. In evolution, benevolence is an indulgence of the well-to-do. Bertold Brecht wrote in *The Three-penny Opera:* "first feed the face, and then tell right from wrong . . . for even noble men may act like sinners, unless they've had their customary dinners!" This "Mack-the-Knife principle" elucidates much of human competitiveness. The awful scenes of aggressive free-for-alls during the distribution of food in disaster areas tell it all.

The point is that aggression is a method of competing, a method that is often utilized when it proves adaptive. Demagogues through-out history have recognized this tendency and used it to manipulate human behavior. When times are hard, people are eager to take out their aggression on whatever scapegoats happen to be available. And, if these scapegoats are easily distinguishable from members of the dominant group (and hence unlikely to share many genes with the aggressors), so much the better. This was the fate of Jews in Nazi Germany and blacks in the American South.

An enormous amount of ink has been spilled over the issue of whether humans are aggressive by instinct. In sociobiological think-ing, this controversy is secondary to the recognition that, in general, aggressive behavior will take place when it maximizes fitness. The first crude theories of instincts claimed that we possess an innate and automatic need to act in a particular manner, and that the discharge of aggression was therefore unavoidable. Thus, ethologist Konrad Lorenz suggests that we redirect our aggressive drives toward goals that are more constructive (or at least less destructive), such as the space race. Sociobiology, however, proposes that our most important need is to maximize fitness. If we want to understand, say, human aggressiveness, we would be better advised to examine the evolutionary costs and benefits of aggressiveness under specific circumstances.

There is little in human behavior that is automatic or the product of extremely simple cause and effect. Aggression is not a result of instinct, nor is it an inevitable outcome of the operation of natural selection. Aggression is a highly risky business for the organism and not something to be undertaken lightly. It is resorted to only after all possible factors are considered. Some of these factors are contained in our genes. Some are in the environment, made available to us through experience. Our genes advise us when aggression is an appropriate (fitness-maximizing) response to our experience. In this sense, and only in this sense, can we be considered "instinctively" aggressive.

We have looked at the way competition and aggression increase when resources become scarce. This holds true for all animals, as long as the resources in question are defendable. For instance, no animals compete for air. Gulls that feed at sea do not defend territories, since the fish schools on which they feed are constantly shifting in location, making marine real estate a poor investment. However, gulls are quite aggressive in defense of their nests, as a nest is a distinct resource, important to fitness, defendable and therefore worth the effort of defense.

The distribution of a resource may also be crucial in determining whether it is worth competing for. The difference between "rural" and "urban" monkeys is interesting to look at. Free-living rhesus monkeys in India live in troops that range over the forested countryside. They eat a variety of fruits and vegetables, and rarely fight with each other. However, rhesus monkeys are also held sacred by many Hindus, and many temple grounds abound with the animals, which show up regularly for handouts. When food is presented in this environment, there is a great deal of fighting and squabbling. It seems clear that these "urban" monkeys are competing for the food because of the concentrated way in which it is presented to them. The food of their rural cousins, on the other hand, is normally spread out in trees and fields, thereby reducing the competition that could occur as each tried to get its share. Of course, the density of monkeys may also be responsible for the increased level of competition, since they tend to concentrate where the food is concentrated.

What is true of rhesus monkeys may be true of humanity as well: rural populations are spread out, as are their resources—game for hunters, grassland for pastoralists or farmland for farmers. But urbanization throws people closely together, and we can expect them to compete for resources that are now concentrated rather than dispersed. The issue should surely not be oversimplified, but it would surprise few sociobiologists if aggression, crime and general competitiveness turn out to be higher among urban *Homo sapiens.*

Evolutionary biology also predicts that the inclination to fight for a resource varies with its value. Of course, one resource will have different value to different people, so that we can expect an individual to fight most tenaciously for those things that "mean a lot" to him. Natural selection has insured that the things that "mean a lot" are those important to fitness.

A subordinate tassel-eared squirrel accustomed to its subordinate role will not usually stand up to a dominant squirrel, at least not for long. However, after the subordinate has been successful in mating with a female, he will defend her quite vigorously from other males, even from some individuals who would normally cause him to turn tail and run. Perhaps the subordinate's gallantry has been stimulated by his recent copulation; perhaps he "loves" his recent lover and protects her for that reason. Whatever flowery words we use, the fact is his new lover does "mean a lot" to him—certainly to his potential fitness. Having copulated successfully, he now stands to gain a great deal by keeping other males away from his female, since he now has a chance of becoming a father. Every additional male who copulates successfully with "his" female makes it that much less likely that genes from the first male will see the light of day in the next generation of tassel-eared squirrels. Because the cost-benefit equation of the would-be father was changed by his successful copulation, the benefit of fighting is higher, making him more willing to incur the potential costs. His "bravery" also has an interesting effect on the other squirrels. Sensing their opponent's motivation, they seem less inclined to risk a battle, and possible injury, than he is.

The implications of this example for humans are profound. We fight most strongly for "what we believe in," and what we believe in is most likely to be closely related to our home and our family, our "basic way of life." Many governments throughout history have underestimated the ferocity and determination with which otherwise peaceful people will defend their homes, a reproductively relevant resource. Napoleon and Hitler might have used a sociobiology lesson and thought twice about invading Russia. And the same, certainly, for America in Vietnam. A good project for one of those rare historians interested in the constants in human affairs would be an examination of invasions and the degree of resistance they have encountered.

•

It's not all that easy being a penguin. You stand all day in the icy winds just to keep an egg warm. Then, when you finally get a break for dinner, you have to jump into the ocean, where voracious leopard seals may be lurking. If they catch you, they'll skin you alive and swallow you whole. As one might expect, penguins are a bit cautious about going swimming. They often crowd together on ice floes, by the hundreds or even thousands, until a few are pushed into the water by the jostling crowd behind. If they are not eaten, the others jump in. Judging from their behavior, these animals seem to care little for each other: they are part of the original "lonely crowd." As with commuters jammed into a subway car, penguins are not likely to know or be related to their neighbors. Accordingly, there is little to inhibit competition, even less to generate "caring," and much to be lost by failure.

Competition makes the heart grow harder—especially if there aren't shared genes to soften the blows. This is true for penguins and, almost certainly, for people as well. One of the strongest human inhibitions deals with aggressiveness toward relatives. The argument for kin selection predicts that we would be less inhibited when fighting with strangers than with our friends or relatives. As a result, we might expect that a good strategy for reducing aggression would be to emphasize genetic relatedness. When relatedness is low (as among penguins on ice floes), we predict fewer inhibitions against competitiveness and aggression, and consequently a lot of pushing and shoving. There are interesting implications in this situation for societies which were founded by immigrants, such as the United States. A high immigration rate means, in general, a lower relatedness between individuals, which in turn means less altruism and more competitiveness. It may be no coincidence that a society in which the average degree of relatedness is low, and in which altruism is predicted to be low and competition high, is the bastion of world capitalism.*

Interestingly, Karl Marx fully expected that the industrialized nations such as England and Germany would be most ripe for communism, while it has in fact been most spectacularly successful in rural, peasant-dominated societies such as Russia and China, societies with settled populations within which competitive inclinations may well have been lower, and where capitalism was not established on a large scale. I am not claiming, certainly, that Russians and Chinese are inherently more altruistic and less competitive than Americans, but it may well be a human trait to be most cooperative and least competitive when one lives in settled networks, consisting largely of relatives and potential reciprocators. To some extent, the value of potential reciprocity may outweigh the exclusivity of kin groups, especially in pioneer settlements. Reciprocity may have tempered the rugged, competitive individualism of frontier America. The neighborly assistance given to a rancher whose barn has burned down is part of frontier lore. And, of course, such aid should be most likely when both reciprocity and kin selection promote it. I would look for more altruism in rural Montana than in Chicago or Birmingham. And when I don't find it—as among the Ik—I would suspect that something is dreadfully wrong.

Bear in mind, however, that there is a complex interplay between genetics and experience. For example, although many animals seem to know instinctively how to fight, they must learn who to fight with. If we isolate a young mouse or rat and then expose it to other mice or rats, the isolated individual will fight with fewer inhibitions than an individual that was socialized by growing up with a normal litter. The hermit simply hasn't learned the rules of the game, and therefore doesn't play fair.

Psychologists have discovered many ways of inducing animals to fight. By controlling its experiences, a "ninety-seven-pound weakling"-type mouse can be made into a terror. If the experimenter rigs a fight in its favor, a "born loser" will increasingly become a winner.

*This thinking, it should be admitted, represents an example of a common problem in "doing" human sociobiology. We can propose and sometimes even demonstrate correlations between what people do and what sociobiology predicts they will do. But what then? Have we shown cause and effect? At this point, no one knows. We are just beginning to find a few correlations. Our next step will be to try to decipher the causes.

For example, if a mouse is placed in an arena with another that has been hobbled, perhaps by having two of its legs tied together, the normal one naturally wins. If he continues to experience victory, he is more likely to win in future battles, even if his opponent is not hobbled. In fact, the very experience of being in a fight makes a mouse more likely to initiate one. It seems that animals learn to fight by fighting and win by winning. A similar pattern may hold for humans. Professional football teams do not like to lose, even during the exhibition season. They want to develop a "winning psychology." The procedure for fashioning a successful rodent gladiator is remarkably similar to the technique used by a canny manager in developing a young prize fighter. Match him with progressively better opponents each time, but bring him along slowly, always choosing someone he can beat. Don't let him face Muhammad Ali in his very first fight.

Social scientists have developed many other explanations of aggressive behavior, all of them variations on the general theme of social learning. Such theories need not be opposed to biological interpretations. Arguing whether learning or instinct produces aggression is like arguing whether the head or the tail is more basic to producing a coin. Evolution is the master engraver of both, and a close examination of various learning theories of aggression shows that they are all remarkably compatible with the theories of evolution. Living things make use of their experiences to produce adaptive behavior; this process is no less valid for aggression than it is for mate selection, parenting or any other behavior.

To take another example, psychologists and psychiatrists have pointed out that frustration is a major cause of aggression. If we place a hungry rat in a tunnel with food at the other end, he runs toward it. If we lower a barrier just before he attains his goal, he is likely to become "angry," that is, he may well start fighting with another rat, if one is present. Certainly frustration is a notable cause of aggression in humans as well, and probably for similar reasons. Since, with humans, it is not usually an artificial barrier but another individual who generally gets in the way, a frustrated individual might not only relieve frustrations by fighting, he may also use the fighting to gain his ends. That frustration produces aggression is almost surely adaptive.

Experiments have shown that if two rats are placed in a cage and one of them is shocked, that individual will be likely to start fighting with its neighbor. Pain apparently increases the likelihood of aggression, and again, for good adaptive reasons. During the evolution of rats, and probably that of people as well, pain was more likely to have been inflicted by another individual than by an electric shock. It should surprise no one that pain stimulates fighting.

Fighting is also likely to occur when social systems deteriorate. One way of recognizing a normally functioning social order among animals is the general absence of destructive fighting. Although it often pays individuals to accept subordinate status rather than to fight losing battles, it also pays them to enhance their position if they can. In a sense, nearly all living things are status seekers, and what better time to step up than when everything and everyone is disorganized? At least some genes may be programmed to stir up trouble when it appears that the established hierarchy is shaky.

Since fighting is a high-risk behavior, we would expect every member of a group to be carefully attuned to its cost and benefits. And among social animals—especially humans—this attuning comes via learning. Play fights and roughhousing teach individuals, in nonthreatening situations, the limits of their abilities and the consequences of overstepping them. This sort of education may be much of what childhood is all about. Humans have the longest childhood of any species, almost certainly because we have the most to learn about the world, about ourselves and about how we relate to others.

Although it may be possible to teach new tricks to old dogs, young puppies are even more eager to learn. Children, too, are acutely aware of their social environment, and they may well be especially tuned in to the occurrence and consequences of aggressive behavior. Their sensitivity may also explain our remarkable fascination with violence, whether rubber-necking at automobile accidents or watching football games or war movies.

In a subtle way, the danger in televised violence may lie in its giving an unrealistic and therefore dangerous perception of the costs and benefits of fighting and aggression. It may be all right for John Wayne or Clint Eastwood to be punched full in the face, but it's a very different thing when it happens in reality. When a child graduates from his regimen of ten thousand or so televised murders, not only is he benumbed to the fact of mayhem, he is also misinformed as to its consequences. Television may prove to be maladaptive for us all.

•

Among the tropical coral-reef fishes known as wrasses, there is at least one species in which individuals are able to change their sex from female to male, when it suits their fitness. Typically a single male maintains a harem of many females, but if that male is removed, the dominant female becomes a male and proceeds to mate with the remaining females. This new male leader is clearly more fit than it was as a female, since it may now mate with each of the remaining females. But what about those other females? Presumably, any of them could be more fit if they were to become males, so why haven't they all done so? Simply because any female who became a male and then lost out in competition with another would-be male would find itself out of luck. Not only would it lose out in the struggle to become a harem master, it would no longer even be eligible for membership in the harem. Under the circumstances, the fish is better off—more fit—to accept subordinate status, biding its time and reproducing as a female until it finds itself the dominant member of the harem. Then, when the male dies or becomes feeble, it moves up into leadership.

These wrasses are extraordinary in their ability to change sexes in midstream, but they are not at all unusual in another aspect of their behavior: if they can't be number one, they settle for number two, or three, or whatever. Some such form of rank ordering occurs in many species, including *Homo sapiens,* any time there are a number of associated individuals competing for the same things. Inevitably, some individuals will be more successful than others, either because they are older, stronger, smarter or perhaps just luckier. We have little trouble anticipating the behavior of the winners. They enjoy the fruits of their victories, and we may call them "dominant" individuals.

What about the losers? There are many options. Most species do not have the convenient flexibility of the wrasses, which can hedge their bets by remaining female rather than becoming subordinate males. In some instances, as among langur monkeys, losers may simply depart, to live alone or perhaps in bachelor groups; as we've seen, such disaffected outcasts may try their luck again later. For many species, however, solitary living is simply not feasible. There are very few solitary baboons, for example, at least for long, since lone individuals are easy prey to leopards and other predators. Even for a baboon that is not an especially successful competitor there may be good reasons for staying put. By accepting its position—which we call "subordinate"—it can, at least, survive.

A social organization based on dominance and subordination is called a "dominance hierarchy." It need not, in fact, be very hierarchical. There may be, for example, a linear graded system, such as is found among barnyard chickens, with A dominant over B, B dominant over C, etc., all the way down to Z, who is dominated by everyone. Or there may be one or several individuals at the top with everyone else below them, as is the case with gorillas. Or there may be a full-scale oligarchy, as with the savannah baboons, in which a small group of aging males help each other retain power by coming to each other's aid whenever one is threatened.

An essential point is that dominance is not an immutable, God-given property of either social systems or of individuals. It is simply the result of everyone's trying to drive the best possible bargain. Furthermore, dominance in one context may not apply in another. A mother may dominate others when it comes to caring for her offspring, but be subordinate when food is being shared.

Social subordination is simply our description of techniques that individuals use to avoid competition that would be disadvantageous to themselves. In some animal species, the consequences of subordinance may be purely behavioral. For example, a recent study of audience effects on the mating of rams has shown that, while subordinate rams were inhibited in mounting a receptive female when a dominant ram was present, the dominant was unaffected by subordinate onlookers. In other cases, subordination can have physiological manifestations, as in so-called "psychological castration." Subordinate male monkeys have been observed to have smaller testes and lower levels of male sex hormones than do dominants; often they are unable to copulate successfully or to produce viable sperm. Conceivably, this diminished sexuality could be a cause of their low social status, rather than being an effect of it. However, this possibility has been disproved by artificially allowing the subordinate animal to become dominant, in one experiment by removing the dominant individuals, in another by disabling them. In both cases, the effects were dramatic: the testes enlarged and both sex hormone levels and viable sperm production were increased. The previously subordinate individuals were in effect "uncastrated."

Yet life isn't all that bleak for the subordinates. As they age and gain experience and strength, they may eventually rise in the pecking order. Apprenticeship, one method of acquiring power, has a long and distinguished history in the natural world. As might be expected, the old bosses try to maintain their leadership as long as they can. Often, they wind up ruling by the reputation of their past prowess. The aged baboon male dominates his troop despite the fact that his canines are worn down, or have perhaps fallen out. When their competitive ability declines, older dominant individuals predictably first concede access to those resources that are least important, relinquishing the crucial ones only when they have no alternative. Anthropologists Irven DeVore and Joseph Popp report that while Kovu, an aging male baboon, ranked last in access to food handouts, he still exercised his authority over mating with females in heat.

The psychiatrist Alfred Adler was particularly sensitive to issues of dominance in human behavior. He coined the term "inferiority complex" and stated that "whatever name we give it, we shall always find in human beings this great line of activity—the struggle to rise from an inferior position to a superior position, from defeat to victory, from below to above." Adler was not a sociobiologist, but he may well have seen the telltale signs of evolution operating on social competition. It might be nice were entrepreneurship and the struggle for social dominance not so basic to human behavior. And it is true that we are so social that the various forms of "altruism" we display have modified these to some degree. However, underneath any cooperativeness there is, unquestionably, a bedrock of uncompromising selfishness that sustains cooperation just as it does acceptance of a subordinate role . . . only insofar as it ultimately serves our fitness.

For a species living in complex social networks, such as early *Homo sapiens,* such evaluative decisions as when to "take a step up" in the social hierarchy must have been terribly important. Even now, we suffer a great deal of trepidation about even asking the boss for a raise. One ethologist has suggested that the importance of deciding on the most opportune time to overthrow the leader may have exerted strong selection for the rapid evolution of our large brain. To paraphrase Marx and Engels, the successful had nothing to lose but their subordinance—and they had a world of fitness to win!

●

To this point, we have spoken about why and when fighting can be expected to occur, but have said nothing about how it comes about. In most cases of conflict, both combatants would be better off if fighting didn't occur at all. Let's assume that there is a real difference in the fighting abilities of two individuals, both of whom want the same thing: a female, a piece of fruit or perhaps simply a comfortable place by the campfire. The less competent individual would be wiser to give way without a fight, since he would probably lose anyway and might become injured in the process. The more competent individual is also better off not fighting, since he would expend time and energy in the struggle and might still be injured even if he were victorious. Assuming that these creatures are able to recognize one another and to remember one another's status, they would both be most fit if they responded to each other according to their past recollections. The less competent should give way to the more competent. If there is a need to reinforce a flagging memory, or if the subordinate doesn't give way quickly enough, it might help if the more competent individual behaved in a manner that reminded the other of his status. Dominant wolves hold their tails straight up; subordinates keep theirs tucked inconspicuously between their legs. Dominant monkeys swagger and loom large; subordinates slink away and look small.

Status advertisement works well so long as all group members know everyone else in the group and each member knows his own "place." But what happens when there is a meeting of strangers, for whom dominance-subordinance relations have not yet been established? At such times, we observe characteristic displays, in which the contestants puff themselves up, erect their fur, bare their teeth, beak or claws, make loud noises and generally seek to impress the stranger with their fierceness. There may be a great deal of bluff and bluster, and, if neither is overly impressed with the other, they may proceed to a stylized "fight." The quotation marks are appropriate here because such fights are really more show than substance. As with medieval knights at a

joust, the opponents generally follow rather precise rules of etiquette.

Mock fighting occurs in many species. It is interesting that rattlesnakes are not immune to each other's venom and can be killed by
a bite. So they fight as if their fangs had been removed, struggling
to push their antagonist backward. Male deer use their sharp antlers
to clash dramatically in combat, but avoid the unprotected flank of
a rival. I have seen films of such a "fight" between roebucks. The two
males pranced side by side, their murderous antlers just a few feet
apart. Periodically, as if in response to a prearranged signal, they
would turn and clash weapons, then disengage and resume prancing.
Once, one of the males turned while its rival was still prancing,
thereby getting a clear shot at its opponent's side and belly. Rather
than pressing home a surprise attack, it simply resumed the stylized
prancing until the other was ready to fight in the accepted manner.
By the way, the females of this species, which lack antlers, also lack
this inhibition; they typically butt each other in the ribs, of course
with little effect.

South American fence lizards have a large bony patch covering
their necks. They "fight" each other by ritually presenting their
necks for their opponents to bite and then alternate biting and receiving bites in a most gentlemanly way. They apparently gauge an
opponent by the strength of his bite, and may also be sensitive to the
opponent's response to being bitten, that is, whether he flinches. In
at least one case that was observed a male lizard conceded defeat
after biting his opponent, without having been bitten in return.
Presumably, having given "his best shot," he knew he was defeated
when the other took it in stride.

Konrad Lorenz reports that a defeated wolf exposes its most vulnerable spot—the soft underpart of its neck—to the victorious animal, which is then somehow inhibited from killing its defeated rival.

When two rival fish meet, they may try to impress each other by
appearing as large as possible, often by swallowing water and literally
puffing themselves up. They may raise their gill covers and try to
present their "best" (that is, their largest) profile. If the issue of
superiority is still in doubt, they may line up side by side, waving
their bodies alternately in pushing a current of water against each
other; the larger and stronger the fish, the better he is likely to be
at making waves. If this ritual still doesn't clarify the relative power

of the opponents, they may open their mouths, but this is rarely to bite; more often they engage in a ritual tug-of-war in which the stronger can prove his prowess. As a last resort, they may fight, but in a match that is usually brief and decisive, with the loser fleeing, often little worse for the experience.

There are many other examples of this type of contest, and the result is usually the same. Animal fighting only rarely results in one individual killing another of the same species.

Early ethologists were entranced by the tournament-like nature of animal fighting, seeing it as an instance of evolution's acting "for the good of the species." If a species has the equipment to kill, their reasoning went, then it had better refrain from using this equipment on fellow species members, or the species would soon go extinct. Although this theory is superficially plausible, it presumes that a sort of group selection has expanded to cover an entire species, which simply does not make biological sense. Let's suppose that my rival, even if temporarily defeated, may eventually succeed in overthrowing me. Accordingly, my refraining from killing my rival when I have the chance may be a truly altruistic act, and, as such, selected against. I would be at a disadvantage compared with others who are less chivalrous and show no mercy, even though their pursuit of a short-sighted selfish benefit might cause the whole group to suffer and perhaps even the species to become extinct.

A more realistic explanation for restraint in fighting is that this too is selfish. If the winner can prove his superiority without pressing home his advantage, he is probably better off refraining, since he otherwise risks possible injury to himself. His opponent might also be a relative or an individual who benefits the victor's group so much that it is selfishly advantageous for the victor to be "magnanimous." In addition, a magnanimous winner might even profit directly in the future through reciprocity. It is probable that, if any genes that induce forbearance exist in animals, they do so because their ulti-mate effect is to support the existence of more copies *of themselves* than would hard-hearted, "thumbs down" genes that showed no mercy for a defeated foe.

Thus far, most of what we have said about the *how* of fighting among animals applies to human beings as well. Some of us are bossy, some of us remember our place, and there's often a great deal of bluster and bluff as we try to impress rivals with our toughness, determination and size. Not only do we bellow with rage and become red in the face, we also puff out our chests and try to appear as large as possible. Many cultures have the equivalents of Heidelberg dueling scars, intended to display courage and ferocity.

But although non-injurious, ritualized fighting may be culturally elaborated in our species, it simply isn't a biological part of us. At least we lack the automatic inhibitions so common among many other animals. This lack may be critical—and very dangerous. A white flag and upraised arms may be "universal" symbols of submission, but My Lai, Auschwitz, Wounded Knee and the St. Bartholomew's Day massacre all suggest that there are no guaranteed inhibitions, even against the killing of children. Why should there be this difference between us and "mere animals"? Are we less civilized than the roe deer or rattlesnakes?

Compared to the wolf, the roe deer or the rattlesnake, human beings lack a well-developed biological capacity for killing. It is quite difficult for a naked, untrained human being to kill another. Our "claws" are mere fingernails, efficient with tools but less than awesome as weapons; our teeth are too small and our jaw is much too receding. Yet, despite these deficiencies, we have become the world's most dangerous animals. Our ability to kill came largely with our cultural development of increasingly efficient and deadly weapons: clubs, spears, bows and arrows, rifles, cannons, bombs and missiles. All these arms are inventions, technologic extensions of our bodies that carry us beyond biology. Cultural evolution advances at a blinding pace compared to biology, so that any potentially non-belligerent, inhibitory instincts we possess have simply been unable to keep pace with our ever-increasing capacity for mutual destruction. The cautions of biological evolution have been heard faintly indeed, as mere whisperings in our headlong rush down the slippery path of cultural evolution.

Of course, animals aren't all that "innocent" either. Killing within a species is not at all as rare as the early students of animal behavior used to believe. It may be, in fact, relatively common, especially when the victims are unrelated to the killer and when their death is unlikely to carry much risk to the perpetrator. But the fact remains that many animals do have strong inhibitions against killing, even though the evolutionary reason for this is probably self-interest rather than true altruism. It is no great surprise that human beings do not seem to be included among these species, since we seem to have less instinctive machinery than other animals in general. But, even if we had some automatic, built-in aggression inhibitor, our ingenuity in inventing means of killing has enabled us to do so at such distance that inhibition would be irrelevant. A defeated foe exhibiting subordination behavior couldn't be seen by a bombardier flying thirty thousand feet overhead, much less by a politician with his finger on The Button.

•

Imagine yourself in this situation: you have volunteered for a psychology experiment in visual perception. You enter a room along with four other people and are shown a straight line. Alongside it are three other lines, one of which is identical in length to the first, the other two of which are different. You are asked to tell which of the three is closest in length to the original. The choice is actually quite simple, and, in fact, embarrassingly obvious. However, you choose last, and incredibly, you hear each of the first four participants give the same (obviously wrong) answer. What do you do? In one such experiment, 35 percent of the subjects agreed with the incorrect judgment of their predecessors. This test was, of course, not really an experiment in perception but Solomon Asch's now-classic study in social psychology. The four other participants were paid stooges of the experimenter, who had told them in advance what to say. Asch's study demonstrates the incredible pressures for conformity. It's hard to stick up for the truth when everyone else is saying otherwise. Significantly, when the same experiment was run with one subject at a time, the correct answer was almost always given.

Although there is something unpleasant about this sort of wishy-washiness, the need to conform is a very real human trait. We are intensely social beasts who are at the same time intensely competitive and selfishly out for our own evolutionary betterment. As a result, we find ourselves in a curious double-bind vis-à-vis our colleagues and our society. While we need society in order to function successfully, society itself cannot work effectively unless its members restrain their self-seeking impulses. Society therefore requires that we set aside at least some portion of our individuality, if the larger human unit is to function at all. The result is conformity, by which we all in a sense perjure ourselves simply because "no man is an island."

An even more chilling demonstration of the power of conformity was conducted by Yale sociologist Stanley Milgram. In an ingenious study, which has been much written about, he told subjects that they were to participate in an experiment in which other subjects were given a learning task. The first subject's job was to administer an electric shock to the learners each time they made an incorrect response. As the learners made more errors, the first subject was expected to increase the voltage of the shock that he administered. The dial began at 15 volts and went up to 450 volts. At 75 volts, the learner was heard to moan, at 150 volts he typically asked that the experiment stop, at 180 volts he would cry out that the pain was too much, and at voltages beyond that he would simply pound on the wall, or, worst of all, would lapse into complete, ominous silence. A scientist in a white laboratory coat stood by the shock giver, instructing him to keep increasing the voltage despite cries from the other subject, who was supposedly strapped into a chair in the next room.

Once again, as you may have expected, the experiment was a sham. It was not a test of the effects of punishment on learning, but rather, a test of people's willingness to obey authority. No one was connected to the electrodes in the other room; a stooge was simply instructed to make the appropriate sounds. But the real subjects didn't know this. What they did know was that they were being told to administer the shocks, and what is truly incredible is that more than 62 percent of the subjects continued to increase the voltage to its upper limit. For every person who did what most of us would doubtless call "the right thing" (that is, refusing to obey the instructions), there were two who did what they were told. It seems that for many of us what we are told is what is right. Milgram's research suggests that there may be some trace of Adolph Eichmann in many of us.

Our tendency to conform apparently includes an inclination to follow orders, an appropriate behavior for a species organized along distinct lines of dominance. This tendency may have been further accentuated by the lengthy portion of our history as hunters, during which coordinated activity was particularly important. Anthropologist W. S. Laughlin has called hunting "the master behavior pattern of the human species," and considers it a way of life, not merely a means of obtaining food. Efficient hunting often requires group coordination, obedience to authority and a high degree of conformity, especially if the prey is large and dangerous.

During this phase of our evolution, those who fitted in and were good "team players" almost certainly left more descendants than those who stubbornly insisted on individual action. In other words, although selection may have conferred benefits on those enterprising enough to somehow distinguish themselves, it also favored conformity and obedience.

While it may be unpleasant to those seeking to draw moral guidelines from our evolutionary history, it seems likely that warfare was also a substantial force in the natural selection of human beings. Armed conflict between bands or tribes may well have exerted a profound influence on our evolution, selecting in part for large brains, efficient use of weapons, ability to communicate complex strategies (and deceit), as well as conformity and obedience to authority.

Waging war is (and probably was) almost an exclusively male pursuit in all human societies. This is not to say that men are therefore smarter than women, but simply that their greater size, strength and aggressiveness—all perhaps the evolutionary result of engaging in warfare—have given the average man a competitive edge over the average woman. Anthropologist Marvin Harris has even suggested that male preeminence in warfare is somehow responsible for the universal social inequality between men and women. As with warfare, hunting is also a sexually differentiated activity—or at least it is a task that men do "normally" and that women undertake only in special circumstances and with much less social sanction. Such exclusion of women from hunting may be traceable to their biological functions of childbearing and nursing, which necessarily tied them more closely to home base, as well as to their anatomical differences, which reduced their effectiveness as hunters of big game.

It is true that among present-day non-Western societies, women do occasionally hunt. Copper Eskimo women sometimes go after seal and even caribou, and among the Ainu of northern Japan, women and children occasionally hunted deer with sticks, ropes and dogs. But these cases are exceptional. Women hunt very rarely and, when they do, their prey is usually small game. Almost never are they permitted to use specially made hunting weapons such as spears, harpoons or bows and arrows. What is pertinent for our discussion is that female exclusion from hunting may well have provided much of the impetus for the elaboration of male-male groups, which proved so important for warfare, politics and other forms of social action as well as competition.*

If we assume that modern non-Western peoples give us some insight into prehistory, we get a rather male chauvinist view of that time in human evolution: hairy-chested hunters and warriors all bloody and brave, bringing home the bacon and an occasional scalp, while the women dug roots, gathered berries and made children. This picture has recently been balanced somewhat by studies showing that, in many cases, gathering is responsible for substantially more calories than is hunting. And since gathering is done primarily by women, feminists point to the importance of women's contribution to prehistoric nutrition and argue that primitive peoples be called "gatherer-hunters." Male chauvinists, of course, emphasize the great value attached to animal protein, and argue for the traditional designation "hunter-gatherers." Regardless of which sex contributed more to survival, an obvious division of labor was in operation, with women gathering and men hunting and fighting.

Let us assume that, as with hunting, primitive war was something of a "master adaptation" for the human species. If so, we can expect that, for better or worse, it was primarily a male activity. In any event, men have come to monopolize the armed forces and public life in virtually all contemporary human societies. This monopoly generally involves a corresponding primary economic and political control, which is often expressed and consolidated via the formation of all-male groups. Anthropological literature is filled with accounts of male secret societies, rituals and meeting places which are "taboo" to women. Of women's secret societies, next to none are reported.

*In one bizarre case of male-male politics, the importance of making allies transcends even the necessity of guaranteeing one's children. The Birom people of northern Nigeria practice "ciscisbeism," a custom in which a wife is permitted to have one or more lovers in addition to her legal husband. Significantly, the lover must pay the husband for this cozy arrangement, and is also expected to help provide for his mistress's children—which may of course be either his own biological offspring or those of the legal husband. Lover and husband become staunch allies through this arrangement: at the turn of the century, outraged missionaries reported that one powerful Birom headman had nine wives and twelve mistresses, and that each of the latter had her own husband as well. As a result, this headman not only had many offspring, but also many allies. Despite the apparent sexual freedom enjoyed by the Birom matron, it is unheard-of for a woman to have more than two or three lovers; men, however, seek to have as many married mistresses as possible, preferring them to unmarried women and accumulating prestige, power and fitness along the way.

The result of this segregation of occupations is that women are systematically excluded from government and other positions of power. On the other hand, it may be more than anecdotal truth that women compensate for their powerlessness by holding "power behind the throne" and also by exercising greater authority in domestic matters. It is a long-standing joke in some families that the father makes all the "important" decisions, such as civil rights policy, the optimum distribution of the federal budget and trade relations with China, while the mother settles the "lesser" issues, such as when to buy a new car, whether to take a vacation (and, if so, where), and when it's time to retire.

Such popular folklore aside, the exclusion of women from major policy roles is an international, species-wide phenomenon. Although women generally make up more than half of the population in every country, they rarely exceed 5 percent of the national parliaments (some examples: France, 4 percent; Norway, 4 percent; Britain, 3 percent; and the United States, 2 percent). Even in the Soviet Union, where as much as 17 percent of the Duma has been female, real power lies in the Supreme Soviet, which has occasionally had one woman member, but most often has none. Of equal interest, successful female politicians have almost invariably been desexed and are generally post-menopausal and rather plain: Indira Gandhi, Golda Meir, Senator Margaret Chase Smith, and Governors Ella Grasso and Dixy Lee Ray. This is not to suggest that a woman should be judged as an effective political force based on her youth and good looks; rather, an unfortunate by-product of our biology seems to be a refusal to accept female politicians unless their femininity is distinctly underplayed.

There is a revealing exception to this generalization: when Ghana's Kwame Nkrumah was criticized for not doing enough for women, he appointed ten female members of Parliament. Many were physically very attractive and there were immediately allegations that a number had used sexual favors to obtain their positions. The point is not whether the accusations were true, but rather that they occurred. It seems that the very appearance of full sexual females in positions of political power disrupts the male-male, hunting-warring-politicking system. We can accept—even adore—a Jacqueline Kennedy as the desirable wife of one of our leaders, but it may be quite a long time before people of either gender can overcome their biology and accept an overtly sexual woman as a leader in her own right.

•

Although men need other men as colleagues in the hunt, in making war, in defending the group and in exercising leadership, they also compete among themselves. Such competition is not limited to peers. There is always a new generation coming along—newcomers who are both needed and feared.

People around the world have devised many different means of dealing with their ambivalence toward the next generation. One of the most common of such coping devices is the rite of passage known as initiation. Graduations, confirmations, and bar mitzvahs are familiar to most of us, and these represent only a small sampling. Sociologists and anthropologists have correctly seen such activities as a necessary stage in passing the reins of power and responsibility from one generation to the next. But a sociobiological perspective suggests that our species-wide passion for initiations may also have selfish, competitive undertones.

Predictably, maturation rites differ according to sex, consistent with an evolutionary view of male and female. In most cultures, as a general rule, girls become women simply by growing up. Initiation ceremonies for women generally *celebrate* the menarche, but this first menstruation (which is usually equated with the onset of womanhood) does not require any direct action on the adolescent's part. Margaret Mead points out:

> The little girl learns that she will have a baby not because she is strong or energetic or initiating, not because she works and struggles and tries, and in the end succeeds, but simply because she *is* a girl and not a boy, and girls turn into women, and in the end—if they protect their femininity—have babies. Her society may enjoin certain precautions on older girls—they may have to observe food taboos, or rub themselves with stinging nettles to ensure that their breasts will grow; but throughout the emphasis is on protecting a natural unfolding, at the most a slight enhancement of breast size, not on effort and struggle. Her sex membership may not be so conspicuous now as her brother's, but she has only to wait, to be, and—some day—she will have a baby.

Of course, boys don't have to *do* anything special to become physically mature either. Their voices deepen and their body hair grows as part of normal maturation. But males, as the biologically more competitive sex, must also demonstrate a *social* maturation, often in hazing ceremonies and strenuous initiation rites, to which women are rarely subjected. These differing conceptions of maturity usually begin very early in life. Again Mead observes:

> The little boy learns that he must act like a boy, do things, prove that he is a boy, and prove it over and over again, while the little girl learns that she *is* a girl, and all she has to do is refrain from acting like a boy.

Young aspiring males must prove themselves on two levels: first, they must compete successfully with other boys for social and eventually reproductive success. Second, they must also compete with males of the previous generation, to whom they often constitute a real threat. Young women are much less of a threat to the fitness of other women, so that competition between them is generally lower and their rites of passage are less intense and less threatening.

While it is typical of the human species that young males must prove their worthiness to be considered men, often through arduous, painful and dangerous tasks, demands are sometimes made on young women as well. For example, African Potok maidens undergo a public cliterodectomy, through which each girl shows her courage. But it is noteworthy that, even in this unusual case, the young women insist that potential lovers prove their devotion through large gifts. The young men are eventually forced to turn to their relatives for help and to raid other villages. In other words, the men still have to prove themselves.

The very few examples of strenuous female initiation do not hold a candle to the common human insistence that boys undergo real trauma, which often includes various forms of circumcision and other types of ritual mutilation, or prolonged and difficult apprenticeships during which they may be expected to prove themselves as hunters, or, perhaps, acquire a vision. A youth among the East African Masai had to kill a lion; an aspiring Crow Indian brave was expected to kill a buffalo and to bring home a scalp; a young New Guinea highlander needed to bring back a human head. Among the Plains Indians, the alternatives were quite clear: become a warrior or, failing this, a "berdache," a "man-woman," who assumed the dress and behavior of a woman, even to the point of marrying as one. In *Tristes Tropiques* anthropologist Claude Lévi-Strauss writes:

Among a great many North American tribes, the social prestige of the individual is determined by the circumstances surrounding the ordeals connected with puberty. Some young men set themselves adrift on solitary rafts without food; others seek solitude in the mountains where they have to face wild beasts, as well as cold and rain. For days, weeks or months on end, as the case may be, they do not eat properly, but live only on coarse food, or fast for long periods and aggravate their impaired physical condition by the use of emetics. Everything is turned into a means of communication with the beyond. They stay immersed for long periods in icy water, deliberately mutilate one or more of their finger-joints, or lacerate their fasciae by dragging heavy loads attached by ropes to sharpened pegs inserted under their dorsal muscles. When they do not resort to such extremes, they at least exhaust themselves by performing various pointless tasks, such as removing all their body hairs, one at a time, or stripping pine branches until not a single needle remains, or hollowing out blocks of stone.

The pattern is undeniable: boys have a more difficult time becoming men than girls do becoming women.

The older adult males controlling each society recognize both their need for the coming generation and their competition with it. They have the resources (such as women) that the younger men want, and since polygyny requires that a number of young men must remain bachelors, competition would surely be expected. The older men have everything on their side except time, and they buy themselves a bit more of that by requiring the younger men to perform in prescribed ways before they can be accepted as men, that is, before they can be considered social rivals. Of course, it does no harm if in the process the young men do something that benefits their elders—such as hunting or serving in the army.

There seems to be a long evolutionary history behind this pattern of rivalry and tension between maturing males and the established adult hierarchy. Among many animal species, youngsters disperse—leave home—when they become sexually mature. Often, maturing males are chased out by the dominant adult males. Primate expert K. R. L. Hall described a case of a family group of patas monkeys accidentally kept together in the same cage: the adult male became dramatically more aggressive toward the juvenile male as soon as the youngster's testes descended and he became a reproductive competitor. The juvenile eventually had to be removed from the cage to save his life.

Maturation is clearly much more complicated in our species, but it may be no coincidence that in Europe young boys were typically apprenticed just before trouble might otherwise have begun brewing at home. Does going away to college, trade school, or the army actually help forestall disruptions and fights within the reproductive unit? Psychoanalysts have long been interested in the Oedipal conflict, believed to result from the competition between father and son for the mother's sexual favors. Sociobiology's view enlarges the focus of that conflict, interpreting the father-son antagonism as a special case of male-male conflict across the generation gap. And, indeed, it does appear that discord and dispersal both peak in *Homo sapiens* about the time that reproductive conflict might be expected to develop.

It makes good biological sense that juvenile delinquency is more common among boys than among girls, and that men are more prone than women to commit violent crime. In the United States, 85 percent of all murderers are men, and 93 percent of all drunk drivers. Automobile insurance is also revealing, with the highest rates being charged to unmarried male drivers under twenty-five years of age. The rates reflect the general recognition that flamboyant, accident-prone behavior is most frequent among males in the up-and-coming generation. They reflect, too, the predictions of evolutionary biology.

The cultural means by which maturing males are traditionally obliged to validate their manhood may vary, but the biological end never does. We can be fairly confident that, in the past, the initiates themselves were willing, and in most cases eager, participants in this process, through the enlightened self-interest that is evolution's bequest to "human nature." But things have changed rapidly. A New Guinea highlander is unpopular with his new Western-style government if he goes headhunting. In the United States, such opportunities for validation of manhood are more diffuse and often greatly delayed. Immediate gratifications are available, of course, but they often require dropping out of school and frequently lead to delinquency and such other socially disruptive behavior as causing unwanted pregnancies. We can legitimately ask whether our society provides satisfying and constructive opportunities for our youth to heed the whisperings within them. The consequences of not doing so are clearly painful.

•

When William Durham was a graduate student at the University of Michigan a few years ago, he expressed interest in the heretical notion that natural selection might have a profound impact on human behavior, and that much of our behavior might therefore be directed to maximizing the propagation of our genes. It was suggested that he straighten himself out by reading about primitive war, since, of all behaviors, making war seemed the most maladaptive. Learn about war, his advisors told him, and you'll see human behavior at its fitness-reducing worst. He came away from his work, instead, with a new appreciation of the adaptive value of human behavior. Unfortunately, the article resulting from his study, "Resource Competition and Human Aggression: A Review of Primitive War," was published in a biology journal, so Durham found himself speaking to those most likely to agree with him, rather than to the social scientists for whom his findings might have come as more of a revelation.

Durham's work is strikingly important for our efforts to view human behavior through the lens of sociobiology. Of all human activities, warfare strikes us as perhaps the most senseless, wantonly destructive and genuinely evil. Therefore, any suggestion that human behavior is ultimately influenced by considerations of fitness maximization must come to terms with the widespread occurrence, the ferocity and the persistence of war. How could there possibly be an adaptive significance to any behavior that is so obviously destructive? Durham's conclusion was that, at least for relatively small, technologically simple societies, aggressiveness between groups may actually be adaptive for the individuals concerned. To understand this view it will be helpful to turn once again to resource competition, the key to so much adaptive aggression among animals.

Durham points out that, even within human groups, a close inverse relationship exists between resources and aggression. When resources are abundant and widely distributed, competition is rare; as resources become scarce, however, competition increases. The "Mack the Knife principle" again.

Competition may, of course, be quite intense for some resources but very weak for others. The Bushmen of Africa's Kalahari Desert are often cited as a peaceful, non-warlike society, and it is true that the Bushmen do not fight over hunting territories. In the Kalahari, the appearance of wild game is unpredictable and shifting in location, so no territory is considered to be owned by an individual or tribe. Consequently territories are not fought over. Individuals seem free to wander or hunt where they please, in an idyllic, if rather dry, Garden of Eden, in which jealous concern over mine versus yours appears, at first sight, to be nonexistent. But, it happens, there are other resources which are defendable and in short supply. These are the objects of much aggressive dispute. Anthropologists who studied the "peaceful" Bushmen report the following:

> The fertile areas in which the principal wild tubers grow, the groves of mangetti nut trees, clumps of berries, fruit trees, and the rare and coveted patches of Tsi—all are known. These important sources of food are owned by the bands with strict definition and jealous concern. There is nothing vague or casual about it.

The Eskimo, another frequently mentioned example of a society that does not wage war, also fit within evolutionary predictions. The opportunities for Eskimos to find food vary dramatically from one period to the next and, given the harshness of their environment, they are forced to migrate when resources become scarce, most notably during the Arctic winter. Not surprisingly, these people do not make war. Instead they make haste—to go where food is available. People living on the razor edge of starvation gain little from warring with each other. Or rather, they would gain much less than they stand to lose, and so maximize their fitness by devoting their energies to survival and its necessities.

A distinction is normally made between aggression within a society and hostilities between societies or groups, and usually only the latter is considered warfare. Although the outcomes of these two sorts of conflict may be different, it may well be that their underlying cause is often the same: resource competition, which, despite the terrible toll in bloodshed and human misery, makes aggression and war beneficial to individual fitness. And it is important to bear in mind that, by its nature, sociobiology has less to say about the behavior of large groups than about the individuals that compose them. It provides more insight into the personal life of a nation's president (whether he has a mistress, how he treats his children, what makes him angry and so on) than it will elucidate the nation's foreign policy. In the same vein, we can expect that evolutionary biology will tell us less about war as waged by societies than about fighting as carried out by individuals. Nonetheless, war has real and direct consequences for the fitness of the individuals involved. Especially in preliterate societies, it is something of a personalized, individual act, at least to a greater extent than in the mass warfare of nation-states.

Durham studied most carefully the Mundurucu of Brazil, a notoriously violent people, for whom "war was considered an essential and unquestioned part of their way of life, and foreign tribes were attacked because they were enemies by definition." Here was a people whose penchant for war seemed to make no adaptive sense whatever. According to one of the first scientists to study this fierce tribe:

> Unless direct, specific questions were asked, the Mundurucu never assigned specific causes to particular wars. The necessity of ever having to defend their home territory was denied and provocation by other groups was not remembered as a cause of war in Mundurucu tradition. It might be said that enemy tribes caused the Mundurucu to go to war simply by existing, and the word for enemy meant merely any group that was not Mundurucu.

The maddening absurdity of Mundurucu warfare had made these people one of the classic cases of utterly maladaptive behavior. How could unprovoked slaughter possibly be reconciled with evolution and maximization of individual fitness?

Durham's closer investigation reveals that war, even among the Mundurucu, may be substantially less capricious than it seems at first glance. In theory, one group may provoke another to war in many ways, the most obvious being outright attack. A less apparent, but no less real reason is that "simply by existing," one group can seriously threaten the resources of another. If groups compete for the same resources, then just as in direct competition between individuals each group can threaten the fitness of the other. An equation linking such statements about groups and those about individual fitness is not difficult. The fitness of individuals within a group suffers most when that group is forced to share resources with individuals of another group. The personal fitness of these individuals could therefore actually be increased by warfare, provided that the cost of waging war is less than the benefits received. We should also bear in mind two additional factors: first, that primitive war is often much less devastating than our "civilized" counterpart. Second, there always seem to be a number of young men who have not yet achieved success within the social system. Such youths are probably most in need of proving themselves, so as to be successful in the competitive male-male social system, and they are therefore most likely to participate in a war. We are already deriving a potent equation.

What is needed is evidence that these people suffered a shortage of some important resource, and that warfare helped solve this shortage. It happens that the Mundurucu were hunters who competed with any neighboring people for the limited supplies of game. The Mundurucu were, in fact, very watchful over their supply of wild game, and severe punishments were visited upon anyone who killed animals "wastefully." It was permissible to kill an unlimited number of jaguars, just as it was permissible to kill an unlimited number of humans—so long as they belonged to another tribe. Jaguars, of course, are predators upon deer and wild pigs, which are also eaten by the Mundurucu. Neighboring tribes, like jaguars, competed with the Mundurucu for wild game. Just as kin selection does not promote altruism between human beings and jaguars, it is similarly much less effective in preventing aggression between groups than in restraining such behavior within a group. We can expect to share more genes with a fellow tribe member than with a member of another tribe, and any existing inhibitions against aggression are further diminished by the fact that different tribes have different customs, speak different languages and so on.

When duck or deer hunting is bad, American sportsmen complain to the Fish and Wildlife Service. In similar situations, the Bushmen move their homes. And the Mundurucu? They wage war. Although they may not consciously realize that by doing so they ultimately increase the amount of game available to them, some of their ritual does in fact suggest a deep-seated awareness of a practical basis for their aggression. Thus, the Mundurucu set great store by the trophy heads of enemies killed in war.

> . . . the most important status was that of a taker of trophy head, who was referred to as Dajeboisi. Literally, the title means "mother of the pec-

cary," an allusion to the Mundurucu view of other tribes as being equivalent to game animals. The "mother" part of the term is derived from the trophy head's power to *attract game and to cause their numerical increase,* and the head hunter was so titled because of his obvious fertility promoting function. [My italics.]

Durham makes a similar argument for the Tsembaga Maring, a New Guinea people who wage war in ten- to twelve-year cycles that occur when their population of domestic pigs becomes so large as to threaten the ecologic resource base on which they depend. The argument should be clear by now: few people admit to liking war, but, throughout history, tens and hundreds of millions of *Homo sapiens* may have been doing little more than heeding the whispering of fitness maximization as they marched off to battle with such horrible and devastating regularity.

●

Sociobiology's discovery that war may have an adaptive side is surely no apology for war, either by the Mundurucu or by modern, technological *Homo sapiens.* The simple fact that some behavior has (or has had) adaptive utility does not imply that is "good." In any event, warfare among non-industrialized peoples is often much closer to skirmishing and is quite different from the war of annihilation currently available to the superpowers. If Mundurucu warfare is adaptive for the individual participants, it must be that the risks of personal injury or death have been low enough to be outweighed by the potential benefits of victory. The consequences of modern war are rather different. There could be no winners of a World War Three, and there is no manner in which the benefits could possibly exceed the costs.

But it may well be that our genetically influenced perception of aggression and war was fashioned during the long millennia when we behaved more like the Mundurucu and less like superpowers endowed with missiles and Joint Chiefs of Staff. Can we recognize that, because of modern technology, the rules of the game have been changed? Can we use our understanding and our reason to overrule our dangerously outmoded whisperings from within? We had better do so.

7

Part I: Toward an Evolutionary Biology of Mind

Sociobiology clearly has a great deal to say about our behavior, but what we *do* ultimately amounts to less than what we *are*. We have not yet considered "mind," that silent and mysterious entity that somehow intervenes between our brain and our actions. Although the mind does not always project itself directly into the world by means of behavior (we are capable of thinking without acting), even our unconscious thoughts may influence what we do. Since evolution is so tightly entwined with our behavior, it should have a great influence on our minds as well. The mind-body problem is an ancient one: a tremendous gap seems to exist between our unique, personal thoughts and emotions on the one hand and the cells, chemicals and electrical circuits that make up our brains on the other. Yet the human mind—its conscious as well as its unconscious aspects, its thoughts as well as its emotions—springs somehow from the concrete, impersonal human brain. And that brain is the product of evolution.

The novelist Samuel Butler, no great fan of the theory of evolution, took Darwin to task for having "banished mind from the universe." Actually, Darwin did nothing of the kind. What he did was show how all living things came to be as they are, not only their anatomies and their physiologies but also the functioning of their minds. Evolution does not banish the mind. Quite the opposite, it makes possible the inclusion of mind in the natural world. It may even help make the study of mind as scientific as the study of bones.

Our bodies, as we have seen throughout this book, are the vehicles created by our genes in the service of themselves. And our minds are among the devices that serve to control those bodies. Both the cellular structure of the brain and the psychic structure of consciousness are the results of millions of generations of evolution, during which genes that were more successful at reproducing themselves prospered at the expense of those that were less adept. Our genes have programmed us and every other living thing to do what is best for them. Our minds are likely to serve that ultimate end no less than are our hands or our kidneys.

Does this claim for a genetic influence on the mind mean that there is no difference between our programming and that of any other animal? Of course not. Although genes program their carriers to behave in ways that maximize their fitness, the techniques used to achieve this goal are different for different carriers. Earthworm genes, for example, appear to be most successful in reproducing themselves if they limit their carriers to a relatively fixed repertoire of behavior; human genes seem to do best if they give their carriers a great deal of freedom of action.

If you're riding a horse down a steep and muddy hill, you're going to have trouble if you insist on controlling every step it takes. There isn't sufficient time to tell your mount when and where to move each leg, and it knows its abilities better than you do in any case. Your best strategy is to give your horse "its head"—allow it to choose its own footing. A similar strategy is followed by human genes, which have "discovered" over time that they are more successful when they give us our heads than if they insist on keeping rigid control. Our genes have given us more freedom than those of any other living thing, yet, just as the horse is still finally controlled by a rider, it is unlikely that we are completely free. Unbridled freedom would probably be a bad strategy: genes have undergone rigorous selection for millions of years, and those that have survived have done so because they had something of value to impart. We are free, it is true, but free only to maximize our fitness and that of our silent genetic riders.

We are now able to program computers to play chess. Generally, this process involves describing the rules of the game and building certain basic strategies into the machine—for example: don't leave your king unprotected; when possible threaten two of your opponent's pieces at the same time; value a queen more than a castle, a castle more than a bishop, and so on. But once the game begins, the machine is on its own. The programmer does not act as a puppeteer, directly controlling each move. We can even design programs that allow a mechanical player to become better with experience, to profit from its own mistakes. Some of these chess-playing machines are remarkably good and can regularly defeat the programmers who constructed them. They behave as if they were independent of their designers, and, in a curious way, they are. But, although their behavior cannot be predicted with complete assurance at any given time, they are in the end nothing but the instructions that created them, and they can do no more than follow the ultimate designs of their builder.

Our builders are our genes. Their strategies derive ultimately from evolution; they have programmed us—with a great deal of flexibility, to be sure—to win the game, to maximize our fitness (and theirs as well). In doing so, we often are sidetracked by some of the lesser sub-programs: in chess, maneuvering to capture a knight; in life, perhaps angling for a promotion or attempting to date someone attractive. We may become so involved in these relatively minor activities that we lose sight of the bigger picture and forget what the game is all about. But satisfaction of subordinate needs is probably adaptive, for just as we do not play chess with our eyes only on the kings (although they are the ultimate goal of the game), we do not live with our eyes only on fitness maximization. In fact, we are often so distracted that our minds may seem anything but devices for achieving it. The evolutionary goal is complicated and not easily defined. Our not knowing the goal, however, has not prevented us from playing the game.

The brilliant and tragic American poet Theodore Roethke may have perceived something of all this when he wrote:

Many arrivals make us live: the tree becoming
Green, a bird tipping the topmost bough,
A seed pushing itself beyond itself . . .
What does what it should do needs nothing more.
The body moves, though slowly, toward desire.
We come to something without knowing why.

The human mind is remarkably flexible—so flexible, in fact, that it delights in bending all the way around and trying to understand itself. Psychologists have been trying to acquire this knowledge for quite some time, and philosophers even before them, but both have met with mixed results. It is now more than two thousand years since Socrates urged, "Know thyself," but the long-standing irony of his advice still persists, and our own mind remains largely a stranger to itself.

It might be useful to compare two major schools of thought concerned with thought. One influential viewpoint was developed in large part by David Hume and a group of French philosophers known collectively as the Encyclopedists. According to their view, there is no innate human nature, and all human knowledge derives instead from the experiences of each individual as he or she lives and grows. At the turn of the seventeenth century, John Locke described the human mind as a piece of "white paper, void of all character, without any ideas; How comes it to be furnished? To this I answer in one word, from *Experience.*" This philosophy of experience had an enormous influence on the early growth of natural science, an influence which continues even now. With their motto "Show me," Hume, Locke and their colleagues could call themselves the first people from Missouri. And in fact they go further yet: "I am only what I am shown; neither more nor less." Although this emphasis on empirical knowledge has been useful in helping us split the atom and conquer space, it has not been especially valuable as a guide to understanding human behavior, largely because it focuses on description while exhibiting little power to explain.*

The second notable philosophy of mind emphasizes its innate qualities. Its most distinguished exponent was Immanuel Kant. Kant's approach differs from that of the philosophers of experience in that it accepts a human nature. According to Kant, and his more recent intellectual descendants such as Sigmund Freud, anthropologist Claude Lévi-Strauss and linguist Noam Chomsky, the human mind does use experience to construct its image of reality, but it does so by using its innate "deep structure" to organize and make sense of that experience.

Kant demonstrated convincingly that the philosophy of experience assumes the existence of certain innate human traits. For example, in order for experience to be interpreted and woven into a mental fabric, there must be pre-existing, *a priori* concepts which

---

*Perhaps the most notable modern descendant of Hume is Harvard psychologist B. F. Skinner, who abhors the word "mind" and insists that all we can discuss about humans is their behavior. He maintains that just about everything we do is a result of whether (and how) we were rewarded for similar actions in the past. His techniques of behavior modification are powerful tools for manipulating behavior, but singularly devoid of any understanding of that behavior.

the mind brings to its encounters with the outside world. These deep structural concepts include the notions of space, time and cause-and-effect. Considering the intellectual poverty of a philosophy based on experience, we might expect that the Kantian approach would have been enormously influential, at least in the sciences dealing with human behavior. But it never acquired this influence, largely because Kant had no way of explaining why the human mind's *a priori* concepts—its human nature—were so well suited to the nature of reality. The philosophical world was finally treated to the spectacle of Immanuel Kant, the ultimate rationalist, conceding that it must all be a "happy coincidence." The only alternative was God.

Perhaps it sounds immodest, but we may now have the answer that eluded Kant: evolution may be the key to explaining why the human mind is so remarkably disposed to deal precisely with the kind of experience that it is likely to receive. Through the sifting and winnowing of natural selection, genes and gene combinations that equipped individuals to deal successfully with the contingencies of life were able to leave more copies of themselves than did others that were less attuned to reality as it has existed for medium-sized organisms living on earth. Of course we have *a priori* mental structures, and of course they accurately reflect the nature of the world: it is adaptive that they do so.

Not only does evolution suggest a convincing reconciliation of Kantian innate philosophy with our craving for scientific explanations, it even reconciles this view with its arch-enemy, the philosophy of experience. If evolution by natural selection is the source of our mind's *a priori* structures, then in a sense these structures also derive from experience—not the immediate, short-term experience of any single developing organism, but rather the long-term experience of an evolving population. It is only through the interaction of living things with their environments that certain individuals came to be more successful than others. Evolution, then, is the result of innumerable experiences, accumulated through an almost unimaginable length of time. The *a priori* human mind, seemingly preprogrammed and at least somewhat independent of personal experience, *is* actually nothing more than the embodiment of experience itself.

The world of our ancestors was clearly different from the one we face today. But still it was a world of time and space, a world in which no two objects could occupy the same spot at the same time and in which events followed one another in a linear sequence. It was, like ours, a world of rocks and trees, of wind and rain, of friends and enemies, children and parents, joy and pain. It was a world in which effect followed cause—strike an animal with a club and it falls down dead. This was and is the world of experiences to which the underlying deep structures of our mind are attuned. By and large, we are very well tuned indeed, yet, as science advances beyond the realm of immediate personal experience—especially in astronomy, theoretical physics and the study of sub-atomic particles—we become disoriented. The human mind has great difficulty grasping distances as immense as light-years or so small that they are literally immeasurable. Because we evolved in a world of medium-sized objects traveling at moderate speeds, we can easily comprehend the apple-falling physics of Isaac Newton. It is intuitively appealing and satisfying. But as we had no prior acquaintance with speeds approaching that of light, there is something more than a little unnerving about Einstein's formulation that matter and energy are interchangeable, or the "fact" that when an object travels at nearly the speed of light it becomes physically shorter and time slows down.

Modern physical science is presenting biologically evolved man with some real paradoxes, which are mind-bending to say the least. An entity can be simultaneously both a wave and a particle, and events can be traced backward in time as well as forward. Antimatter annihilates matter, and electrons exist as clouds of probability rather than as discrete objects. We are simply finding ourselves out of our depth, as bewildered and out of place as a deep-sea fish suddenly dumped on the Mojave Desert.

Biologist-mathematician-philosopher J. B. S. Haldane expressed our bewilderment well when he wrote: "The world is not only queerer than we imagine, it is queerer than we *can* imagine." In the formation of the basic, *a priori* nature of our mind, evolution not only provided us with a starting point, it may also have set limits on how far we can go—literally, how much we can imagine.

Having ranged from Kant to Darwin, from our Paleolithic origins to a world of relativistic physics, let us conclude with a glimpse at the eyeball of a frog. It may have a great deal to tell us about ourselves. In a wonderful paper titled "What the Frog's Eye Tells the Frog's Brain," several MIT scientists discussed an experiment in which they allowed frogs to look at different types of objects under different patterns of illumination, using electrodes to record the firing of the optic nerves that sent messages from the frog's eye to its brain. They were literally spying on what occurred in the passage from reality to the animal's mind. As it turns out, the frog's brain receives a very distorted picture of its environment—at least, distorted from our viewpoint. There are only five different cell types in the middle layer of the frog's retina, and each responds only to a limited stimulus: one is sensitive to changes in illumination, another to an abrupt shift from light to dark, another to moving edges (possible frog predators such as herons or snakes?), another to small moving dots (bug detectors?) and so on. The frog's-eye view of the world is simply the total of these rather narrow perceptions, and nothing else.

Of course, a frog is not a towering intellect and, because its sensory requirements are limited, it receives from its sense organs only the information that its limited brain can handle. The frog has no use for a complete picture of the real world, even though such a picture might be a more accurate one than what it actually receives. Humans, on the other hand, see the world very differently. We are not frogs, limited to narrowly focused bug detectors. In fact, we have constructed sophisticated sensory devices such as radar and infra-red sensors to extend our sensitivity far beyond the range of our biological equipment. Presumably, what our biology and our machines tell us is true—or is it? No less than the frog, we are the product of evolution by natural selection, outfitted with a human nature and certain qualities of mind. Frogs probably don't spend much time pondering the nature of their minds, but humans who think about theirs may come to the conclusion that, in some ways, they are not really as different from the frogs as they might hope.

●

If we look hard enough at the varieties of human behavior, can we reduce what Henry James called life's "blooming, buzzing confusion" to the simplicity of biological species obeying natural laws? "Reductionism" of this sort is a dirty word to most social scientists, the majority of whom still believe with Emile Durkheim, one of the founders of sociology:

There is between psychology and sociology the same break in continuity as between biology and the physico-chemical sciences. Consequently, every time that a social phenomenon is directly explained by a psychological phenomenon, we may be sure that the explanation is false.

Social facts, according to Durkheim, are to be understood through other social facts and not by reducing them to the facts of psychology or biology. Of course, Durkheim lived before the advent of biochemistry, molecular biology and biophysics, or it is unlikely that he would have made the first part of his statement, so obviously untrue today.

I suspect Durkheim was equally incorrect in claiming that psychological phenomena are unable to explain sociological events. But the issue is finally not whether human behavior can be reduced to psychology or evolutionary biology or, for that matter, to cells or even molecules or atoms. Rather, we should be asking to what extent we increase our understanding by recognizing that we are biological as well as cultural beings.

Efforts to reduce human behavior to some single explanatory factor began long before sociobiology. In the fifteenth century, Scotland's King James IV isolated several children at birth to prevent them from hearing any human speech. His goal was to discover whether humans possessed an innate, God-given language. Unfortunately, the children all died before they could speak at all, much less confirm King James's pious hope that they would naturally begin speaking Hebrew.

The nineteenth-century social philosopher John Stuart Mill took a very different position from that of Durkheim:

> The laws of the phenomena of society are and can be nothing but the laws of the actions and passions of human beings gathered together in the social state. Human beings in society have no properties but those which are derived from, and may be resolved into, the laws of the nature of individual men.

The "laws of the nature of individual men," according to Mill, are the laws of nature, neither more nor less.

Pioneer psychoanalyst Carl Jung reduced the unconscious human mind into two parts: the personal unconscious, the product of an individual's private experiences, and the collective unconscious, which contains the experience that our species has accumulated during its evolutionary history. This collective, species-wide wisdom supposedly guides much of our unconscious behavior, and often emerges in myth, legend and particularly dreams as universal "archetypes." To my knowledge, no one has attempted to analyze Jungian archetypes with an eye specifically toward evolutionary biology, but it would almost certainly be an interesting project.

More recently, there has been a trend toward "humanistic psychology," under the influence of such students of human behavior as Abraham Maslow and Carl Rogers. Maslow identifies a hierarchy of "organismically-based needs," which include (1) physiology (hunger, thirst, sex etc.), (2) safety, (3) love and belonging, (4) esteem (largely as a result of accomplishment) and (5) self-actualization. The individual seeks to satisfy whichever of these needs have been frustrated; it is significant that each of us supposedly begins with the lowest in the hierarchy and works up to the highest. Certainly, this scheme makes profound evolutionary sense, reflecting as it does a hierarchy of human needs that does not differ significantly from those opted for by natural selection.

Linguist Noam Chomsky has been a pioneer in the field of "structural linguistics," a discipline that seeks to distinguish a common, underlying deep structure in the extraordinary diversity of human languages. According to Chomsky, that deep structure is expressed in every language by a series of rules that govern the transformation of deep structure into the apparent, surface structure—language itself. When we "understand" the speech or writing of another person we use the converse of these rules to transform the surface structure back into our own deep structure. While our deep structure is very personal and owned privately and unconsciously by each of us, it is also something we share with all other people. In thus reducing one aspect of the human mind, Chomsky and his school emphasize our relationship to biology as well as our kinship with each other.

The great Swiss child psychologist Jean Piaget was particularly concerned with the strategies employed by children to understand their environments, and wrote many meticulously researched volumes on topics such as the child's conception of time, space, physical reality and moral principles. His prodigious output should be examined in the context of his greater concern with epistemology, the study of the nature and legitimacy of knowledge: that is, how do we, as humans, come to know the world? What is the unfolding process by which the human mind comes to grips with reality? And to what extent do we err in our perceptions because of our limitations as biological creatures? Piaget was originally trained as a biologist, a specialist in the scientific naming of snails and clams. His reductionistic thinking is quite apparent in his human research, where it provides insights into the developing minds of children. Piaget has shown that children pass through discrete and predictable stages in which they develop an ability to interpret and respond to their world.

Finally, Clyde Kluckhohn, an anthropologist, and Henry Murray, a social psychologist, introduced a useful framework for reductionism when they pointed out that

> Every man is in certain respects
> a. like all other men,
> b. like some other men,
> c. like no other man.

This is not a multiple choice test. All of the above are true, a fact which makes humanity so interesting yet so difficult to study. We are like no one else both because each of us is genetically distinct and unique, and because our individual life experiences are always different as well. However, since all people grow up within one culture or another, they therefore share a great deal with the others in their society. In that sense we are all like some other men. Beyond this, as *Homo sapiens* we share a common core of humanity, making us like all other men. It is in this final realization that sociobiology makes its most powerful contribution, although we could supplement the Kluckhohn-Murray propositions with the additional statements that every person is also in certain respects

> 1. like all living things,
> 2. like all animals,
> 3. like some animals.

Reductionism is very much a mixed bag. True, it narrows our perspective and appears to impoverish our view of ourselves, but it also enables us to see more clearly our relatedness to all of life and thereby to enrich ourselves immeasurably.

•

A reductionistic view of the human mind, sprinkled liberally with evolutionary biology's theory of fitness maximization, may well provide some new insights into old ideas. Our conscience, for example, flashes warning signals when we have overstepped our limits and stepped on someone else's toes, perhaps because in pursuing our own fitness we have intruded on someone else's like-minded pursuit. What we call conscience may actually be our own adaptive recognition that, having gone too far, we are in danger of being caught; it may be a means of warning ourselves—in our own interest—to proceed cautiously and be more heedful of society's rules and expectations.

Similar suggestions can be made for nearly all our mental processes. Love may insure that fitness-enhancing investments will be made in appropriate individuals such as one's mate, parents, children, other relatives and friends. Jealousy may be the consequence of a mental reckoning leading to the conclusion that another person is deriving an "unfair share" of fitness-related benefits. Anger can be seen as a state of high arousal in which one's body prepares itself for vigorous, aggressive interaction and at the same time communicates that state to others. It thereby informs others of the extent of one's displeasure and in many cases makes them more likely to modify their behavior so as to avoid a confrontation. Sadness, or grief, is another conspicuous behavioral state, one generally associated with needfulness; it is brought on by personal loss or some other difficulty and can usually be alleviated if not cured by the solicitous behavior of others. Just as infants cry in response to needs that are then often gratified, adults also cry or mourn when in distress, and assistance is usually forthcoming. Happiness may be seen as a state of joy that celebrates fitness enhancement. When the happy individual is alone, his or her behavior is more likely to be restrained; it reminds us that we have done something to benefit ourselves. When in public, a happy person's behavior is more likely to be loud and attention getting. In this context, happiness is an advertisement that we have done well and, since everyone loves a winner, probably an effective device to increase the likelihood of continuing to do well.

If all these interpretations sound crassly mechanistic and therefore unpalatable, it might be worthwhile to consider whether our very reluctance to accept the fitness-enhancing aspects of our own behavior might not also be fitness-enhancing in itself. Since we all learn quite early in life that people don't like us to behave too selfishly, it might reduce our fitness to admit that we are actually quite concerned with increasing our own well-being.

It is even possible that the persistent, biologically generated conflict between personal and societal benefit has produced two powerful aspects of the human mind: morality and the unconscious. As regards morality, ever since Darwin, some biologists and philosophers have argued that we can, and should, base our ethical system on the theories of evolution. Nineteenth-century apologists of colonialism and laissez-faire capitalism transformed "survival of the fittest" from a biological description of how the natural world operates to a social prescription of how it ought to be. To some twentieth-century biologists, appalled by earlier misuse of Darwin's work but determined, nonetheless, to develop a system of evolutionary ethics, "survival of the fittest" meant giving a positive value to whatever encouraged living things to evolve. They supported diversity and the fullest possible expression of genetic potential, while opposing anything that led to extinction of any species. Both these efforts seem to be ill founded, and the nineteenth-century version, with its proponents of Social Darwinism, was quite perverse.

There is nothing inherently good or bad about a rattlesnake's venom, although I imagine a rattlesnake and a field mouse would probably take issue with each other on this point. Similarly, mutation, which helps organisms evolve by creating more genetic diversity, is not in any sense better than selection, which narrows the range of diversity. Evolution *is*. It is a fact, but so are extinction, defecation, typhoid and Hamburger Helper. As thinking human beings, we may choose to attach "ought" or "ought not" to these or to anything else, but there is nothing in their mere existence that automatically makes them good or bad.

Although the connection between evolution and ethics is more subtle than one's simply deriving from the other, it may nonetheless be real. Evolution will not tell us what is good or bad, but it may suggest a great deal about what we humans have come to consider to be good or bad, and why. While all human societies have definite ideas about right and wrong, it is possible that all human beings experience individually a definite conflict between what they privately feel is correct for themselves and what they publicly announce is right for themselves and others. Personal human morality may therefore ultimately be based on fitness considerations, with behavior that maximizes fitness generally valued over that which reduces it. At the same time, however, behavior that maximizes my fitness may well reduce yours, and vice versa, so that individuals who are excessive in their selfish pursuit of fitness are likely to be discriminated against by the rest of society, their actions ultimately leading to a net loss on their part, in the form of fines, injury, imprisonment or even execution. On the other hand, society is likely to support individuals who publicly renounce selfish gain or somehow show by their behavior that they are "ethical" in their dealings with others. The stage has been set for several conflicts: we may say one thing and do another, urging our colleagues to follow a moral system which actually maximizes our fitness exclusively.

This is not to say that there may not be genuine ethical leaders, men and women who personally espouse the morality they preach. After all, the human population is large enough to produce an incredible variety of people—within recorded history we have learned from leaders such as Confucius, Moses, Christ, Buddha and Muhammed. But I can't help wondering whether the public acclaim given to preachers of noble sentiments doesn't derive in large part from an individual's recognition that if *everyone else* behaved in the approved way, he or she would then be better off.

We may use a similar approach to gain a new perspective on the human unconscious mind. There seems little doubt that the unconscious, although poorly understood, is real, and that in certain obscure ways it influences our behavior. We can therefore predict that it is a product of our evolution, and, especially insofar as it is widespread and "normal," that it should be an adaptive product as well. What can we conclude about the evolution of the unconscious and its adaptive significance?

Thomas Hobbes wrote in the seventeenth century that human beings are "by their nature" unrelentingly selfish, and warned of the continuing and unavoidable "warre of each against each" unless society would mediate. In Hobbes's view, the role of society is to restrain those biological tendencies that may be beneficial to individuals but potentially ruinous for the whole. As social creatures, we each have a very low fitness unless we associate with our fellows; we therefore live in social groups, for our personal gain. At the same time, these social groups must, for the survival of the society, restrain our more flagrantly self-centered acts. We are placed in a frustrating bind: we need the society of others for our benefit, but successful functioning within that society requires us to renounce conspicuous pursuit of that benefit.

If human society requires that each of us sublimate our selfish fitness-maximizing strategies, then much of our social behavior is greatly constrained and actually a complex web of lies and deceptions. "The self," wrote Reinhold Niebuhr, "is tempted to hide its desire to dominate behind its pretended devotion to the world. All mature conduct is therefore infected with an element of dishonesty and insincerity. The lie is always intimately related to the sin of egoism." Lying, of course, is not a deed we advertise or are generally proud of. In fact, the best liars are those who are not aware of their lying; they can put up the most convincing front, not betrayed by signs of internal struggle. The product of this repression is the unconscious, an internal core of biologically evolved, ravenous selfishness (similar to Freud's concept of the id), which has combined with our personalized coping devices. Because it is usually inaccessible to our conscious minds, the unconscious enables us to retain fitness-maximizing, highly self-centered behavioral strategies, without our being aware that we do so.

This theory of the adaptive significance of the unconscious suggests that we reexamine our understanding of both consciousness and the unconscious in human beings and animals as well. Opinions have differed over whether animals have minds, souls, and consciousness. Most of us are accustomed to thinking of *Homo sapiens* as unique in our possession of a conscious mind. Yet we may in fact be unique in possessing an *un*conscious, or at least, unique in the degree to which our unconscious has developed. Thus, while deceit is not especially common among animals, it is rampant in human beings. Animals may therefore lack an unconscious in proportion as their social behavior is not constrained by externally imposed social rules. Insofar as animals can be considered "honest," we can also expect them to be conscious. There is probably little occurring in animals' minds beyond what meets the eye, since there is minimal adaptive value in hiding anything. But, because human beings have elaborated complex and restrictive social rules, they may in so doing have set the stage for the evolution of one of our distinguishing features —not consciousness, but the existence of the unconscious.

To conclude this obviously speculative excursion, try to imagine what someone would be like if he or she did *not* have an unconscious.

There are two ways this situation may be interpreted: either the qualities normally present in the unconscious would instead appear in this person's consciousness and directly influence his or her behavior; or these qualities would be absent altogether. The result? Individuals in the former case would be discriminated against by society, quite possibly locked up, hurt or even killed. Clearly, their fitness would be low. Those of the latter case would simply lack a fitness-maximizing component to their behavior and accordingly their fitness would also be low.

Leibnitz wrote that if God didn't exist we would have to invent him. It appears likewise that if the unconscious hadn't existed we would have had to evolve it.

●

Sigmund Freud was the foremost pioneer in the mapping of the inner workings of the human mind. Although many of his ideas are open to dispute, they at least provide a starting point for understanding our hidden selves. As with Piaget, Freud began his career as a biologist, and there are several interesting parallels between his thought and the theories of modern sociobiology.

In *Civilization and Its Discontents,* Freud maintained that "our civilization is, generally speaking, founded on the repression of the instincts." Many other belief systems have been founded on this notion: rationalism, epitomized by the thought of Immanuel Kant, held that reason intervened between us and our instincts. For rigid New England Protestants, it was Divine Grace that preserved us from our otherwise sinning selves. And for Freud it was the superego that had to contravene the id.

In the Freudian scheme of things, the function of the nervous system is not so much to produce excitation as to minimize it. The external world continually impinges on us, causing disruption and hence discomfort. Our nervous system responds by helping us avoid all this unpleasantness and by keeping itself in as low a state of stimulation as possible—on an even keel. It is true that human beings, even infants, often seek mild stimulation, for if too intense, it creates tensions. Human behavior, then, functions to minimize tensions within the human mind.

Freud's view is entirely compatible with sociobiological thinking, and we can add sociobiology's insight that mental tension may well be generated by situations that are not conducive to fitness maximization. Let us assume, with Freud, that the human mind is programmed to reduce tension, whenever it is felt; such tension may be greatest when we are in fitness-reducing situations. The result is a scheme whereby the mind is programmed to avoid these fitness-reducing situations and hence to seek fitness-enhancing ones.

In general, sociobiology is concerned with the adaptive value of behavior. It offers a perspective of normalcy and health, viewing most traits as the evolutionary consequence of individuals' having followed those strategies that maximized their fitness. It may also suggest a perspective on mental health quite different from anything Freud ever imagined. If the result of natural selection is that we seek to behave so as to maximize our fitness, then those who successfully do so may well experience a state of mental health. Such individuals will probably be perceived by others as healthy. However, when healthy individuals find themselves unable to behave in a fitness-maximizing fashion, they modify their own behavior or their surroundings so as to bring things more closely in line (or, to use Freud's image, to reduce the internal tension that results). The converse may also hold: perhaps we regard fitness maximization in others as an indication of their mental health or illness. Whether we are aware of it or not, we may in effect tend to define mental illness as a behavioral state in which fitness is not being maximized. Certainly behavior that is grossly antisocial or self-destructive is generally judged to be "sick" in virtually all human societies.

This argument is not intended as a claim that all healthy human behavior must always be directly fitness enhancing. In some societies, although "normal" behavior may even be somewhat maladaptive, it still functions well enough to permit the success of its practitioners, and an individual's failure to do what others are doing may reduce his or her fitness even more than going along with them would do. So great is the power of conformity and our need for the social group that failure to conform to even a "mad" society may itself be a symptom of madness!

For example, among the Koryak of Siberia it was taken as an article of faith that dogs had to be sacrificed in large numbers to propitiate the animal gods and insure good hunting for the coming year. This custom seems strange when we consider that the Koryak lived on the verge of starvation. Despite their insistence on destroying one of their most valuable resources, one on which they depended for their very survival, the Koryak survived; they obtained new dogs from their neighbors (who impiously refused to sacrifice theirs) in exchange for meat and furs. While Koryak culture may appear "crazy" to the Western observer, we don't consider individual Koryak to be crazy. Each was conforming to the norms of his culture and was perhaps no less sane than is the American who spends $6,000 for a car that can go 120 miles per hour yet rarely goes more than 35 because the roads are so clogged with other cars!

However, if your next-door neighbor began sacrificing dogs in order to assure success in his business, he might well end up in an institution, diagnosed as psychotic. And his confinement would probably be a correct response by society. In Seattle, a young woman was recently arrested for kidnapping. It happened that she also drank cat blood and had developed her own magical religion. She was confined, rightfully, by our standards, in a mental institution. On the other hand, the Masai of East Africa have been drinking cow blood for generations, yet no one suggests that they should be institutionalized. The point is that if one person does something bizarre we are likely to consider him crazy. If a handful do it, we describe them as a cult (like the snake handlers of the southern Appalachians, who believe that rattlesnakes will bite only those who waver in their faith). If many do it, they have formed a culture, by which point the issue is no longer one of sanity versus insanity. The insane person lives in a highly maladaptive culture of one, and we may therefore be justified in calling him insane. After all, humans are social, conforming creatures and, in such a system, solitary "cultures" are likely to be very unfit.

•

It seems odd that an illness can actually be adaptive. Certainly there is nothing adaptive about being stricken with pneumonia, and we don't expect to hear a rousing cheer from our genes if we are hit by a truck. There may, however, be a great deal that is fitness enhancing about the body's response to these unfortunate events. For example, we are accustomed to thinking of fever as an unfortunate accompaniment to being ill. When most people find they have a fever, they take aspirin to treat it. But consider a high temperature from an evolutionary viewpoint. If living things consistently elevate their body temperatures when bacteria or viruses invade them, then couldn't this response be part of a fitness-maximizing strategy? Isn't it possible that individuals who respond to disease organisms by raising their body temperatures are actually more successful in combating the infection than are individuals who don't? Recent research has suggested that this hypothesis is true.

The study in question involved desert iguanas, lizards which are cold-blooded and which therefore cannot normally elevate their body temperature by means of fever. However, they can employ behavior to elevate their temperature, by moving to a warm environment. Since they are cold-blooded, the lizards quickly assume the temperature of their surroundings. In the study, the experimental iguanas were injected with dangerous bacteria. Some were then kept in a constant-temperature environment, while others were placed in an environment containing a range of possible temperatures from which to choose. The results showed that lizards given the bacteria chose to have a warmer body temperature than did the healthy individuals, and that infected lizards which had the option of giving themselves a fever recovered much better than those unable to respond in this manner. In addition, iguanas whose fever was reduced by injections of an aspirin-like drug actually had a lower survival rate than did those who were left untreated. Fevers, then, may be adaptive, and perhaps we should think twice before reaching for the aspirin.

If physiological responses such as fever can be adaptive, it seems possible that behavioral responses can also enhance fitness, even behaviors that appear to be "sick." Of course, the extreme forms of even an adaptive response can be maladaptive. A fever above 105 degrees can be very dangerous. And, similarly, certain extreme behaviors may be self-destructive and clearly maladaptive. But, just as research on the adaptive value of fever helps us understand its occurrence, an evolutionary approach to mental illnesses may help us discover the origin of these puzzling behaviors.

Depression, for instance, is the most common adult psychiatric illness. In its milder neurotic form, it may simply be the "blues"—a profound sadness, a great deal of complaining and a feeling of hopelessness. In more severe cases, there may be disturbances of sleeping and eating, refusal or inability to act effectively, and attempted or actual suicide. How could a behavioral pattern that seems so clearly to be fitness reducing in fact be fitness maximizing?

Suppose that mild depression is actually a cry for help. During normal life experiences, there are times when assistance is required from parents, friends, spouse, even from one's children. All social animals have a repertoire of "care-eliciting" behaviors, actions they can take to increase the likelihood that they will be attended to. Significantly, friends and relatives usually do respond with care-giving behaviors when a human shows symptoms of mild depression. Such aid will be offered so long as the demands are not excessive and the help offered is in fact doing some good. More severe depression typically generates more pronounced efforts of assistance, in this case from the medical community as well.

By combining the "cry for help" aspects of depression with our knowledge of the sociobiology of male-female differences,* a great deal that was puzzling about depression now becomes clear. From biological considerations alone, we would expect that women especially are attuned to males' competence as "good providers," certainly more so than men are attuned to women in this regard. This difference helps explain the fact that, in all societies, depression is significantly more common in women than in men. Their biology makes it more likely that women should be the sex to attempt care-eliciting behaviors. Males are supposed to be the care providers. Depression is also frequently associated with marital strife, a finding consistent with the suggestion that depression represents an unconscious effort to mobilize concern, attention and resources, in this case from an unresponsive or insufficiently responsive husband.

In general, although depression is more common among married than among unmarried women, the opposite holds for men. The discovery that unmarried men are more likely to be depressed than are married men has been an important weapon for radical feminists, since it suggests that marriage itself is a male-designed phenomenon, tending to free men from depression while depressing women, presumably because of the emotionally stressful, sexist demands made

*As a brief summary of the relevant male-female differences, recall that males produce a large number of small, inexpensive sperm which do not necessitate a large parental investment, while females produce a smaller number of expensive eggs, which call for a relatively large investment. Males are therefore selected to compete among themselves for access to females. Furthermore, since females are selected to choose males who contribute maximally to their fitness, males are selected to seek access to reproductively relevant resources.

upon a married women in today's society. There may be much truth
in this claim, but the male-female differences in depression associated with marriage also fit well with the sociobiological hypothesis. If men are the resource-providing sex and women are biologically
predisposed to be resource receiving, and if depression is in fact a
petition for resources (emotional, financial, etc.), it seems reasonable
that unmarried men who showed depressive inclinations would be
considered unattractive mates, while depressive tendencies in
women would not be nearly as undesirable. As a result, depression
may be more common in married women and in unmarried men
simply because unmarried men who incline toward depression are
discriminated against by marriageable women, while unmarried
women with comparable tendencies are not as likely to be avoided
by a man seeking a mate.

We would also predict that if depression is a care-eliciting behavior, then it should be especially common following the birth of a
child, a period when a woman is likely to be especially needful and
therefore especially sensitive to her mate's behavior toward her.
"Post-partum depression" is a significant mental health problem,
well known to psychiatrists.

What implications does this discussion have for suicide, the most
drastic solution to severe depression? It seems clear that anyone who
truly wants to commit suicide can do so and there is little that society
can do to prevent it. Most suicide attempts are regarded as dramatic
gestures, appeals for help. While women expectedly attempt suicide
much more often than do men, men actually kill themselves more
frequently. It has been widely observed that suicide in women will
often involve an overdose of pills, which can frequently be treated
successfully by hospital emergency rooms. Men tend to take their
lives by putting a bullet in their heads. In Seattle, women who jump
off the Aurora Bridge often land in the water and may well survive;
when men jump off the bridge, they are more likely to land on an
asphalt parking lot. Again, this disparity is predictable: men have less
to gain than women by signaling their need. After all, they are supposed to be the provid*ers*, and not the provid*ed to*. Women who
attempt suicide may do so as a last-ditch, desperate attempt to dram-
atize their problem; when men reach that state, they often have
nowhere to turn.

As with virtually all issues in human sociobiology, this speculation on male-female differences in depression does not deny the role of social learning or culture. Women everywhere may express more depression than men at least in part because they are "socialized" to do so. Human societies generally teach men that they must solve their own problems ("Return with your shield or on it"), while women are brought up to be passive and to expect help from others. But these explanations reinforce each other, and are not mutually exclusive. First of all, it is by no means certain that such male-female differences are solely due to different socialization, and secondly, even for those that are, we are entitled to ask why so many human societies have independently arrived at the same basic pattern of socialization.

A similar evolutionary perspective may help us understand other male-female differences in mental illness. For example, statistics have shown that women outnumber men in depression, neuroses and hypochondria, and men exceed women in disorders such as drug addictions, wild and uncontrollable manias, and a range of antisocial, often quasi-criminal behaviors generally described as "sociopathy." Again, these findings are anticipated by the basic evolutionary biology of maleness and femaleness. As the riskier, more competitive sex, males are expected to engage more frequently in flamboyant, eye-catching behavior. But the fact that we can catch a glimpse of the possible adaptive function of these illnesses should not imply that the sufferers are any the less ill. Mild depression in women may be entirely adaptive, just as is mild flamboyance in men, but when either becomes grossly exaggerated, something is clearly wrong, if only because the behaviors themselves have become counterproductive and the people involved are often dreadfully unhappy.

In general, mental illness may reflect an inadequate or ill-conceived effort to chart an adaptive course in stormy seas. If the sufferer's behavioral corrections appear to be leading in the right direction, we say the individual is "coping," "well-compensated," "becoming adjusted" and so forth. For example, grief is considered an appropriate response to loss of a loved one, while depression is not. Although neuroses (such as compulsiveness) might be thought of as coping devices, possibly useful to the individual, they are often seen as rather peculiar, since they are not shared by the majority of "healthy" others in the society. As a result, the neurotic may also become unhappy as he perceives himself as different from the majority, a situation with which gregarious, social and conforming *Homo sapiens* is not comfortable. The neurotic's unhappiness may finally be adaptive, insofar as it induces him to seek help and thus to correct his deviation.

In extreme cases, individuals may find themselves in such difficult circumstances, either because of their family life or perhaps some real, organic disability, that they may create artificial worlds in which they are somehow better off. These are the "fixed delusional systems" of many psychotics. For someone whose behavioral functioning is greatly out of tune with evolutionary biology, the pain may be too severe to bear, and constructive therapy may seem a Herculean, if not impossible task. As with those lizards that develop a fever in order to cure themselves, some people may "go crazy" in order to "keep sane"!

Part II: Notes on Biology and Culture

The great nuclear physicist Niels Bohr once wrote, "The opposite of a correct statement is a false statement. But the opposite of a profound truth may well be another profound truth." It is a profound truth that human behavior is culturally influenced, symbolic and learned—the product of experience. But it is also profoundly true that human behavior has its origins in biology, that it is the product of evolution. As the Eastern mystics have long held, opposites are complementary. Culture is, in fact, one of our most important biological adaptations, and it therefore need not be opposed to biology. In behaving culturally, we are also behaving biologically. Our culture is natural to us, just as quills are natural to a porcupine.

There exists convincing fossil evidence that the increased size of our brains and the development of culture are closely linked. However, the initial, rapid evolution of a large brain occurred after we had already achieved certain rudimentary cultural systems. Recent findings indicate that fossil australopithecines, relatives of our ancestors, had relatively small brains at the same time that they were making and using weapons. A rudimentary ability to manufacture and use weapons and other tools rendered primitive humans who were better at it more fit than those who were less adept. This increase in fitness resulted in very rapid selection for large brains, and a very finely organized, interdependent system. Our minds evolved in the context of culture, just as culture has always been produced by the action of our minds.

Because of this close connection between biology and culture, a great many of our activities that seem to be learned are also fitness enhancing as well. For example, many human societies enforce a post-partum sex taboo, which forbids a woman to have intercourse for some period, often several years, after giving birth to a child. Different peoples rationalize the taboo in different ways, and rarely offer a biological explanation: intercourse at this time is "immoral" and offensive to the gods, the husband's semen will spoil the mother's milk, and so on. Regardless of the local justification, such behavior appears highly adaptive, since it reduces the likelihood of another conception's following too closely on the first. A correlation also exists between this technique of adaptive birth spacing and the protein content of the local diet. Post-partum sex taboos are strongest in tropical areas, where protein is less abundant and childbearing and nursing are consequently more stressful. In temperate regions, where protein is more plentiful, birth control methods of this sort are less widely practiced.

Parents everywhere provide educational experiences for their children. In our culture, we give our youngsters toys. We have learned this behavior from others; we probably received toys from our own parents, and we (and our children!) often observe people giving toys to other children. But is the fact that it is a learned behavior the only reason for toy giving? It is clearly beneficial to our fitness when our children have useful learning experiences, and it seems very likely that we were either selected for behaviors that provide such opportunities to our offspring or that we recognized the benefits such behavior would bring. We find it "sweet" to make our children happy, just as children are made happy by things that enhance their fitness—such things are sweet to them.

As another example of the adaptiveness of cultural behavior, we may consider the incest taboo, a prohibition that in some form or other is universal. All societies forbid sex and marriage between close relatives, and may or may not include additional explicit requirements concerning the degree of relatedness within which individuals may not wed. The taboo deals most strongly with relations between mother and son, between siblings and between father and daughter. Its prohibitions are only rarely violated, the exceptions being within certain royal families such as those of the Peruvian Incas or the pharaohs of Egypt. In these cases, brother-sister matings were common, and served to keep power and privilege within a narrow group.

Freud considered that the incest taboo, like the Oedipus complex, reflected a conflict basic to all humanity. Anthropologist Claude Lévi-Strauss maintains that inhibition of incestuous sex marked the emergence of a distinctly human society (although, in fact, a proscription similar to the incest taboo operates among many animals as well). To Lévi-Strauss, the differences between human societies are greatest at the surface. Beneath it, their common features reflect the common features of the human mind itself. The universality of the taboo against incest may therefore suggest that it says something real about human nature and, presumably, about the evolutionary process that gave rise to it.

From a biological standpoint, matings between close relatives often lead to a substantial depression in fitness. Offspring born of such unions have significantly higher rates of mental retardation, dwarfism, deaf-mutism and similar disabilities. Not surprisingly, although "inbreeding depression" is not often cited as a justification for the incest taboo, most people obey it nonetheless.

Many non-Western people use "exogamy"—marriage outside the closest kin group—as a means of solidifying political, social and economic relationships. "We marry our enemies" (to make them our friends) is an oft-quoted tribal maxim. In avoiding incest, people therefore often enhance their fitness in two different ways: they are able to use marriage bonds to benefit themselves by means of the social arrangements they establish, and they can also avoid inbreeding and its fitness-reducing consequences. In addition, they may well thwart the disruptive effects of sexual competition within the family, a situation that could occur if the incest taboo were not heeded.

Most animals also avoid incestuous matings. Mice reared in the same litter show a reduced frequency of mating together when they are adults, regardless of whether they are biological siblings. In this case, play patterns established early in life apparently interfere with later sexual patterns. A very similar process may occur among people. Sociologist Joseph Shepher has studied marriage patterns among members of the Israeli collective settlements known as *kibbutzim*. In these social units, children who are not related biologically are reared communally in nursery groups and later in day-care centers. Shepher found that out of 2,769 marriages between second-generation kibbutz adults, only six took place within the peer group of any one kibbutz, and this despite the fact that such marriages were actively encouraged by authorities. Growing up together apparently causes children to see each other as brothers or sisters, thus somehow inappropriate as potential mates. The ultimate fitness-enhancing biological basis for their behavior seems clear, even though in this case the individuals are not even related.

The reluctance of human beings to have sex with someone with whom they grew up is highly adaptive, serving as it does the ultimate goal of fitness by reducing the likelihood of incest. A form of traditional Chinese marriage known as "Shim-pua" is a good test case. The social norm for wealthy Chinese families was to adopt prospective daughters-in-law while they were still young girls and to raise them alongside their future husbands. An interesting study by anthropologist Arthur Wolf indicates that this arrangement was not very successful. In nineteen of such adoptions that took place in one Chinese village, seventeen would-be happy couples refused to consummate their marriages, despite the urging of family and friends. In the two successful marriages, the girls were older than usual when adopted (almost adolescent rather than young children) and so apparently did not develop sibling relationships with their future husbands. So, familiarity may or may not breed contempt, but seemingly it does not lead to breeding.

The correspondences observed between cultural practice and evolutionary wisdom may, of course, be mere coincidence. But, alternatively, they may exemplify the results of a process similar to natural selection operating on customs rather than on genes. Customs that reduced the fitness of their practitioners would eventually become less common, and would be replaced by fitness-enhancing customs, customs that increased the population of those people who practiced them. Although this explanation makes no assumptions regarding biology, it is possible that there exists a direct, genetically influenced tendency to engage in adaptive behaviors. While this seems a possible if unlikely interpretation of most complex customs, there may nonetheless be a devious but real connection between genes and adaptive human behavior.

Our lack of a genetically mediated tendency to engage in a specific behavior might be compensated for by tendencies to recognize which customs contribute to our fitness and to adopt them accordingly. In other words, we may use fitness as an important criterion (either acknowledged or unacknowledged) in deciding whether to adopt a specific custom, whether in the realm of food preparation, courtship ritual or child-care techniques. Certain behaviors are, of course, clearly more relevant to fitness than are others—child-care customs, for example, versus the ornamentation of bathroom mirrors. Because we are more likely to use fitness considerations in evaluating the former than the latter, we would expect to find much more variability between human societies in regard to relatively trivial customs than in regard to those that are critical for biological success.

The working out of some relationships between genetics and culture may be quite unsuspected. Milk drinking, for example, may not seem very remarkable to us, but to my knowledge, we are the only species in which adults ever drink milk. It is equally extraordinary that we drink the milk produced by another animal, the cow. Yet milk drinking is by no means as common as we might think. Cow's milk is frequently consumed by many European peoples and those derived from them—such as Americans—as well as by such cattle-raising people as the Masai of East Africa. But this practice is virtually unknown among Polynesians, Eskimos, Native Americans, Native Australians and most Orientals; the great majority of human beings simply do not drink cow's milk, and many consider it positively barbaric.

As it happens, in order to digest milk efficiently, humans require the enzyme lactase, which breaks down the milk sugar lactose. For adults who lack this enzyme, drinking milk often leads to cramps, gas and diarrhea. All human beings can produce lactase at birth, but among non-milk-drinking people, the ability to do so disappears after several years of age, to coincide with weaning. There is a very close correlation between the presence of lactase among adults and the persistence of milk drinking in the culture. Not surprisingly, peoples who lack lactase are those who don't drink milk, while dairying cultures, such as those of the northern Europeans and the Masai, have been drinking milk products for generations, and retain their ability to produce lactase as adults.

We may justifiably question which of the variables was the cause of the other. Did the gene for lactase in Europeans and the Masai somehow give rise to their fondness for milk, or did the use of milk by these people somehow lead to an increase in lactase genes? Either alternative is possible. It may be that, within those human populations that had the opportunity to raise cattle, individuals who could profit from the high nutrition of milk had a selective advantage over others, and therefore genes for lactase spread. On the other hand, the initial chance presence of lactase genes in certain populations may have made those populations more likely to persist in keeping dairy cows while other people discarded the notion after their attempts were followed by severe indigestion. We simply do not know how milk drinking developed, and perhaps we never will. It is important, however, to realize that there is almost certainly some sort of connection between the rather straightforward gene for lactase and the much more complicated human custom of dairying and milk drinking (clearly, there are no genes for milking cows). Although an ability to produce lactase does not force us to drink milk, because of some as-yet-unknown mechanism it does make us more likely to do so.

Similarly, we don't have genes for walking, although all normal human beings are eventually able to walk. Our genetic makeup insures that we develop the anatomy that will make walking possible, and in fact unavoidable. Is there a similar mental anatomy that makes certain customs likely to develop?

●

Perhaps evolution doesn't always win. While we seem to do much to enhance our fitness, we also do a great deal that doesn't make much biological sense. Anthropologist Weston LaBarre has made the following observation:

> An instructive example . . . may be taken from the folk belief of the Cassubians, a peasant group in Poland of Balto-Slavic speech. This is the belief in the mysterious flower of the fern, which blooms only at midnight on Midsummer Night. The uncanny blossom is a strange red in color and appears to be glaring at the onlooker with the unnerving glitter of a glass eye. If a person sees it, he must not stand still, or speak, or look around —even if fearful voices or howls are heard behind him—lest he die by the hand of a witch. The flaming fern-flower may be picked up with a red silk cloth, but this is very difficult, since access to it is barred by thorns, or by the Evil One in the form of a monkey, bull or wolf; or a late wanderer may ask the way, and the flower vanishes in an instant if one replies to him. If a man does succeed in plucking the fern-flower, however, he will be able to understand the language of animals and to see great hoards of hidden treasure in the ground, and he will live hale and

hearty to a great age. But no one has ever seen it. This fact will not surprise botanists—since all ferns are non-flowering plants. The botanist may, however, be puzzled as to how the legend of a fern-flower ever could have arisen, since it has no possible referents in the objective plant world . . . what is surprising to the non-anthropologist is that the Cassubians have so much detailed and circumstantial knowledge about the fern-flower—when no man has ever seen it!

Psychiatrists may have more to say than sociobiologists about this paradox. Every culture has its puzzling "fern-flower," which seem to defy logic, both evolutionary and otherwise. A few examples will be useful in determining whether these riddles fit—or don't fit—into an evolutionary view of human behavior.

Sparganosis is an eye infection widespread in southeast Asia. The folk remedy for this disease is to apply split frog poultices or compresses made of frog tissue to the inflamed area. According to theories of ancient Chinese medicine, this procedure should cure such inflammations for two reasons: first, infections are hot and frogs are cold, therefore, frog tissue should heal inflammations just as cold, wet yin balances hot, dry yang; second, it is well known that eye inflammations are often caused by worms, which are eaten by frogs. What the Indo-Chinese don't realize is that sparganosis is, in fact, caused by an embryonic worm normally parasitic in frogs; by applying frog tissue, they are actually spreading the illness rather than curing it! If a patient doesn't have sparganosis when he begins the cure, he is much more likely to suffer it afterwards. For more accessible examples we might consider that bleeding was practiced by Western physicians for hundreds of years, and it seems only yesterday that tonsils were (needlessly) removed from children on the slightest pretext.

In another unusual case of "fern-flowers," the Dinka of Africa believe that membership in the crocodile clan will safeguard them against being eaten by crocodiles, and they therefore confidently swim crocodile-infested rivers, even at night. Although no supporting data are available, it would seem likely that crocodiles don't really distinguish between Dinka who have the crocodile as their totem and those who do not. While belief in crocodile-clan protection is probably maladaptive, it is worth noting that lion-clan Dinka do not believe that such membership protects them against known man eaters, but only against the common normal animal-eating variety; in this case, reality intervenes, at least to some extent.

The natives of the Fore region of New Guinea have long suffered from a mysterious disease known as *kuru,* which strikes adult women and young children of either sex, and causes a substantial mortality. Only recently, the origin of this disease has been revealed to be a virus that lives in the human brain. By eating the brains of their victims, New Guinea headhunters infect themselves with the virus. Since women and children are responsible for food preparation, they are especially likely to contract the disease, apparently because they nibble on dinner while it is still not quite ready! By our standards eating raw human brains is rather unpleasant, and by any standards it also appears to be maladaptive. As with the frog cure for sparganosis and crocodile clanism, it is a cultural trait that seems to diminish the fitness of those practicing it.

The Marquesas Islanders and the Maori of early New Zealand used oceangoing canoes that sported enormous vertical tail vanes. Not only would those structures have been more useful as keels, they actually robbed the canoes of sailing efficiency, making them more difficult to maneuver and more likely to capsize. The Polynesian sailors compensated for their self-generated difficulties by affixing magical sea-bird feathers to these outlandish poop fins. Such talismans may have provided peace of mind, but not a great deal of actual stability.

A more familiar example of maladaptive human behavior is the eating and exercise habits of the average American. Most of us overindulge in foods that are high in saturated fats and cholesterol, despite the fact that these materials are clearly harmful and may in fact be life threatening when consumed in sufficient quantities. Fats cause our arteries to clog up and lead to heart disease, the foremost killer in the United States today. This dietary imprudence is aggravated by our tendency to avoid exercise. We drive when we could walk, use the elevator when we could take the stairs and so on.

How can we explain these and other apparent deviations from fitness-maximizing behavior? Frankly, I don't know. It seems likely, however, that each case would have to be considered individually, as there may be no single explanation that applies to all. Dangerous Western eating and exercise habits may well be the effects of our cultural developments outstripping our biological evolution. Human beings evolved as part-time carnivores, probably on the African savannah. There is every reason to suspect that we are programmed to relish animal fat, a very concentrated food source and, not surprisingly, one that is prized by all meat-eating animals. Most wild game is actually quite lean, and a fatty meal would therefore be a rare and sought-after treat. Because we undoubtedly got more than enough exercise during our long African evolution, any opportunity to avoid exercise and to leave ourselves with enough physical activity to keep our bodies in good order would be seized upon.

But nowadays we fatten our livestock in feedlots; slather butter and oils on everything; and compound the problem by adding unnecessary calories through sugar, candies and other worthless confections. For a savannah-bred protohuman, this diet would be heaven. For us, it may well be lethal. Having provided us with an opportunity to satisfy (in excess) our primitive needs, modern culture then adds to the villainy by designing all sorts of "labor-saving devices" that enable us to avoid the exercise that might otherwise be our bodily salvation. Only recently has there been a sizable recognition of the problem, if not of the cause, of poor physical maintenance: jogging and running are popular, most people are to some extent calorie conscious, and low-fat foods are even gaining acceptance.

The other examples of apparently maladaptive behaviors are more difficult to interpret, perhaps because we simply don't understand them as well. Customs that apparently reduce fitness could bear a closer examination: anthropologist Marvin Harris has suggested that a great deal of human behavior that appears maladaptive (such as the veneration of "sacred cows" in India) may actually reflect a long-term ecological wisdom. There may yet be a functional value to much that on first impression appears useless or even harmful. This certainly seems true of primitive war, as we saw earlier.

Yet there is always room for error, even in evolution. Natural selection does not produce the best possible solution to any problem, only the best solution offered by the mutations and genetic combinations that become available to it in each generation. The human knee and lower back, for example, could have been designed by a good structural engineer to be much more efficient. As they are, they work well enough, but nonetheless give us no end of trouble. Someday a better construction may evolve. The human species, like any other, is bedeviled by a Pandora's box of disadvantageous genes that regularly beset us with Down's syndrome ("mongolism"), cleft palate, clubfoot, juvenile amaurotic idiocy, dwarfism, hemophilia, sickle-cell disease and many others. There are some good—that is, understandable—reasons why natural selection has not eliminated these traits. Describing them all is beyond the scope of this book, but the simple fact remains: though evolution does not produce the best of all possible worlds, it has clearly produced ours.

Just as certain disadvantageous genes are selected against and may eventually disappear, harmful cultural traits, once they are identified as such, often suffer a similar fate. Bleeding and unnecessary tonsillectomies have been "selected out" of modern medicine. The frog treatment for sparganosis is disappearing, along with Dinka crocodile clanism, although the elimination of these practices may actually be due as much to the worldwide homogenization of cultures as to native recognition of a disadvantageous cultural trait. Kuru is nearly extinct, thanks to the Nobel-prize-winning research of American virologist Carleton Gajdusek. The Polynesian poop fin has already vanished, oceangoing canoes having been replaced by gasoline- and diesel-powered boats. It is clear that cultural traits, like biological traits, may be replaced by new ones. And as older cultural traits are superseded, biology will continue to play a real, although still not fully analyzable, role in producing, maintaining and eventually replacing these behaviors we call our own.

8

Politics: A Tangled Bank

When Alice was lost in Wonderland, she came upon the Cheshire Cat and asked:

> "Would you tell me, please, which way I ought to go from here?"
> "That depends a good deal on where you want to get to," said the Cat.
> "I don't much care where—" said Alice.
> "Then it doesn't matter which way you go," said the Cat.
> "—so long as I get *somewhere*," Alice added as an explanation.
> "Oh, you're sure to do that," said the Cat, "if you only walk long enough."

I have been trying throughout this book to show that a path leads from evolutionary biology to human behavior. The journey may have been rocky and the path rather indistinct in places, and it is not entirely clear where we have gotten. Certainly there is more yet to see and it is equally certain that not all of it will be pretty. In the final paragraph of *The Descent of Man*, Charles Darwin indicates his painful awareness that evolution does not necessarily tell us what we want to hear. "But," he wrote, "we are not here concerned with hopes or fears, only with the truth as far as reason permits us to discover it." Obviously, his conclusion still applies.

Nevertheless, sociobiology's path is far from trouble free. And the trouble seems to be not so much with the infant science itself as with its possible implications. My own feeling is that sociobiology has very few political, ethical or moral implications. However, to some people it is as much a social issue as a scientific one.

Practically from the moment that it first became known, sociobiology has been under fire, largely from the political left. Accordingly, it might be helpful to list the main social criticisms that have been leveled against it, and provide a response to each. In many cases these will repeat points already made, so I will be brief:

1. *Sociobiology is racist.* This is utter nonsense. The bare mention of behavior in conjunction with genetics seems to evoke the specter of racism for those unable to distinguish science from politics. If anything, sociobiology is an antidote to racism, since it emphasizes those universals that underlie racial and cultural differences. In so doing, it shows the biological oneness of the human species. We are a single species. We can, and do, exchange genes with each other. Our behavior is the product of natural selection, and this is equally true of every one of us, whether Wall Street executive, Amazonian warrior or Kalahari Bushman. Color varies and so does culture, but our basic biology stays the same.

Nonetheless, there is at least some basis for concern. In the past, biology was greatly abused in support of racist doctrine. The pattern was fairly consistent. Differences between the races—usually black *versus* white—were interpreted as "proof" that one—always the white—was better. For example, Étienne Serres, a French anatomist of the nineteenth century, seriously proposed that black males were inferior to white because the distance between penis and navel in black boys increases less rapidly as they get older than it does in white boys. Apparently, then, an elevated belly button was supposed to indicate elevated racial quality. Undoubtedly, if the facts had been the other way around, and white males had had lower belly buttons, this finding instead would have been used to prove white superiority.

For a time, whites were described as more "highly evolved" than blacks because they were thought to be "more different" from monkeys and apes—conveniently ignoring evidence that points with equal justice the other way. It was also claimed that blacks were inferior because they retained juvenile traits throughout life (such as less body hair). Then, when "neoteny" became the rage in explaining human evolution (the idea here is that we are fetalized apes, who somehow developed the ability to reproduce), all this was forgotten and it was argued with equal conviction that whites, with their shorter skulls, smaller jaws and so forth, are superior because they are more juvenile!

I suppose there is a similar risk that the facts and theories of sociobiology will be misused today. But there is no racism "in" sociobiology, just as there is no racism in belly-button height, head shape, or jaw size. The fact is sociobiology is no more racist than anatomy.

2. *Sociobiology is genetic determinism.* True, sociobiology does rely heavily on the notion of genetic influence but this is far from determinism. In fact, misplaced worries about the dangers of genetic determinism ignore the dangers of the opposite (and equally exaggerated) alternative: environmental determinism. After all, if human nature is entirely determined by culture and social learning, then there is no human nature and, accordingly, no yardstick by which we might measure any social system. How can we describe tyranny, for example, as "inhuman" if we deny that "human" has any inherent meaning? If people have no essential nature, why shouldn't they be coerced and controlled by anyone who has the ability to do so? If human nature is non-existent, a major psychological barrier is removed against the manipulation of the weaker by the stronger.

The fact is, by identifying the biologically evolved, fitness-maximizing core of human nature, sociobiology describes what we are and helps us to understand ourselves. It is not genetic determinism.

3. *Sociobiology abolishes free will and thereby robs us of our human dignity.* Again, evolutionary biology is not deterministic, except as it describes certain limits placed on us by the natural world in which we operate. But, then, we are all subject to lots of limits. For example, we cannot exceed the speed of light, and in that sense our personal freedom is limited. I can't say I feel especially angry with Einstein for pointing this out, and it may actually be a useful sort of thing to know. The interchangeability of matter and energy, the inevitability of increase in entropy, the law of gravity—all these realities restrict our freedom, but more realistically what they do is define our world. To put it another way, they set the boundary conditions for existence. And, as can be seen in Schoenberg's twelve-tone music or in closely defined poetic forms such as the Japanese *haiku,* limits do not preclude art or creativity. They may, in fact, be essential for it.

Free will may actually be greatest when everyone is able to behave in accordance with his or her inclinations, whether these result

from early experience, social learning, cultura
tion. Sociobiology is simply a concerted effort t
contribution. There is, of course, the danger
become something of a "self-fulfilling prophe
ences our behavior because it predicts certair
happens, it will be a misuse of evolution,
notion that what is, is necessarily good, an

By defining much of human behavior ir
zation—love, for example—sociobiology t
this is true of any attempt to look rationa
Freud's explanation of love: "a state sugge
sion, which is thus traceable to an impo
respect of libido in favor of the love-ob
cold-blooded about being too analytic at

also something wonderfully exciting about learning why we do what
we do and finding out what we are. Human freedom and dignity
result from the fact that deep inside we are something. We cannot
be packaged and processed like TV dinners or prefabricated break-
fast cereals.

4. *Sociobiology is sexist.* If the identification of evolved male-
female behavioral differences is sexist, we probably must conclude
that sociobiology is sexist. However, I think it is more useful to re-
serve the term "sexism" for differential valuing of one sex over the
other, which often results in society's discriminating against one sex
—usually women. It is true that sociobiology may be misused for such
purposes, but this is not the fault of the discipline. As with yin and
yang, neither female nor male is complete in itself, and both are
equally valued in evolution. When a new generation is produced,
both are winners.

5. *Sociobiology is support for the status quo.* Some critics are
concerned that sociobiologists will use their science to legitimize
social institutions as they are now. Sociobiologists, they feel, will
argue that social systems arose through evolution and therefore must
be good.

We have already dealt specifically with this fallacy of legitimation.
Typhus evolved; that does not necessarily make it good. Human
behavior has also evolved; it also is not necessarily good. Certainly,

it is not good *because* it has evolved! It is also misleading to think that evolution might serve as an argument against change. Considering that change is what evolution is all about, this is a most astonishing notion. Specifically, evolution is the change in genetic makeup of a population over time. When Darwin first proposed his ideas in the mid-nineteenth century, they were seen as revolutionary, and literally so. Indeed, Karl Marx was so impressed with natural selection that he supposedly wanted to dedicate *Das Kapital* to Darwin. To the entrenched European aristocracy, on the other hand, evolution was a dangerous and fearful doctrine, specifically because it was a theory of change rather than support for the status quo. It would be truly ironic if modern evolutionists are now accused of opposing change.

6. *Sociobiology offers excuses for injustice and a rationale for social inaction.* The danger suggested here is that some people will argue that we are as we are because of our biology, thereby somehow relieving us of the responsibility for correcting injustice. Injustice is our judgment of the way things are in the world. Certainly there are many injustices and it is our right and duty to point them out when we see them, and to attempt some correction. Sociobiology helps us identify some of the possible roots of our injustice—male dominance, racism and so forth. It surely has not created them. If any change is to occur, whether radical or merely cosmetic, we would do well to understand the biological nature of our species—what we really are.

One rather hopeful aspect of our nature is that traits especially important to our fitness are likely to be resistant to change. A child psychologist has recently described this resistance as a "collusion of genes" designed to hit the adaptive target despite a variety of possible experiences for each individual. A human being can absorb a great deal of punishment and still turn out remarkably well. This helps to explain why human populations show no detectable differences in intellectual function, despite the fact that they have very different experiences and clearly are genetically different as well. It also shows how well buffered we are against inappropriate and potentially damaging environments.

In Shakespeare's *The Tempest,* Prospero describes the evil, malformed Caliban as "a born devil, on whose nature Nurture can never stick." This is unlikely. Since all behavior results from the joint action of genes and experience (nature and nurture), there is no nature upon which nurture cannot stick. And, therefore, there is no evolutionarily-based excuse for refusal to engage in remedial programs for the underprivileged, who have had "inadequate" early experiences. In short, the genetically-influenced side of our nature is both resilient and responsive to its environment. There is no basis whatever for giving up on someone because "it's in his genes." Evolution does not support social inaction.

•

Although it is not politically motivated, sociobiology nonetheless paints a picture of human nature that Marxist ideologues have some reason to dislike, since natural selection is essentially a process of genetic selfishness, and selfish individualism does not bode well for the selfless communism envisioned as humanity's ideal state. Thus, Marx bitterly attacked "those passions which are at once the most violent, the basest and the most abominable of which the human breast is capable: the furies of personal interest." And half a century later, a somewhat more mellow Leon Trotsky had this to say: "The powerful force of competition . . . will not disappear in a socialist Society, but . . . will be sublimated."

If we grant, with sociobiological theory, that at the heart of human behavior there lies a germ of genetic selfishness, Marxists may have a great deal of work to do if they really expect to create their version of an ideal society. Clearly, this says nothing whatever about whether socialism—or any other "ism"—is good or bad.

Tertullian, a church father writing in the third century A.D., pronounced that "It is unnatural to act in plays, to paint the Face, or to wear dyed cloth." What if Tertullian was right? Is it also unnatural to speak (we have to learn it), to form a government, to watch television, to fly to the moon? It seems absurd to prohibit something because it is "unnatural," in part because it is so difficult to determine natural from unnatural where human beings are concerned. If something really is unnatural, then stronger efforts may be needed to get people to do it, but the result could still be worthwhile. After all, as the descendants of cavalier arboreal primates whose feces fell to the ground and out of their treetop homes, toilet training does not seem to come naturally to us. But no one argues against such unnatural training.

Herbert Marcuse has written: "Glorification of the natural is part of the ideology which protects an unnatural society in its struggle against liberation." The problem as he sees it is that repressive social systems have been justified as being "natural." This may be. Marxist philosophers such as Marcuse would remake society in the interests of personal liberation. Presumably, liberated people in such an ideal state would then be free of the constraints of "unnatural" societies. But isn't this also a "glorification of the natural"? The moral is simply this: people with a social or political axe to grind will call what they don't like "unnatural" and what they do, "natural." Let us all beware.

●

There is, unfortunately, at least one sense in which evolution is a natural target for political activists. Evolutionary biology has a long and dismal history of misuse, much of it to support the patterns of racism, imperialism and social exploitation prevalent in the late nineteenth century. This was Social Darwinism, a doctrine that attempted to justify exploitation as the working out of "survival of the fittest." Even before the publication of Darwin's *Origin of Species*, Herbert Spencer argued against the eradication of poverty by social welfare programs, since it was, he said, only natural that some people be deprived and underprivileged.

> . . . the poverty of the incapable, the distresses that come upon the imprudent, the starvations of the ideal . . . are the decrees of a large, far-seeing benevolence . . . under the natural order of things society is constantly excreting its unhealthy, imbecile, slow, vacillating, faithless members.

It is a variant on Jesus' observation "the poor shalt always be with thee"—perhaps with a somewhat different motive.

No question, evolution has been used to support unpleasant political and social doctrines. For example, in 1900, the enormous German armaments firm of Alfred Krupp, later the bulwark of Nazi militarism, offered a cash prize to the winner of an essay contest on "What does the theory of descendence [evolution] teach us in regard to the internal political development and legislation of states?" And later John D. Rockefeller informed a Sunday school class that "the growth of a larger business is merely a survival of the fittest . . . the working out of a law of nature and a law of God."

Actually, just as beauty is in the eye of the beholder, the social and political implications of evolution were and still are in the eyes of the social activists, whatever their persuasion. As historian Gertrude Himmelfarb describes it, Social Darwinism was all things to all people:

> In the spectrum of opinion that went under the name of social Darwinism almost every variety of belief was included. In Germany it was represented chiefly by democrats and socialists; in England by conservatives. It was appealed to by nationalists as an argument for a weak state. It was condemned by some as an aristocratic doctrine designed to glorify power and greatness, and by others, like Nietzsche, as a middle-class doctrine appealing to the mediocre and submissive. Some socialists saw in it the scientific validation of their doctrine; others the negation of their moral and spiritual hopes. Militarists found in it the sanction of war and power of intellectual and moral persuasion. . . . Some complained because it exalted men to the level of supermen or gods; others because it degraded them to the status of animals. Political theorists read it as an assertion of the need for inequality in the social order corresponding to the inequality in nature, or alternatively as an egalitarian tract in which men as well as animals were in an undifferentiated state of equality. Bertrand Russell did not see how a resolute egalitarian could resist an argument in favor of "Votes to Oysters."

Of course, Social Darwinism has now been totally discredited. It ignored the crucial fact that natural selection operates by differential reproduction not head-on competition, and, furthermore, it attempted to derive ethics and morality from nature. They simply do not mix.

During the period 1930–1960, the Soviet Union participated in one of the most remarkable and tragic episodes in the history of modern science. Genetics in Russia was essentially rewritten under the direction of one T. D. Lysenko, who falsified data, imprisoned leading Soviet geneticists and set back Russian agriculture a whole generation by his insistence that hereditary changes could be induced by exposure to controlled environments (that is, modern-day Lamarckism). Incredibly, it was only in post-Khrushchev Russia that Lysenko was stopped and sanity returned to Soviet genetics.

What was Lysenko's appeal? Scientifically he was dead wrong, but politically he was on target. For one thing, the emphasis on competition in Darwinian natural selection tends to make Marxists rather uncomfortable. As we have seen, sociobiology reads very much like laissez-faire capitalism operating in the realm of genes. Just as Adam Smith argued that well-balanced and harmonious economic systems will emerge when each individual looks out for its own best interests, sociobiology predicts that human beings (or genes) have been selected to maximize their own fitness . . . selfishly. Adam Smith:

> . . . every individual . . . by directing [his] industry in such a manner as its produce may be of greatest value, intends only his own gain, he is in this as in many other cases led by an invisible hand to promote an end which was no part of his intention . . . by pursuing his own interest he frequently promotes that of society more effectively than when he really intends to promote it.

To evolution, of course, it does not matter whether individuals or genes act in a capitalistic manner. Insofar as they do, the political metaphor is a convenient way of describing the process. But "genetic capitalism" does not justify a particular political system any more than the fact that fire is a convenient metaphor for human metabolism provides a rationale for arson!

However, Stalin and his colleagues saw Lysenkoism as politically convenient. The fact that it was scientifically wrong was either unnoticed or deemed irrelevant. Furthermore, Lysenko was appealing because his approach promised rapid improvement in the socialist masses. Under his scheme several generations of the "right" political system could be expected to generate the perfect socialist citizen. Lysenkoism is now history, but this saddest tale of twentieth-century science lives on as a warning of what could happen when science is perverted for political ends. Responding to the polemics of a Boston-based group calling itself Science for the People, sociobiologist E. O. Wilson wrote: "Knowledge humanely acquired and widely shared, related to human needs but kept free of political censorship, is the real science for the people."

To some extent, both sociobiologists and their opponents have tended to go beyond pure objective science, especially where human beings are concerned. And, as we have just seen, political considerations have often loomed large, although so far this seems to motivate the opponents rather than sociobiologists themselves. Actually, there is another reason for resistance, especially among the hard-line social scientists, who have long been firmly committed to an environmentalist or "blank state" approach to human behavior. Basically, sociobiology is a radical doctrine, in every sense of the word. It not only presents a new view of the roots of behavior, it also radically undermines the traditional approach and training of many professional experts in human behavior.

Perhaps such experts fear that sociobiology threatens to make their training—and themselves—obsolete. This fear is not well grounded. Sociobiology comes to upgrade social science, not to bury it. Evolutionary considerations taken alone will never suffice to explain our behavior completely. Thus, if human sociobiology ever becomes a successful discipline in its own right, it will require massive inputs from the existing social sciences. At the very least, however, sociobiology offers a breath of fresh air and a new way of looking at things. But scientists, underneath it all, are just *Homo sapiens* themselves. Most of them tend to resist new ideas, any new ideas, often for no other reason than because anything new must conflict with whatever they had previously been taught. As the great physicist Max Planck put it: "A new scientific truth does not triumph by convincing its opponents and making them see the light, but rather because its opponents eventually die, and a new generation grows up that is familiar with it."

•

It seems increasingly clear that sociobiology will cause us to revise our own self-image, just as the works of Copernicus, Darwin and Freud have done. But, as with its predecessors, sociobiology will not by itself tell us what is good, or what we should do with our lives. Evolution is not a program for social or political action. It is less a message than it is a mirror: gaze in it and you will see your own biases and preconceptions. Do not look to it for advice or guidance, for it will only reflect what is already in you.

Are you a counter-culture enthusiast, convinced that modern technological society is deadly, joyless and basically unhealthy? Would you like scientific support for organic, grow-your-own gardening, unmedicated childbirths and the simple life with a minimum of artifice? You surely will be able to find it in sociobiology. Think about the lack of synchrony between cultural change and evolutionary change. The first is so fast and the second so slow that the gap between the two is necessarily large and ever-growing. "Obviously," the route to personal happiness lies with narrowing that gap and embracing our biology.

On the other hand, are you excited about recent advances in technology? Are you turned on by space exploration, high-speed digital computers and the remarkable discoveries of particle physics and medical science? Sociobiology can be for you too. We are not separate from nature and, indeed, human behavior appears to follow paths of fitness maximization. Certainly culture is our most important biological adaptation, so let's use it for all it is worth. Doing less would be denying our humanity.

The not-so-simple fact is we just don't know how fast evolution operates in human populations and we have no idea whether we are "out of synch" with our own biology or, if so, how much. And, even if we did, this wouldn't provide any sound guidelines for our own behavior. In fact, maybe part of our biology is that we must always be strangers to ourselves.

On the other hand, whereas we know next-to-nothing about the fit between our own biology and our culture, we do know something about culture and also about evolution. And there is no doubt that the former is having a very real effect on the latter. We are interfering dramatically in our own evolution—the first species ever to do so consciously. We do this every time we take medicine, whenever we plan our parenthood or decide on a spouse. And, just like evolution itself, there is nothing wrong or right in this; it just is.

There is a popular misconception that the human being of the future will have a very large head and a small body. Presumably this is because we use our heads so much these days and our bodies so little. The fact is, this is pure Lamarckism, the inheritance of acquired characteristics—and it doesn't work. The only way our children's children will look like disembodied brains is if people with big brains and small bodies (and a genetically-mediated tendency to be this way) have more offspring than the rest of us. And I see no evidence of this happening. There are similar claims around—that we are losing our appendixes or our little toes, or our ear lobes, all because we are not using them. Again, this will happen only if it is

favored by selection, call it natural or artificial, whatever you please.*
The point is that the future evolution of *Homo sapiens* will be determined solely by the differential reproduction of individual *Homo
sapiens* and the effect this has on the distribution of genes in future
generations.

There is evolution in our future, just as there was in our past.
There is simply no way of avoiding it. And if sociobiology has any
validity, our human nature will doubtless change, just as it has
changed during our evolutionary history thus far. And similarly, insofar as sociobiology helps us understand what we are, it may also help
us understand what we will be. But, like the Cheshire Cat, sociobiology cannot advise us which road to take. Once we have decided,
however, it may have much to tell us about what we are likely to
meet along the way.

●

Yes, there is a human nature, just as there is evolution, natural selection and sociobiology—as well as those who might wish to pervert
them all. It will be as foolish to exaggerate the political implications
of this fact as to ignore them, but the greatest error of all would be
to substitute ignorance, convenience or ideology for scientific evidence and our own very real biology. If sociobiology seems complicated when we apply it to the understanding of human behavior, the
human uses and misuses of sociobiology seem even more complicated—a truly "tangled bank." This was Darwin's imagery, in the
final paragraph of *The Origin of Species:*

> It is interesting to contemplate a tangled bank, clothed with many
> plants of many kinds, with birds singing on the bushes, with various
> insects flitting about, and with worms crawling through the damp earth,
> and to reflect that these elaborately constructed forms, so different from
> each other, and dependent upon each other in so complex a manner,
> have all been produced by laws acting around us. . . . There is grandeur
> in this view of life, with its several powers, having been originally

---

*Interestingly, we may actually be losing our appendixes, but not because we
don't use them. Rather, we shall evolve into an appendix-less species if individuals
lacking appendixes or having smaller ones (and with a genetic basis for this trait), leave
more successful offspring than those with full-sized appendixes. This may be occurring, with selection operating via appendicitis, since there is a mortality associated
with this disease that is not trivial. On the other hand, since culture now intervenes,
via appendectomies, we may be slowing whatever "natural" trend may have existed
for smaller appendixes.

breathed by the Creator into a few forms or into one; and that, whilst this planet has gone cycling on according to the fixed law of gravity, from so simple a beginning endless forms most beautiful and most wonderful have been, and are being evolved.

Now, with sociobiology, we can at last contemplate ourselves within that tangled bank.

References and Notes

1. Introduction: Hottentot Gods and the Strange Case of the Plucked Ocelot

The opening discussion was suggested by a statement of Margaret Mead's, which was cited by Clifford Geertz in his chapter in Platt (1965).

For a scholarly, comprehensive treatment of sociobiology, the interested reader could not do better than Wilson (1975). Another classic, enormously influential in the development of sociobiological thinking, is *Adaptation and Natural Selection,* by evolutionary biologist George C. Williams (1966). My own book (Barash, 1977a) is essentially a primer, intended for non-specialists at the freshman or sophomore level. Wilson's more recent book *On Human Nature* is directly concerned with human sociobiology. Valuable articles with a sociobiological perspective to anthropology can be found in the volumes edited by DeVore (1978), and Chagnon and Irons (1979). For biologically-oriented critiques of modern social science, see especially *The Imperial Animal* by Tiger and Fox (1971), a controversial and thought-provoking book for the non-specialist, and Pierre van den Berghe's *Man in Society* (1975), an iconoclastic introduction to the role of biology in sociology. Maddi's discussion of core versus peripheral elements appears in his solid book *Personality Theories* (1968). The Evans-Pritchard quotation is from a collection of BBC radio talks on anthropology titled *The Institutions of Primitive Society* (1954); this and other collections of anthropological material provide happy hunting grounds for the aspiring human sociobiologist. The Geertz quotation is from his chapter in Platt (1965), another wide-ranging volume; I also thank Geertz for pointing out the Johnson and Racine quotations. Weston LaBarre (1954), for whom culture is "the immortality of dead men," is a leading anthropologist, currently at Duke University. Whether you agree with him or not, whatever he says is generally said so well that it is a pleasure to read! The tragic mistranslation of *mokusatsu* is described by William J. Coughlin's "The Great *Mokusatsu* Mistake" (1953). I am grateful to Lionel Tiger (1969) for the information concerning the movie version of *Lord of the Flies.*

2: Where We Stand: Alcoholic Mice and Why Sugar Is Sweet

Richard Dawkins is an Oxford ethologist (specialist in animal behavior) whose recent book, *The Selfish Gene* (1976), is a lively account of how living things are just that—each seeking to maximize its own reproductive success. This book, although not intended as a text, has received a great deal of attention from professionals as well. The reader desiring more basic information on evolution could consult any of several excellent texts, such as Maynard Smith (1966), Moody (1970) or Dobzhansky (1974). My information on Huntington's chorea comes from Bruyn (1968) and from the devoted souls at the Clinical Research Center, Palo Alto Veterans Hospital, especially Drs. Ken Davis and Phil Berger. Behavior genetics is a burgeoning field; an up-to-date summary can be found in the excellent text by Ehrman and Parsons (1976). Although both the authors specialize in the behavior genetics of *Drosophila* (the fruit fly), their book draws examples from all animal species, including *Homo sapiens.* Daniel Janzen is an ecologist at the University of Pennsylvania; he has been notable in applying sociobiological principles to the "behavior" of plants. His technical paper in 1977a talked about rape, coyness etc. in plants, while another one (1977b) dealt with the evolutionary strategy of molding, spoiling and rotting. Cornell University ethologist William Dilger had an excellent piece in *Scientific American* (1962) describing the behavior of hybrid lovebirds, complete with many illustrations. Nebraska ethologists Roger Sharpe and Paul Johnsgard (1966) reported on the genetics of courtship in mallards.

There are several excellent introductions to ethology: the one by Eibl-Eibesfeldt (1975) is beautifully illustrated and strongly pushes the "classical European" position, which emphasizes a historical rather than a functional approach to the use of evolution in studying behavior; there is also material on "human ethology." Jerram Brown's text, *The Evolution of Behavior* (1975), is much more sociobiological in its outlook, although sadly it omits human beings altogether. K. and M. Breland, who describe the penny-pinching raccoons, were students of Harvard psychologist and chief apostle of conditioning B. F. Skinner. Their article on "The Misbehavior of Organisms" (1961) is humorous as well as informative, and an obvious parody of Skinner's very influential book of the 1930s, *The Behavior of Organisms.* That work was actually about the bar-pressing behavior of white rats. The contribution of Beethoven to my thinking on human genetics is due to an article from the *London Times,* October 18, 1977. Pupil dilation was reported scientifically by Chicago psychologists Hess and Polt (1960). Anthropologist Napoleon Chagnon (1968) has written a vivid description of the Yanomamo. These inhabitants of the Amazonian rain forests are among the fiercest people on earth, and they seem to exemplify many of the human traits predicted by sociobiologists; I doubt, however, that this is because of their aggressiveness *per se,* but rather because Chagnon is one of the very few anthropologists to point out the similarities between expectations based on evolution and the reality of what many peoples actually do. Similar scrutiny of other ethnographies would likely turn up similar parallels. Astronomer Carl Sagan's (1977) speculative account of the origins of human intelligence contains a very readable treatment of the human brain in computer and evolutionary terms. In writing his book, he stepped even further outside his field than I did in writing this one! The Laughlin quotation is from his chapter in Lee and DeVore (1968), a goldmine collection of pieces all dealing with hunting and gathering peoples. The observations on Arapesh menstruation are from *Male and Female* (1949) by one of America's favorite anthropologists, Margaret Mead. Her book is written with detail, sensitivity and no small amount of poetry as well.

3. Sexism: Strategies of Reproduction, or When Is Beeswax Like a Ferrari?

The Mead quotation is from *Male and Female* (1949) once again, and the comparison of male and female attitudes toward sex was drawn from the book by Smith and Smith (1974). Sigusch and Schmidt (1971) compare male and female attitudes toward sex among lower-class Germans. My technical papers reported on bluebird adultery (1976) and mallard rape (Barash, 1977b). Robert L. Trivers is a brilliant sociobiologist who has made several major contributions to the field, with important theoretical papers during the 1970s. His work on parental investment and its influence on mate selection (1972) is already a modern classic. Burney LeBoeuf, a professor at the University of California at Santa Cruz, was originally trained as a psychologist. He subsequently saw the light and began biological studies of social behavior in a spectacular mammal, the elephant seal. His technical account (1974) is a valuable reference on competition in these oversized animals, and Cathleen Cox and LeBoeuf (1977) describe the female's role in inciting this competition. Johns Hopkins University researcher John Money is one of our foremost experts on the hormonal aspects of male-female differences. His book, *Man and Woman, Boy and Girl* (1972), written with psychiatrist Anke Ehrhardt, especially emphasizes the role of hormones during child development. For homosexual rape in worms, see the technical report by Abele and Gilchrist (1977). Plug popping in Japanese monkeys was described in the detailed account of their sociobiology written by Penn State anthropologist Jeffrey Kurland (1977). The LaBarre quotation is from his book *The Human Animal* (1954), which has the distinction of discussing anthropology from both a biological and a psychoanalytic standpoint. Trivers and Willard (1973) pioneered the suggestion that natural selection might favor parental ability to vary the sex ratio of offspring, although the classic work on sex ratios and evolution is found in Sir Ronald Fisher's small but potent book, *The Genetical Theory of Natural Selection* (1930). The Marvin Harris quotation is from his article (1977b) in the *New York Times,* titled "Why Men Dominate Women." I think he is wrong about why, although clearly right about whether. His ideas of "cultural materialism" are actually quite close to sociobiology in that they look at the adaptive value of seemingly non-adaptive traits. Female infanticide among upper-class Chinese and Hindus is discussed by Sonoma State University (California) anthropologist Mildred Dickeman, in her chapter in Chagnon and Irons (1979). A good reference for animal polyandry is the manuscript by University of Montana ethologist Donald Jenni (1974). This paper appeared in a very important symposium titled *The Ecology and Evolution of Social Organization,* held at Washington, D.C., in 1972. Had the word been in current usage at the time, it probably would have been titled *Sociobiology* instead.

University of Washington ecologist Gordon Orians is probably the world's expert on the red-winged blackbird. He also pioneered the application of natural selection to animal social systems, emphasizing the role of female choice in his paper "On the Evolution of Mating Systems in Birds and Mammals" (1969). For hummingbird prostitution, see the report by Syracuse University biologist Larry Wolf (1975), and for the important role of beeswax in determining the mating system of Himalayan honeyguides, see Cronin and Sherman (1977). Stephen Emlen and Lewis Oring (1977) presented a technical account of resource-based mating systems in general, emphasizing that social systems may well be predictable from the local pattern of environmental resources. For gerontocracy and polygyny among Australian aborigines, see Rose (1968). New Mexico entomologist Randy Thornhill (1976) discusses cannibalism of the male by the female as an especially dramatic aspect of parental investment.

The strange courtship of empid flies was described by Kessel (1955). For menstrual cycles and cognitive performance, see Kopell *et al.* (1969); homosexual pairing in gulls—U.C. Irvine biologists George and Molly Hunt (1977); courtship in ring doves and male avoidance of cuckoldry—Duke University psychologists Erickson and Zenone (1976); and divorce in kittiwake gulls—the British biologist Coulson (1966). Ethologist Randall Eaton discussed lion sexuality in a manuscript published as part of a symposium on the sociobiology, ecology and conservation of the world's cats. Virginity inspectors among the Buhaya are described in F. Lorimer's book *Culture and Human Fertility* (1954).

4. Parenting: Murderous Monkeys, Paternal Marmots and Sexism (Continued)

Margaret Mead's description of the Arapesh nightmare and the later quotations are from her *Male and Female* (1949). Colin Turnbull is an anthropologist who specializes in African peoples. His account of the Ik (1973) is fine reading, although it is unlikely to enhance one's faith in humanity. University of Texas ecologist Eric Pianka (1970) has written a good technical discussion of r- and K-selection, and University of Michigan biologist Richard Alexander wrote a lengthy and wide-ranging article for the 1974 issue of the *Annual Review of Ecology and Systematics.* Titled "The Evolution of Social Behavior," Alexander's piece suggested the possibility of parental manipulation and also discussed the evolution of menopause and many other issues relevant to this chapter and book. Anthropologist Marvin Harris discusses the apparent correlation between infanticide and war, both in his *New York Times* article (1977b) and in his recent book *Cannibals and Kings* (1977a).

Wodinsky (1977) reported on the optic gland, reproduction and longevity in octopuses. For the evolutionary significance of "spontaneous" abortion see the technical chapter by William Bernds and David Barash (1979) titled "Early Termination of Parental Investment: A General Theory for Mammals, Including Humans." Harry Power's important 1975 study of non-parenting by non-parental bluebirds may have been the first to demonstrate that parental care is closely tied to the occurrence of shared genes. All the gory details of langur infanticide, plus color photos, can be found in the fascinating book by Harvard University anthropologist Sarah Hrdy, *The Langurs of Abu* (1977). My own technical manuscript "The Ecology of Paternal Behavior in the Hoary Marmot: An Evolutionary Interpretation" (1975) discusses the adaptive flexibility of marmot fathering behavior. A somewhat similar pattern was reported for orang-utans one year earlier (1974) by British ethologist John MacKinnon, while ten years before that Jared Verner's manuscript "The Evolution of Polygyny in the Long-billed Marsh Wren" (1964) had established the practical and theoretical significance of flexibility in male parenting behavior.

British ethologists Deag and Crook (1971) first suggested the term "agonistic buffering" to refer to the selfish use of infants by male Barbary macaques (often incorrectly called Barbary "apes"). Rothchild and Wolf's book *The Children of the Counterculture* (1976) describes the rather negative consequences of "liberated" child rearing. Similarly, Alice Rossi (1977) shows that not all women sociologists deny that biology has something to do with male-female differences in behavior. Her manuscript "A Biosocial Perspective on Parenting" appeared in a fascinating issue of the scientific journal *Daedalus* devoted entirely to "The Family." Sex roles in Israeli kibbutzim are described in the book by maverick sociologists Lionel Tiger and Joseph Shepher (1975). My information on African fertility rituals came from Turnbull's *Man in Africa* (1977), an overview of African anthropology.

I believe that Richard Alexander (1974) was the first to suggest an evolutionary approach to the avunculate system—he exemplifies those sociobiologists turning increasingly to the study of *Homo sapiens.* Israeli ethologist Amotz Zahavi seems to come up regularly with imaginative and challenging ideas. It was he who suggested (1977) that pair bonds are "tested" behaviorally. He also once proposed that male sexual adornment in animals has been selected specifically because it constitutes a *liability* to success: a male peacock, for example, who can make it through life carrying his huge albatross of a tail must be a high-quality peacock indeed, and accordingly perhaps females are selected to prefer such males!

Robert Trivers' technical report "Parent-Offspring Conflict" (1974) is one of the most important and stimulating works of theoretical sociobiology. It should be consulted by anyone interested in the subject. In her review of

"Mammals in Which Females Are Larger than Males" (1976) ethologist Katherine Ralls of the National Zoo in Washington, D.C., also discusses the "super-mom" hypothesis. Finally, extra parental devotion to the youngest child is discussed by sociologist Bert Adams (1972) and in the book by psychologists Sears, Macoby and Levin, *Patterns of Child Rearing* (1957).

5. Altruism: Kin, Karma and Kamikazes

The milestone, pioneering work on the genetics of altruism was by British entomologist and evolutionary geneticist William D. Hamilton (1964), currently at the University of Michigan and a welcome example of the brain drain! More recent extensions of this work appear in his 1975 book chapter titled "Innate Social Aptitudes of Man: An Approach from Evolutionary Genetics." In addition, Mary Jane West Eberhard, a student of Michigan's Richard Alexander currently at the University of Valle, Cali, Colombia, wrote a valuable review in 1975 titled "The Evolution of Social Behavior by Kin Selection." Strong quantitative evidence for the validity of kin selection in ants was presented by Trivers and Hare (1976). For alarm calling in round-tailed ground squirrels see Dunford (1977), and for an especially impressive study of kin selection and alarm calling, this time in Belding's ground squirrels, see the manuscript by Paul Sherman "Nepotism and the Evolution of Alarm Calls" (1977). Florida State University geneticist Glayde Whitney (1976) suggested that female mammals are genetically predisposed to be more altruistic than males, and wildlife biologists David Hirth and Dale McCullough (1977) compared altruistic alarm calling in male and female deer. Penn State University anthropologist Jeffrey Kurland (1977) studied the social behavior of Japanese monkeys for his doctoral dissertation, presenting the most detailed report thus far concerning kin selection among a free-living primate species.

For wife sharing in the Tasmanian native hen, see Maynard Smith and Ridpath (1972) and for human polyandry and a survey of world social systems, see Murdock (1957). Pierre van den Berghe and David Barash (1977) discuss human family structure in the light of inclusive fitness considerations. Polyandry among the Tibetan Tre-ba is described by Goldstein (1971) and among the Pahari of India by Berreman (1962). The quotation concerning traditional Chinese family structure is from Margery Wolf (1968); I thank Gary Becker for bringing it to my attention. His forthcoming book on the economics of human families will have a distinctly sociobiological flavor. The book by distinguished anthropologist Evans-Pritchard (1940) is the classic work on the Nuer people of Sudan. Data showing the increase in auto-immunity with aging appear in a manuscript by Whittingham *et al.* (1969), in the little-known *Australasian Annals of Medicine;* I thank Gene Roberts for bringing this to my attention.

Dutch sociologist Harry Hoetink (1973) proposed the idea of "somatic norm image" as part of his studies of racism in the Caribbean; I thank University of Illinois historian George Frederickson for pointing out to me the possible parallels between Hoetink's work and the predictions of kin selection. (Although George is less impressed with these parallels than I am.)

For reciprocal altruism, Trivers (1971) is a must. So is Alexander (1975), who makes a strong case for the role of selection operating on individuals in shaping human behavior. Alexander's manuscript, published independently of, and about the same time as, E. O. Wilson's *Sociobiology*, reviews the weakness of other approaches to natural selection and behavior and further indicates that by the mid-1970s sociobiology was an idea whose time had clearly come. For a very readable discussion of group selection, a theoretical possibility whose arguments have become increasingly obscured in computer models, see E. O. Wilson's 1973 article in the semi-popular magazine *BioScience*. A good discussion of the "helpers at the nest" phenomenon is found in Jerram Brown's excellent book (1975).

Ruth Benedict described Kwakiutl potlaches in her very influential book *Patterns of Culture* (1934), which also serves as a popular introduction to the "culture and personality" school of anthropology. Bronislaw Malinowski's massive book *The Argonauts of the Western Pacific* (1922) is the classic reference for the *Kula* exchange. The research on altruism in the Cook Islands by anthropologists Ted and Nancy Graves was reported in an award-winning paper they presented at the 1975 meeting of the American Anthropological Association. Richard Alexander's 1971 paper speculated on the role of cannibalism and warfare in human evolution, especially the rapid evolution of the human brain. The quotation from Michael Ghiselin comes from his scholarly *The Economy of Nature and the Evolution of Sex* (1974). For the "midwife" hypothesis of human brain evolution, see the book chapter by Dartmouth University political scientist Roger Masters (1979). Social psychologist Donald Campbell speculated that the sociobiology of human selfishness may have necessitated social constraints in his presidential address to the American Psychological Association, "On the Conflicts Between Biological and Social Evolution and Between Psychology and Moral Tradition" (1975). The May, 1976, issue of *American Psychologist* published a number of responses to this provocative idea.

6. Competition: Fighting, Male Groups and War

Nobel prize-winning ethologist Konrad Lorenz presents the classical ethological view of aggression, complete with "species benefit" and other errors, in his popular book *On Aggression* (1966). Singh (1969) discusses urban monkeys of India in a *Scientific American* article, while Robert Farentinos reports on "Social Dominance and Mating Activity in the Tassel-Eared Squirrel" (1972). The book by ethologist John Paul Scott (1958) reviews the role of experience in animal aggression, whereas Yale psychiatrist Dollard *et al.* (1939) considers the role of frustration. Sex reversal in wrasses is described by Australian biologist D. R. Robertson (1972) and the quotation from psychoanalyst Alfred Adler comes from his 1932 book with the arresting title *What Life Should Mean to You.*

An excellent discussion of aggressive competition and social dominance in a sociobiological framework appears in the book chapter by Harvard anthropologists Joseph Popp and Irven DeVore (1979). Hall and Mayer (1967) report on "Social Interactions in a Group of Captive Patas Monkeys" and ethologist Eibl-Eiblsfeldt (1961) describes the ritualized, tournament-like nature of animal fighting. British evolutionary biologists John Maynard Smith and G. R. Price (1973) pioneered the use of game theory in analyzing aggressive encounters, just as social psychologist Solomon Asch (1951) pioneered the experimental study of conformity and sociologist Stanley Milgram (1963) initiated research on obedience to authority. The quotation from anthropologist William Laughlin is from his book chapter "Hunting: an Integrating Biobehavioral System and Its Evolutionary Importance" (1968).

Lionel Tiger's controversial book *Men in Groups* (1969) also discusses the under-representation of women in politics, and the Nkrumah episode as well. The curious practice of ciscisbeism among the Birom of Nigeria was described in a paper presented at the controversial American Anthropological Association in Washington, D.C. (Smedley, 1976). The Mead quotations are from her book (1949); the Kalahari quote is from Marshall (1960) and the two Mundurucu quotes are from Murphy (1957). William Durham's article (1976a) is valuable reading for anyone interested in relating sociobiology and primitive war.

7. Toward an Evolutionary Biology of Mind and Notes on Biology and Culture

"What the Frog's Eye Tells the Frog's Brain" is a now-famous article by MIT biologist Jerome Lettvin *et al.* (1959). Kluckhohn and Murray suggest the hierarchies of human uniqueness in the volume they edited, *Personality in Nature, Society and Culture* (1948). After writing on Immanuel Kant and sociobiology, I showed the manuscript to historian of science Carolyn (Iltis) Merchant; she pointed out that Berkeley molecular biologist Gunther Stent (1975) had raised many similar points. For the effects of fever on survival, see Bernheim and Kluger (1976) and Kluger *et al.* (1975). Stengel's book *Suicide and Attempted Suicide* (1964) is a basic reference, including male-female differences. Tasmanian psychiatrist Scott Henderson (1974) independently suggested that depression is a care-eliciting behavior in human beings; I thank Maggie Scarf for directing me to this reference. Weissman and Klerman (1977) review the evidence for male-female differences in depression, concluding that the differences are real and universal. (Gerald Klerman is currently director of the U.S. Alcoholism, Drug Abuse and Mental Health Administration.)

I thank E. O. Wilson (1977) for the quotation from Niels Bohr. Iconoclastic anthropologist Robin Fox (1975) describes culture as a biological human adaptation in his book of essays. Israeli sociologist Joseph Shepher (1971) reports on "incest avoidance" among kibbutz residents. The notion that "familiarity breeds contempt" as a mechanism of incest avoidance was first proposed by Westermarck in 1891. Anthropologist Arthur Wolf describes the sexual failures of "Shim-pua" marriages—involving childhood adoption of a would-be bride—in his article "Childhood Association, Sexual Attraction and the Incest Taboo." (1966). See LaBarre (1954) for Cassubian fern-flowers, sparganosis, crocodile-clan Dinka, Polynesian poop fins and the Siberian Koryak. A *Scientific American* article by N. Kretchmer (1972) gives a good review of lactose and lactase. Humanistic psychologist Abraham Maslow discusses his ideas of hierarchical human needs in his book *Toward a Psychology of Being* (1962). Anthropologist William Durham (1976b) develops the notion that humans preferentially adopt behavior that enhances their fitness in his article on "The Adaptive Significance of Cultural Behavior," appearing in the scientific journal *Human Ecology*.

8. Politics: A Tangled Bank

For some polemical critiques of sociobiology, see Allen *et al.* (1975, 1976), and for responses, see Wilson (1976) and Barash (1978). University of Michigan anthropologist Marshall Sahlins criticizes sociobiology in his book *The Use and Abuse of Biology* (1976). Harold Fishbein is the child psychologist who discussed the "collusion of genes," in his book *Evolution, Development and Children's Learning* (1976). The quotation concerning Social Darwinism is from Himmelfarb's *Darwin and the Darwinian Revolution* (1959). The Marcuse quotation is from his book *One Dimensional Man* (1964). Medvedev's *The Rise and Fall of T. D. Lysenko* (1969) documents that extraordinary tragedy of Soviet science, a lesson of what can happen if politics and science are allowed to mix too freely.

Bibliography

Abele, Lawrence G., and Sandra Gilchrist. "Homosexual Rape and Sexual Selection in Acanthocephalan Worms." *Science,* 197:81–83, 1977.

Adams, Bert N. "Birth Order: A Critical Review." *Sociometry,* 35:411–439, 1972.

Adler, Alfred. *What Life Should Mean to You.* London: Allen & Unwin, 1932.

Alexander, Richard D. "The Search for an Evolutionary Philosophy of Man." Proceedings of the Royal Society of Victoria, 84:99–120, 1971.

_____. "The Evolution of Social Behavior." *Annual Review of Ecology and Systematics,* 5:325–383, 1974.

_____. "The Search for a General Theory of Behavior." *Behavioral Science,* 20:77–100, 1975.

Allen, L., *et al.* "Against Sociobiology," *New York Review of Books,* November 13, 1975.

_____. "Sociobiology—Another Biological Determinism." *BioScience,* 26:-182–186, 1976.

Asch, Solomon. "Effects of Group Pressure upon the Modification and Distortion of Judgment," in *Groups, Leadership and Men* (Guetzkow, ed.). Pittsburgh: Carnegie Press, 1951.

Barash, David P. "The Ecology of Paternal Behavior in the Hoary Marmot *(Marmota caligata):* An Evolutionary Interpretation." *Journal of Mammalogy,* 56:612–615, 1975.

_____. "The Male Response to Apparent Female Adultery in the Mountain Bluebird, *Sialia currucoides:* An Evolutionary Interpretation." *American Naturalist,* 110:1097–1101, 1976.

_____. *Sociobiology and Behavior.* New York: Elsevier, 1977a.

_____. "Sociobiology of Rape in Mallards *(Anas platyrhynchos):* Responses of the Mated Male." *Science,* 1977:788–789, 1977b.

_____. "Sociobiology: Evolution as a New Paradigm for Behavior," in *Sociobiology and Human Nature: An Interdisciplinary Critique and Defense* (Gregory and Silvers, eds.). San Francisco: Jossey-Bass, 1978.

Benedict, Ruth. *Patterns of Culture.* Boston: Houghton Mifflin, 1934.

Bernds, William P., and David P. Barash. "Early Termination of Parental Investment: A General Theory for Mammals, Including Humans," in *Evolutionary Biology and Human Social Behavior* (Chagnon and Irons, eds.). North Scituate, Mass.: Duxbury, 1979.

Bernheim, Harry A., and M. Kluger. "Fever: Effect of Drug-Induced Anti-Pyresis on Survival. *Science,* 193:237–239, 1976.

Berreman, G.D. "Pahari Polyandry: a Comparison." *American Anthropologist,* 64:60–75, 1962.

Breland, K., and M. Breland. "The Misbehavior of Organisms." *American Psychologist,* 16:681–684, 1961.

Brown, Jerram L. *The Evolution of Behavior.* New York: W. W. Norton, 1975.

Bruyn, G. "Huntington's Chorea: Historical, Clinical and Laboratory Synopsis." *Handbook of Clinical Neurology* (Vinken and Bruyn, eds.), vol. 6. New York: Elsevier, 1968.

Campbell, Donald T. "On the Conflicts Between Biological and Social Evolution and Between Psychology and Moral Tradition." *American Psychologist,* 30:1103–1126, 1975.

Chagnon, Napoleon. *Yanomamo: The Fierce People.* New York: Holt, Rinehart & Winston, 1968.

———— and W. Irons (eds.). *Evolutionary Biology and Human Social Behavior.* North Scituate, Mass.: Duxbury, 1979.

Chomsky, Noam. *Language and Mind.* New York: Harcourt Brace Jovanovich, 1972.

Connell, Joseph H. "The Influence of Interspecific Competition and Other Factors on the Distribution of the Barnacle, *Chthamalus stellatus.*" *Ecology,* 42:710–723, 1961.

Coughlin, William J. "The Great *Mokusatsu* Mistake." *Harper's Magazine,* CCVI:31–40, 1953.

Coulson, J. C. "The Influence of the Pair-Bond and Age on the Breeding Biology of the Kittiwake Gull, *Rissa tridactyla.*" *Journal of Animal Ecology,* 35:269–279, 1966.

Cox, Cathleen R., and Burney J. LeBoeuf. "Female Incitation of Male Competition: a Mechanism in Sexual Selection." *American Naturalist,* 111:317–335, 1977.

Cronin, Edward W., and Paul W. Sherman. "A Resource-Based Mating System: the Orange-Rumped Honeyguide." *The Living Bird,* 15: 5–32, 1977.

Dawkins, Richard. *The Selfish Gene.* London: Oxford University Press, 1976.

Deag, J. M., and J. H. Crook. "Social Behavior and 'Agonistic Buffering' in the Wild Barbary Macaque, *Macaca sylvanus.*" *Folia Primatologica,* 15:183–200, 1971.

DeVore, Irven (ed.). *Sociobiology and Human Behavior.* Cambridge: Harvard University Press, 1978.

Dilger, William. "The Behavior of Lovebirds." *Scientific American,* 206:-88–89, 1962.

Dobzhansky, Theodosius. *Genetics of the Evolutionary Process.* New York: Columbia University Press, 1974.

Dollard, J., *et al. Frustration and Aggression.* New Haven: Yale University Press, 1939.

Dunford, Christopher. "Kin Selection for Ground Squirrel Alarm Calls." *American Naturalist,* 111:782–785, 1977.

Durham, William H. "Resource Competition and Human Aggression, Part I: a Review of Primitive War." *Quarterly Review of Biology,* 51:-385–415, 1976a.

――――. "The Adaptive Significance of Cultural Behavior." *Human Ecology,* 4:89–121, 1976b.

Eaton, Randall L. "Why Some Felids Copulate So Much," in *The World's Cats* (Easton, ed.). Seattle: Carnivore Research Institute, 1976.

Ehrman, Lee, and Peter Parsons. *Behavior Genetics.* Sunderland, Mass.: Sinnauer, 1976.

Eibl-Eibesfeldt, I. "The Fighting Behavior of Animals." *Scientific American,* 205:112–121, 1961.

――――. *Ethology, the Biology of Behavior.* New York: Holt, Rinehart & Winston, 1975.

Emlen, Stephen T., and Lewis W. Oring. "Ecology, Sexual Selection, and the Evolution of Mating Systems." *Science* 197:215–223, 1977.

Erickson, Carl J., and P. G. Zenone. "Courtship Differences in Male Ring Doves: Avoidance of Cuckoldry?" *Science* 192:1353–1354, 1976.

Evans-Pritchard, E. E. *The Nuer, A Description of the Modes of Livelihood and Political Institutions of a Nilotic People.* Oxford: Clarendon, 1940.

――――. *The Institutions of Primitive Society.* Glencoe, Illinois: Free Press, 1954.

Farentinos, Robert C. "Social Dominance and Mating Activity in the Tassel-Eared Squirrel *(Sciurus abeati)." Animal Behaviour,* 20:316–326, 1972.

Fishbein, Harold D. *Evolution, Development and Children's Learning.* Pacific Palisades, Cal.: Goodyear, 1976.

Fisher, Ronald A. *The Genetical Theory of Natural Selection.* Oxford: Clarendon, 1930.

Fox, Robin. *Encounter with Anthropology.* New York: Harcourt Brace Jovanovich, 1975.

Ghiselin, Michael T. *The Economy of Nature and the Evolution of Sex,* Berkeley: University of California Press, 1974.

Goldstein, M. C. "Stratification, Polyandry and Family Structure in Central Tibet." *Southwestern Journal of Anthropology,* 27:64–74, 1971.

Hall, K. R. L., and B. Mayer. "Social Interactions in a Group of Captive Patas Monkeys." *Folia Primatologica,* 5:213–236, 1967.

Hamilton, William D. "The Genetical Theory of Social Behavior: I. and II." *Journal of Theoretical Biology*, 7:1–52, 1964.

———. "Innate Social Aptitudes of Man: An Approach from Evolutionary Genetics," in *Biosocial Anthropology* (Fox, ed.). New York: Wiley, 1975.

Hardin, Garrett. *Nature and Man's Fare*. New York: Holt, Rinehart & Winston, 1959.

Harris, Marvin. *Cannibals and Kings*. New York: Random House, 1977a.

———. "Why Men Dominate Women." *New York Times Magazine*, November 13, 1977b.

Henderson, S. "Care-Eliciting Behavior in Man." *Journal of Nervous and Mental Disease*, 159:172–181, 1974.

Hess, Eckard H., and James Polt. "Pupil Size as Related to Interest Value of Visual Stimuli." *Science*, 132:349–

Himmelfarb, Gertrude. *Darwin and the Darwinian Revolution*, New York: Doubleday, 1959.

Hirth, David H., and D. R. McCullough. "Evolution of Alarm Signals Ungulates with Special Reference to White-Tailed Deer." *American Naturalist*, III: 31–42, 1977.

Hoetink, H. *Slavery and Race Relations in the Americas*. New York: Harper & Row, 1973.

Hrdy, Sarah B. "Male-Male Competition and Infanticide Among the Langurs *(Presbytis entellus)* of Abu, Rajasthan." *Folia Primatologica*, 22:19–58, 1974.

———. *The Langurs of Abu*. Cambridge, Mass.: Harvard University Press, 1977.

Hunt, George L., and Molly W. Hunt. "Female-Female Pairing in Western Gulls *(Larus occidentalis)* in Southern California." *Science*, 196:1466–1467, 1977.

Janzen, Daniel. "A Note on Optimal Mate Selection by Plants." *American Naturalist*, 111:365–371, 1977a.

———. "Why Fruits Rot, Seeds Mold and Meat Spoils." *American Naturalist*, III:691–713, 1977b.

Jenni, Donald A. "Evolution of Polyandry in Birds." *American Zoologist*, 14:129–144, 1974.

Kessel, E. L. "The Mating Activities of Balloon Flies." *Systematic Zoology*, 4:97–104, 1955.

Kluckhohn, Clyde, and H. A. Murray (eds.). *Personality in Nature, Society and Culture*. New York: Alfred A. Knopf, 1948.

Kluger, Matthew J., D. Ringler, and M. Avner. "Fever and Survival." *Science*, 188:166–168, 1975.

Kopell, B. S., *et al.* "Variations in Some Measures of Arousal During the Menstrual Cycle." *Journal of Nervous and Mental Disease*, 148:180–187, 1969.

Kretchmer, Nathan. "Lactose and Lactase." *Scientific American*, 227:70–78, 1972.

Kurland, Jeffrey A. "Kin Selection in the Japanese Monkey." *Contributions to Primatology,* 12:1–145, 1977.

LaBarre, Weston. *The Human Animal.* Chicago: University of Chicago Press, 1954.

Laughlin, William S. "Hunting: an Integrating Biobehavioral System and Its Evolutionary Importance," in *Man the Hunter* (Lee and DeVore, eds.). Chicago: Aldine, 1968.

LeBoeuf, Burney J. "Male-Male Competition and Reproductive Success in Elephant Seals." *American Zoologist,* 14:163–176, 1974.

Lee, Richard, and Irven DeVore (eds.). *Man the Hunter.* Chicago: Aldine, 1968.

Lettvin, J. Y., *et al.* "What the Frog's Eye Tells the Frog's Brain." *Proceedings of the Institute of Radio Engineers,* 47: 1940–1951, 1959.

LeVine, Robert. *Culture, Behavior and Personality.* Chicago: Aldine, 1973.

Lévi-Strauss, Claude. *Tristes Tropiques.* New York: Atheneum, 1974.

Lorenz, Konrad Z. *On Aggression.* New York: Harcourt, Brace and World, 1966.

Lorimer, F. *Culture and Human Fertility.* Zurich: UNESCO, 1954.

McGregor, D. *The Human Side of Enterprise.* New York: McGraw-Hill, 1960.

MacKinnon, J. "The Behavior and Ecology of Wild Orang-utans *(Pongo pygmeus)." Animal Behavior,* 22:3–74, 1974.

Maddi, Salvadore. *Personality Theories.* Homewood, Ill.: Dorsey, 1968.

Malinowski, Bronislaw, *Argonauts of the Western Pacific.* New York: E. P. Dutton, 1922.

Marcuse, Herbert. *One Dimensional Man.* Boston: Beacon Press, 1964.

Marshall, L. "Kung Bushmen Bands," in *Comparative Political Systems* (Cohen and Middleton, eds.). Garden City: Natural History Press, 1960.

Maslow, Abraham. *Toward a Psychology of Being.* Princeton: Van Nostrand, 1962.

Masters, Roger D. "Of Marmots and Men: Human Altruism and Animal Behavior," in *Sympathy, Altruism and Helping Behavior* (Wispe, ed.). New York: Academic, 1979.

Maynard Smith, John. *The Theory of Evolution.* Baltimore: Penguin, 1966.

_____ and M. G. Ridpath. "Wife Sharing in the Tasmanian Native Hen, *Tribonyx mortierii:* A Case of Kin Selection?" *American Naturalist,* 106:447–452, 1972.

_____ and G. R. Price. "The Logic of Animal Conflict." *Nature,* 246:15–18, 1973.

Mead, Margaret. *Male and Female.* New York: Morrow, 1949.

Medvedev, Z. A. *The Rise and Fall of T. D. Lysenko.* New York: Columbia University Press, 1969.

Milgram, Stanley. "Behavioral Study of Obedience." *Journal of Abnormal and Social Psychology,* 67:371–778, 1963.

Money, John, and Anke A. Ehrhardt. *Man and Woman, Boy and Girl.* Baltimore: Johns Hopkins University Press, 1972.

Moody, Paul A. *Introduction to Evolution.* New York: Harper & Row, 1970.

Murdock, George P. "World Ethnographic Sample." *American Anthropologist,* 59:664–687, 1957.

———. *Culture and Society.* Pittsburgh: University of Pittsburgh Press, 1965.

Murphy, R. F. "Intergroup Hostility and Social Cohesion." *American Anthropologist,* 59:1018–1035, 1957.

Orians, Gordon H. "On the Evolution of Mating Systems in Birds and Mammals." *American Naturalist,* 103:589–603, 1969.

Pianka, Eric R. "On r- and K- Selection." *The American Naturalist,* 104:-292–297, 1970.

Platt, John R. (ed.). *New Views on the Nature of Man.* Chicago: University of Chicago Press, 1965.

Popp, Joseph L., and I. DeVore. "Aggressive Competition and Social Dominance Theory," in *Perspectives on Human Evolution,* 1979.

Power, Harry W. "Mountain Bluebirds: Experimental Evidence Against Altruism." *Science,* 189:142–143, 1975.

Radloff, L. "Sex Differences in Depression: the Effects of Occupation and Marital Status." *Sex Roles,* 1:249–269, 1975.

Ralls, K. "Mammals in Which Females Are Larger than Males." *Quarterly Review of Biology,* 51:245–276, 1976.

Robertson, D. R. "Social Control of Sex Reversal in a Coral-Reef Fish." *Science,* 177:1007–1009, 1972.

Rose, Frederick G. G. "Australian Marriage, Land-Owning Groups and Initiations," in *Man the Hunter* (Lee and DeVore, eds.). Chicago: Aldine, 1968.

Rossi, Alice S. "A Biosocial Perspective on Parenting." *Daedalus,* 106:1–32, 1977.

Rothchild, J., and S. B. Wolf. *Children of the Counterculture.* New York: Doubleday, 1976.

Sagan, Carl. *The Dragons of Eden.* New York: Random House, 1977.

Sahlins, Marshall. *The Use and Abuse of Biology.* Ann Arbor: University of Michigan Press, 1976.

Scott, John P. *Aggression.* Chicago: University of Chicago Press, 1958.

Sears, Robert R., E. Macoby and H. Levin. *Patterns of Child Rearing.* Evanston, Ill.: Row Peterson, 1957.

Sharpe, Roger, and Paul A. Johnsgard. "Inheritance of Behavioral Characteristics in F2 Mallard and Pintail Hybrids." *Behaviour,* 27:259–272, 1966.

Shepher, Joseph. "Mate Selection among Second Generation Kibbutz Adolescents and Adults: Incest Avoidance and Negative Imprinting." *Archives of Sexual Behavior,* 1:293–307, 1971.

Sherman, Paul W. "Nepotism and the Evolution of Alarm Calls." *Science,* 197:1246–1253, 1977.

Sigusch, V., and G. Schmidt. "Lower-Class Sexuality: Some Emotional and Social Aspects in West German Males and Females. *Archives of Sexual Behavior,* 1:29–44, 1971.

Silvers, Anita, and M. Gregory (eds.). *Sociobiology and Human Values.* San Francisco: Jossey-Bass, 1978.

Singh, S.D. "Urban Monkeys." *Scientific American,* 221:108–115, 1969.

Smedley, A. "Birom ciscisbeism." Paper presented to the American Anthropological Association, Washington, D.C., 1976.

Smith, J. R. and L. G. *Beyond Monogamy.* Baltimore: Penguin, 1974.

Stengel, E. *Suicide and Attempted Suicide.* Middlesex, Eng.: Penguin Books, 1964.

Stent, Gunther. "Limits to the Scientific Understanding of Man." *Science,* 187:1052–1057, 1975.

Thornhill, R. "Sexual Selection and Parental Investment in Insects." *American Naturalist,* 110:153–163, 1976.

Tiger, Lionel. *Men in Groups.* New York: Random House, 1969.

————— and Robin Fox. *The Imperial Animal.* New York: Holt, Rinehart and Winston, 1971.

————— and Joseph Shepher. *Women in the Kibbutz.* New York: Harcourt Brace Jovanovich, 1975.

Towers, B. E. "Parental Adjustment to Childhood Leukemia." *Psychosomatic Medicine,* 18:9–14, 1974.

Trivers, Robert L. "The Evolution of Reciprocal Altruism." *Quarterly Review of Biology,* 46:35–57, 1971.

—————. "Parental Investment and Sexual Selection," in *Sexual Selection and the Descent of Man* (Campbell, ed.). Chicago: Aldine, 1972.

————— and D. E. Willard. "Natural Selection of Parental Ability to Vary the Sex Ratio of Offspring." *Science,* 179:90–92, 1973.

—————. "Parent-Offspring Conflict." *American Zoologist,* 14:249–264, 1974.

————— and H. Hare. "Haploidiploidy and the Evolution of the Social Insects." *Science,* 191:249–263, 1976.

Turnbull, Colin. *The Forest People.* Garden City: Doubleday, 1967.

—————. *The Mountain People.* New York: Simon & Schuster, 1973.

—————. *Man in Africa.* New York: Doubleday, 1977.

Van den Berghe, Pierre L. *Man in Society.* New York: Elsevier, 1975.

————— and D. P. Barash. "Inclusive Fitness Theory and Human Family Structure." *American Anthropologist,* 79:809–823, 1977.

Verner, J. "The Evolution of Polygyny in the Long-Billed Marsh Wren." *Evolution,* 18:252–261, 1964.

Weissman, M. M., and G. L. Klerman. "Sex Differences and the Epidemiology of Depression." *Archives of General Psychiatry,* 34:98–111, 1977.

West Eberhard, Mary J. "The Evolution of Social Behavior by Kin Selection." *Quarterly Review of Biology,* 50:1–33, 1975.

Westermarck, E. *The History of Human Marriage.* New York: Macmillan, 1891.

Whitney, Glayde. "Genetic Substrates for the Initial Evolution of Human Sociality. I. Sex Chromosome Mechanisms." *American Naturalist,* 110:867–875, 1976.

Whittingham, Senga, *et al.* "Autoantibodies in Health Subjects." *Australasian Annals of Medicine,* 18:130–134, 1969.

Williams, George C. *Adaptation and Natural Selection.* Princeton: Princeton University Press, 1966.

Wilson, Edward O. "Group Selection and Its Significance for Ecology." *BioScience,* 23:631–638, 1973.

————. *Sociobiology: The New Synthesis.* Cambridge: Harvard University Press, 1975.

————. "Academic Vigilantism and the Political Significance of Sociobiology." *BioScience,* 26:183–190, 1976.

————. "Biology and the Social Sciences." *Daedalus,* 106:127–140, 1977.

————. *On Human Nature.* Cambridge: Harvard University Press, 1978.

Wodinsky, Jerome. "Hormonal Inhibition of Feeding and Death in *Octopus:* Control by Optic Gland Secretion." *Science,* 198:948–951, 1977.

Wolf, Arthur. "Childhood Association, Sexual Attraction and the Incest Taboo." *American Anthropologist,* 68:883–898, 1966.

Wolf, Larry L. "Prostitution Behavior in a Tropical Hummingbird." *Condor,* 77:140–144, 1975.

Wolf, Margery. *The House of Lim.* New York: Prentice-Hall, 1968.

Zahavi, Amotz. "The Testing of a Bond." *Animal Behaviour,* 25:246–247, 1977.

Index